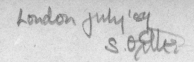

Marx: the First Hundred Years

David McLellan is Professor of Political Theory at the University of Kent. His latest book is *Karl Marx: the Legacy* (1983), based on the BBC TV series.

Raymond Williams is Professor of Drama at Cambridge University and a Fellow of Jesus College. His most recent book is *Culture* (1981).

Victor Kiernan is Emeritus Professor of History at Edinburgh University. Among his books are *Marxism and Imperialism* (1974) and *European Empires from Conquest to Collapse, 1815-1960* (1982).

Tom Bottomore is Professor of Sociology at the University of Sussex. Among his recent books is *Political Sociology* (1979).

Ernest Mandel is Professor of Political Science at the Free University of Brussels (Flemish section). His works include *Marxist Economic Theory* (1968), *Late Capitalism* (1975) and *Revolutionary Marxism Today* (1979).

Roy Edgley was Professor of Philosophy at the University of Sussex from 1970 until early retirement in 1981. His publications include *Reason in Theory and Practice* (1969), and he is now working on books on violence and on Marxism and philosophy.

Marx:
the First Hundred Years

Edited by David McLellan

Fontana Paperbacks

First published in Great Britain by Fontana Paperbacks 1983
Second impression May 1983

Set in Linotron Times
Made and printed in Great Britain by
The University Press, Oxford

A hardback edition is published by Frances Pinter Ltd

Contents

Editor's Introduction

The range of the six essays that comprise this book demonstrates the amazing breadth of Marx's interests and of his contributions to an understanding of our world. In the intellectual sphere at least (an important qualification) Marx was himself the prototype of communist man – the 'all-round individual' of the *Paris Manuscripts* or the 'social individual' of the *Grundrisse*. For him, one of the main evils of societies past and present was the division of labour:

> as soon as the distribution of labour comes into being, each man has a particular, exclusive sphere of activity, which is forced upon him and from which he cannot escape. He is a hunter, a fisherman, a shepherd, or a critical critic, and must remain so if he does not want to lose his means of livelihood; while in communist society, where nobody has one exclusive sphere of activity but each can become accomplished in any branch he wishes, society regulates the general production and thus makes it possible for me to do one thing today and another tomorrow, to hunt in the morning, fish in the afternoon, rear cattle in the evening, criticize after dinner, just as I have a mind, without ever becoming hunter, fisherman, cowherd, or critic.[1]

In similar vein Marx had himself produced a critique of political economy, turned Hegel upside down, and produced a materialist theory of history without ever becoming economist, philosopher or historian. For the most novel and interesting work is often done by people who are exploring the frontiers between two 'disciplines' which are not left to sleep peacefully side by

[1] *The German Ideology*, in K. Marx, *Selected Writings*, ed. D. McLellan (Oxford, 1977), p. 169.

side but are engaged in fruitful intercourse. As a man who would relax from his intensive social and historical studies by fiddling with problems of higher calculus or delving into the Greek of Aeschylus, Marx was excellently equipped to preside over a veritable interdisciplinary orgy.

But the very richness of Marx's mixture has entailed digestive difficulties for those accustomed to thinner fare. And the huge development of the social sciences in the century since Marx's death has often brought with it results that are thin in two respects: first in the vertical sense of being produced inside a narrow specialization by scholars who know more and more about less and less, and secondly in the horizontal sense that they spring from a preoccupation with the surface phenomena of society so easily available for observation and quantification. The upshot has been the construction of specialized procedures more or less restricted to a single discipline or field whose narrow-gauged tracks have been unable to encompass the breadth of Marx's enterprise. For him, as for his master Hegel, 'the truth is the whole' – a perspective which eluded even Marx's own followers in the decades following his death but was brought back into focus by Lukács and has since remained the inspiration of much Western Marxism.

Considering this emphasis on totality, it is not surprising that Marx's work remains dramatically unfinished, a fact which compounds the difficulty of deciphering his work. More than half of Marx's published work consists of *ad hoc* newspaper articles which Marx himself considered to be of little value. 'The continual newspaper muck annoys me,' he wrote, 'it takes a lot of time, disperses my efforts, and in the final analysis is nothing ... Purely scientific works are something completely different.'[2] In the 'purely scientific' field Marx's *magnum opus* is undoubtedly *Capital*, but a close study of his twenty-year struggle to complete the first volume shows that even the three volumes that were eventually published (and the last two were put together by Engels who took considerable editorial liberties) represent only a fragment of what Marx intended. He

[2] Marx to Cluss, in K. Marx and F. Engels, *Werke* (Berlin, 1957ff), vol. 28, p. 592.

specifically expressed a desire to write works on philosophy (Hegel) and on political theory (the state) which he considered indispensable for a clear understanding of his project. But these – along with so much else – remained unwritten. Ill health, self-imposed exacting standards of scholarship, and a congenital reluctance to publish all stood in Marx's way.

A third problem in interpreting Marx is created by the fact that a considerable portion of what Marx *had* undertaken was left in unpublished draft form. The *Paris Manuscripts* of 1844, *The German Ideology* of 1846, and the rough draft of *Capital* known as the *Grundrisse* of 1857/8 – as well as a lot of *Capital* itself – were all left unfinished in Marx's illegible manuscript and thus occupy an ambiguous status in his *oeuvre*. Although they are obviously more than random thoughts scribbled on the back of an envelope, they do not possess the clear, final authority of published work. Moreover, the fact that these manuscripts were finally published only at lengthy intervals after Marx's death is one of the main reasons for the radically changing picture of Marx's work that has been available over the last hundred years. As the various manuscripts have emerged from obscurity, they have illuminated different aspects of Marx's work and offered a different focus. In particular, the *Paris Manuscripts* published around 1930 provided the framework for a 'humanist' perspective on Marx, and the appearance of the *Grundrisse* in the West in the mid-1950s made possible a fundamental re-evaluation of the methodology inherent in *Capital*.[3] One reason for the rather economic determinist readings of Marx, popular in the decades after his death, was that little of his work was widely available apart from *The Communist Manifesto* and *Capital*. Marx tended therefore to be considered simply as a great economist whose work consisted in showing with scientific rigour the inevitability of capitalist collapse and the victory of the working class. Until very recently, therefore, people could still plausibly write books with such titles as *The Unknown Karl Marx*.[4]

When reading what fragments remain of Marx's mighty torso

[3] Cf., for example, R. Rosdolsky, *The Making of Marx's 'Capital'* (London, 1977).
[4] Cf., for example, *The Unknown Karl Marx*, ed. R. Payne (London, 1972).

it is important to remember that their author was, among other things, a member of the Victorian middle classes. The story of his painful efforts to maintain a facade of bourgeois respectability, to give his daughters an education that would do credit to any young lady of the time, to investigate carefully the social and financial backgrounds of their prospective husbands, and so on, is well known and should come as no surprise. As Hegel remarked, 'It is just as absurd to fancy that a philosopher can transcend his contemporary world as it is to fancy that an individual can overleap his own age.'[5] But this applied to Marx's intellectual, as well as to his social universe. Mid-Victorian England was a time and a place of comparative stability and great confidence in the future. The progress of the natural sciences – not perceived, then, as a mixed blessing – was particularly striking. This attitude was epitomized in the Great Exhibition of 1851 and Liebknecht reports how Marx at the time spoke enthusiastically of the revolutionizing potential in the replacement of steam by electricity: 'The way Marx spoke of the progress of science and mechanics showed so clearly his world outlook, especially what was later to be called the materialist conception of history, that certain doubts which I still entertained melted like snow in the spring sun.'[6] Linked to this optimism about scientific progress was a confidence in the values of rationality, democracy and freedom that was common to all progressive intellectuals of that epoch but much more difficult for our divided and disoriented time to appreciate.

It is equally important to note that, at the time Marx was writing, Europe was the centre of the world and England – 'the demiurge of the bourgeois universe' as he called it – was the centre of Europe. Marx was by intellectual tradition and geographical location a Westerner convinced that the main revolutionary crises would develop in the Western heartlands of capitalism. But Marx's ideas, originating in the West, have been applied in the East, and in contexts that it would have been impossible for Marx to envisage. The combination of Marxism and underdevelopment has created political problems, and

[5] G. Hegel, *Philosophy of Right*, tr. T. Knox (Oxford, 1967), p. 11.
[6] *Karl Marx: Interviews and Recollections*, ed. D. McLellan (London, 1981), pp. 43f.

particularly a tendency to authoritarian government, that bear little relation to Marx's own conceptions. For Marx, communism would be the inheritor of all the positive tendencies inherent in Western capitalism, particularly its political liberties (albeit very partial) and its economic wealth. It is difficult, therefore, to see much connection between Third World socialism or Chinese communism and the ideas of Marx. In many developing countries a version of Marxism combined with nationalism serves as little more than an ideology to encourage mass participation in the modernization process.

Finally, the very success of Marx's ideas as the inspiration for mass political movements has led to their being systematized, rigidified and distorted. This process began with Engels who survived his friend for twelve crucial years and helped popularize a version of Marxism (as in *Anti-Dühring*) whose very comprehensiveness and clarity made it more accessible than the works of Marx himself. It is well known that Marx, in a protest at the simplification of his ideas by French followers, claimed not to be a Marxist.[7] When the term Marx*ism* first emerges it is in the context of a political battle with the Bakuninists in the First International.[8] And it has been used as a political football ever since. As the Marxist movement grew and split into antipathetic groups, each tended to produce an interpretation of Marx favourable to their own policies. Indeed some of the leading Marxist practitioners adopt an attitude to Marx's message that strikingly resembles that of Dostoievsky's Grand Inquisitor.

The appeal to Marx to solve interfactional disputes is, of course, misguided. To search for what Marx 'really meant' is necessarily forlorn. Even if one could overcome the obstacles, outlined above, that impede an approach to Marx's writings, it is by no means clear that his views on many questions were either always coherent or always univocal. But although it may be impossible to recover Marx's answers with any precision, he

[7] Engels to Bernstein, in K. Marx and F. Engels, *Werke* (Berlin, 1957ff), vol. 35, p. 388.
[8] See M. Manale, 'Aux origines du concept de "marxisme"', *Economies et Sociétés, Cahiers de l'ISEA*, series 5, no. 17, October 1974.

has at least left us with a fruitful set of questions which fall into three main categories.

The central question in the study of human society – historical, cultural, sociological, economic – is how to divide society up, and then, having divided it, how to describe the relationship between the divisions. In Marx's effort to explain the development of society, he sometimes used the metaphor of (economic) base and (political, ideological) superstructure. Others found this too simplistic and preferred to talk of different factors, different spheres or different sorts of relations. Then the problem was how the relationship between these 'bits' (however conceptualized) should be described. Did some determine, condition or simply correspond to each other? And if some were relatively autonomous, how relative was the autonomy? It was all very well to urge 'the concrete analysis of concrete circumstances' (in Lenin's rather concrete phrase) but some general theory of the primacy of the economic was evidently necessary for Marxism to conserve its identity.

Secondly, there was the political question. All hitherto existing human enterprises had tended to divide people into leaders and led. Yet Marx's prognosis for revolution had suggested that the proletariat were in the process of forging a society in which that would no longer be the case. But could any revolutionary organization avoid, in contemporary society, the iron law of oligarchy? And if it could not, how could it point the way to a society whose principles it did not itself embody? Marx himself did not belong to any political party, and any subsequent Marxist – from a Leninist proposing a highly centralized 'vanguard' party leading the workers to a libertarian socialist who believed that political power should be vested directly in workers' assemblies – could claim, without fear of refutation, that they were in the true Marxist tradition.

Finally, there is the larger philosophical question of the relationship of Marx's thought – and indeed any sociology – to the general problems of epistemology and ontology. The problems of the ultimate nature of reality and of the criteria for genuine knowledge are as old as mankind. Marx's account of society did not seem to deal directly with such questions. Many thought that their solution was at least implicit in Marx's work or else that they were rendered thereby irrelevant. Yet they have continued to haunt many of his successors – and been answered in very diverse ways. The neo-structuralist readings of Marx have sought philosophical backing in Spinoza, there has been a strong revival recently within Marxism of a 'return to Kant', and the Lukácsian tendency to read Marx through Hegel is still strong. The perennial questions remain perennial.

It is, of course, true in a sense that Marx will always remain 'unknown' and his intentions irrecoverable; but if, as the currently fashionable deconstruction theory has it, texts are to be evaluated according to their ability to generate new interpretations and lines of thought that go far beyond anything that the original author could have conceived, then Marx's writings clearly deserve the deconstructionist prize. For the essays that follow demonstrate that Marx's work, a hundred years on, is as capable as ever of producing fresh and relevant lines of inquiry.

Culture

Raymond Williams

1

There is an initial paradox. Few would now remember Karl
Marx for any direct contributions he made to cultural theory.
Yet it is clear that the contribution of Marxism to modern
cultural thought is widespread and influential.

This problem can be interpreted in very different ways. Thus
it is often said that the influence of Marxist cultural thought is
a by-product of the success of Marxism as a critique of the
capitalist social order and as the decisive philosophy of
revolutionary socialism. This can then be either a recognition
or a dismissal: an acknowledgment of the major effects which
this body of thought and this transforming movement have had
on an area of human practice to which they have always, in fact,
given considerable attention; or, conversely, a rejection of the
distortions which this primarily political, economic and sociological theory and practice have imposed on works and interests
which they can only misunderstand and damage.

Or again it is said that while the practical success of Marxism
has for obvious and integral reasons been primarily in the
political and economic spheres, its central contribution has
always been much wider and indeed that the distinctive effects
of its political and economic influence can only be understood
when it is seen that these are the expression of a much more
general interpretation of all human activity and of ways of
understanding and changing it. From this emphasis it follows
that Marxist cultural theory is not a by-product of a political and
economic movement but one of the main areas of the theory and
practice as a whole. It can then of course still be rejected as
wrong, and even among those who are broadly in sympathy
with it there can be divergent attitudes. There have been many,
including too many in power, who, while repeating the most

general claims, have in practice reduced cultural theory to a relatively dogmatic application of political and economic positions. There have been others who have seen the preoccupation with cultural theory, which has been a feature of Western Marxism since the 1920s, as an indication of the (temporary) failure, in such societies, of the central revolutionary political and economic movement. On the other hand, an increasing number of Marxists now believe that cultural theory has become even more important, in modern social and cultural conditions, than it was in Marx's own day.

Finally it is said that the evident influence of Marxism in modern cultural thought is indeed a *contribution*, whether welcome or unwelcome: that it has, in combination with some other intellectual and social traditions, established certain distinctive positions and interests but has in practice combined these with other forms of thought which have no particular basis in Marx but which can still be swept up in the general Marxist classification. This would be one kind of explanation of the fact that there are now not only divergent but contending and incompatible schools of Marxist cultural thought. On the other hand, from either of the earlier positions outlined, what is emphasized is not the combination with other forms of thought but this or that *interpretation* of what Marx really said or meant, and the consequent argument against other interpretations. This happens even in areas in which Marx wrote extensively and systematically, so it is not surprising that it also happens in relation to the more scattered and less systematic indications of a cultural theory.

It is not likely that any of these problems can be authoritatively resolved in a relatively brief essay. Yet perhaps something can be done, if its purposes are declared and its limits acknowledged. My main interest will be in what Marx himself wrote in this general area. Yet this is not an interest determined by some wish to provide legitimacy for any subsequent position. Necessarily, as a way of understanding what Marx wrote, I shall refer to what others have understood him to have written, but I am not attempting, here, a history of the Marxist tradition of cultural thought, which is not only a vast subject in itself but in which there are writers who, on these matters, are at least as important as Marx himself. If all were in one way or another inspired by Marx, still the most important of them looked to his work not for legitimation of their own, or for some title of authority, but as to a great colleague, in a social and intellectual enterprise much wider than any individual contribution. That enterprise is now part of a continuing and necessarily conflicting world history. We look at Marx in that context but still primarily, for present purposes, at Marx himself.

2

We can define three aspects of Marx's contribution to cultural thought. First, there are his own incidental but very extensive comments on a wide range of writers and artists. Second, there is the effect of his general position on human development, which can be taken as at least the outline of a general cultural theory. Third, there are the unfinished problems, the questions raised and set aside or only partly answered, some of which are still important in their own right.

The first aspect needs emphasis, against many hostile or merely ignorant accounts. It is not only that he was an intense and lifelong reader of so many of the great works of world literature. Professor Prawer's *Karl Marx and World Literature*[1] gives extraordinary evidence of this, of a kind to impress even those who knew the general fact. It is also that much of his early writing was directly concerned with literary and aesthetic subjects, and that as late as 1857, with other major work in progress, he planned and read for an essay on aesthetics, though he did not write it.

What has then to be asked is how these facts bear on his more general work. It is a difficult question to answer. The student poems, the fragment of a novel, the sketch of a Platonic dialogue, the projected but unrealized journal of dramatic criticism, are too slight and local to sustain any positive

[1] S.S. Prawer, *Karl Marx and World Literature* (Oxford, 1976).

indications. They testify to his intense interest in writing and can be said to show two characteristics – a Promethean daring and an irrepressible critical irony – which are central in the mature writer. On the other hand it is too easy to read back such characteristics, from the later achievement. There must have been thousands of student writers who did as much but did not go on to the very different work of the mature Marx.

Can we say the same of the lively early journalism, and in particular the *Rheinische Zeitung* articles on censorship and freedom of the press? Not really. The attack on the Prussian censorship is rather more than conventional liberal protest:

> The law permits me to write; it asks only that I write in a style other than my own! I am allowed to show the face of my mind, but, first, I must give it a *prescribed expression*![2]

This becomes a shrewd analysis of the familiar pressure or demand for 'moderation' of tone:

> Freely shall you write, but let every word be a genuflection toward the liberal censor who approves your modest, serious good judgment.[3]

Or again, in a far-reaching comment:

> The moderation of genius does not consist of the use of a cultivated language without accent or dialect; it lies rather in speaking the accent of the matter and the dialect of its essence. It lies in forgetting about moderation and immoderation and getting to the core of things.[4]

Similarly, in his observations on the freedom of the press, an important but relatively familiar position –

> In no sense does the writer regard his works as a *means*. They

[2] Cit. *Marx and Engels on Literature and Art*, ed. L. Baxandall and S. Morawski (St Louis, 1973), p. 59.
[3] Ibid., p. 60.
[4] Ibid., p. 59.

are *ends in themselves*; so little are they means for him and others that, when necessary, he sacrifices *his* existence to theirs[5]

– is set in the context of a more original and still relevant argument:

It is startling to find *freedom of the press* subsumed under ·*freedom of doing business*. . . *The first freedom of the press consists in its not being a business.*[6]

There is shrewd insight, also, in the essay on Sue's *Les Mystères de Paris* which Marx contributed to *The Holy Family*. The essay works, with some inconsistency, at several levels of analysis, but is especially interesting in the use of analysis of vocabulary to clarify what would later be called the ideology of the tale, and in analysis of its internal contradictions.

These are the more isolable pieces of Marx's early literary and cultural writing. They are still, at their best, important now only because of the later work of their author. The same is true, really, of the evidence of Marx's wide knowledge of world literature, not only from documentary records but in the long use of allusions, quotations and references, and in the use of certain writing techniques in his major philosophical and historical works. That Marx was such a man, learned and cultivated, deeply devoted to literature, is a fact against certain ignorant travesties. But the centre of the argument about Marx and culture cannot be displaced to such a dimension. Marx himself would have been among the first to say that it doesn't primarily matter how well-read a man is, a fact that is often only the indication of his social and cultural position and mode of life. What matters much more is what is done with that reading and knowledge, at levels more decisive than learned and apt allusion and habits of style. If Marx was, indeed, an exceptionally cultivated *bourgeois*, he gave most of his energy to becoming or making possible something different: never in a

---

[5] Ibid., p. 61.
[6] Ibid., pp. 60–1.

renunciation of reading and learning, but always in the transition from a possession of knowledge to its transforming use.

One further observation on this aspect of Marx is necessary. It has been so widely alleged against Marxism, both as theory and as some twentieth-century practice, that it is an enemy of culture, especially in respect of the freedoms of its creation, that it has been tempting for some Marxists to produce the old man himself, reading and re-reading Aeschylus and Ovid and Dante and Shakespeare and Cervantes and Goethe and so on, as if that were sufficient answer. But it would be a guilty admission of the faults of Marxist cultural theory and practice if the central argument were shifted to the private or semi-public cultivation of their founder. On the other hand it is true that it should be necessary for some of those who claim the authority of Marx, either for their own bureaucratic illiberalism or for that reduced version of Marxism which treats culture as a *priori* marginal or dependent, to come into contact with his mind in this vigorous, uncompromising and persistent part of its range. Except, of course, that the early work especially can be conveniently diagnosed, by friends and enemies, as pre-Marxist, with special bearing on the fierce (and in fact lifelong) assertions of the liberty and autonomy of cultural work. There is a serious question waiting there, as the mature theory is seen to develop, but it cannot in any case be solved, from any position, by the assembly of facts about his reading or by the tactical use of this or that quotation. It will be solved, if at all, by direct inquiry into the long, massive, unfinished, often contradictory work which we now call Marx.

3

There is a preliminary problem, of wider import than either Marx or Marxism. I have been using the term *culture*, in this essay, in one of its predominant twentieth-century senses, as a general term for artistic, literary and intellectual work. There is no comparably adequate general term, so the use can be readily justified. But it is well known that *culture* is also used, in anthropology and sociology but also more generally, to describe a distinctive way of life, then including arts and learning but also much more general practice and behaviour. The complexities of the word are in fact even wider than this, and have been explored elsewhere.[7]

Now from certain positions it can be objected that any particular use of *culture* is misleading: too broad, too narrow, or simply too confusing. Yet the difficult history of the word is in fact an indication of a very general and complex intellectual movement, which happens to be especially though by no means exclusively relevant to Marx and Marxism. The variations and conflicts around the meaning of *culture* are central elements of a long, specifically modern inquiry. It is precisely the relations between, on the one hand, the arts and learning, and on the other hand a more general way of life, that are argued through, beyond and behind this term, in what in any local instance can seem intolerably confusing ways. Moreover the relations between *culture*, either as the arts and learning, or as a more general way of life, and that state or process widely defined as *civilization*, have also been intensively explored and argued, again through, beyond and behind the vital words. There has been the use of *culture* as inner spiritual development, best externally exemplified in the arts and religion and responses to them, in contrast with the external and material achievements of *civilization*. On the other hand the distinctiveness of particular ways of life, in their more general aspects but including their arts and ideas, has been emphasized as the diversity of *cultures* by contrast with the often unilinear and uniform version of *civilization* (or as some would now say, *development*). Again, however, and in fact in the work of a German contemporary of Marx, G.F. Klemm in his *Allgemeine Kulturgeschichte der Menschheit* (1843–52), the general progress of mankind was traced through phases of *cultural* history, in which basic forms of social life were seen as rooted in historically changing and developing conditions.

[7] R. Williams, *Keywords* (London: Fontana, 1976), pp. 76–82.

Such phases were also traced through the key word *Society*, as in the American Lewis Morgan's *Ancient Society* (1877), which so impressed and directly influenced both Marx and Engels.

This actual history quickly shows us that it is not possible, in any simple way, to answer or even ask the question: what does Marx say about culture? Yet at the same time it shows us that the questions he actually asked, in this initially indeterminate area, belong to a very widespread and active area of philosophical, aesthetic and historical inquiry, which undoubtedly preceded him and which has certainly continued after him, not only 'inside' and 'outside' the Marxist traditions but of course primarily as a central issue in itself, where the effects of any particular intellectual tendency are for obvious reasons difficult to disentangle.

What this means in practice, for the study of Marx himself, is that the real history is not one of isolated innovative work: that it finds, in Marx, certain strikingly original questions and answers, but finds also his answers to the questions of others, questions persistent from work with which he otherwise disagrees, to say nothing of borrowings, provisional syntheses, notes and sketches. This in no way diminishes him, but it restores, as against the isolated authoritative master, that which he was himself always concerned to show: a concrete, shifting, at times contradictory historical process, temporarily and provisionally highlighted in this great and singular figure.

4

'There is no history ... of art.' Or, to give the sentence in full, 'There is no history of politics, of law, of science etc., of art, of religion.'[8] This is a manuscript note, rather than a considered

[8] K. Marx and F. Engels, *Werke* (Berlin, 1957ff), vol. 3, p. 539.

statement, but it at once introduces a major emphasis in Marx's thought and raises a central problem in interpretation. The intended emphasis becomes clear in its full context. It had been and is still commonplace to generalize certain human activities as if they were distinct and autonomous, and from this to assert that they can be regarded as having their own independent history. And this had been especially the case in cultural activities, which had been regarded not only as the originating, directive impulses of all human development but also, in certain powerful intellectual traditions, as themselves originated, by revelation or by inspiration, by forces beyond human beings. The whole thrust of Marx's reading of history was then, first, to insist that all cultural processes were initiated by humans themselves, and, second, to argue that none of them could be fully understood unless they were seen in the context of human activities as a whole. That is the initial and least controversial sense of the argument that 'there is no history ... of art': that the real history is always of human beings making art, from their own human resources, as distinct either from the history of a 'reified' Art – the sum of certain human activities seen as if it were a self-evolving product or an internally developing abstraction or a result of extra-human direction – or, where these more extreme projections were not in question, from that kind of specializing history which deliberately ignored the general conditions within which the specialized activity was practised. It is an important part of the legacy of Marx, but then also of a wider movement of modern thought, that these initial emphases are now very widely accepted.

But there are then further and more controversial senses of Marx's argument. These can be seen from the way in which the argument was put by Marx and Engels in *The German Ideology* (1845–6):

> Morality, religion, metaphysics, and other ideologies, and their corresponding forms of consciousness, no longer retain therefore their appearance of autonomous existence. They have no history, no development; it is men who, in developing their material production and their material

intercourse, change, along with this their real existence, their thinking and the products of their thinking.[9]

It is here that the central problem is joined. But we should first be clear about a problem of formulation, which is potentially very misleading. It is easy to read such sentences as 'they have no history, no development' or 'there is no history . . . of art' in the irrelevant and obviously untrue sense that these activities do not change and develop and thus have no history. This would be directly contrary to what Marx meant, but the rhetorical form of the statements, made as they were within explicit polemic against those who taught that the history of these 'spiritual' activities was the essential history of all human development, can in some respects mislead. What is at least initially being argued is that these activities are not separate and autonomous, and that they have all been carried out by actual human beings, in the whole real conditions of their existence.

Yet this readily acceptable sense of the argument is also, evidently, not Marx's whole sense. This can be seen in the sentences which immediately precede those quoted:

> We begin with real, active men, and from their real life-process show the development of the ideological reflexes and echoes of this life-process. The phantoms of the human brain also are necessary sublimates of men's material life-process, which can be empirically established and which is bound to material preconditions.[10]

Sympathetically read, this can be taken as little more than a strong form of the argument that all human activities, including the 'cultural' and the 'spiritual', have their origins in the whole real conditions of human existence. This general argument would be widely accepted. Yet it is obvious that other distinctions are being made: notably between 'real' on the one hand, and 'reflexes', 'echoes', 'phantoms' and 'sublimates' on the other.

[9] K. Marx and F. Engels, *Historisch-kritische Gesamtausgabe* [MEGA] (Moscow, 1927–35), vol. 1, part 5, pp. 15–17.
[10] Ibid.

There are again strong and weak senses of this argument. The weak sense offers little more than the argument that the most refined forms of human thought necessarily occur within more general human activities in definite material preconditions: that human beings have to gain the resources for physical existence as a condition of doing anything else. In this weak sense there is no room for serious doubt. Yet the language of at least this early formulation indicates a stronger and more controversial sense. The language of 'reflexes', 'echoes', 'phantoms' and 'sublimates' carries the inescapable implication of a secondary activity, and then, it would seem, of 'consciousness' as a secondary activity. We have again to remember that this was part of a polemic against the assumption that the whole of human history was determined by ideas, whether human or extra-human in origin: an assumption which complacently and cruelly ignored the long history and present facts of human labour, through which the necessary physical existence and survival of human beings were gained and assured. The counter-emphasis, that human labour is central, necessary and thus genuinely originating, remains as Marx's major contribution to modern thought. But what can then be seen as happening is a way of formulating this emphasis which, ironically, is in danger of converting human labour – its 'material preconditions', 'material production' and 'material intercourse' – to, in its turn, a specialized and even reified element of human totality.

This comes out clearly in the next preceding sentences in *The German Ideology* (the argument is being deliberately read backwards, as a way of progressively analysing its assumptions):

> In total contrast to German philosophy, which descends from heaven to earth, we here ascend from earth to heaven. That is to say, we do not set out from what men say, imagine, or conceive, nor from what has been said, thought, imagined or conceived of men, in order to arrive at men in the flesh. [We begin with real, active men . . . etc.][11]

[11] Ibid.

As a statement of philosophical presupposition this is clear and admirable. It is wholly consistent, in its general emphasis, with the argument that we must begin any inquiry into human development and human activities from actual human beings in their actual conditions. But then rather more than this is actually said. The rhetorical reversal of metaphysical thought, in the proposal to 'ascend from earth to heaven', has the extraordinary literal effect, if we are reading it closely, of shifting 'what men say, imagine or conceive' and 'what has been said, thought, imagined or conceived of men' from earth to . . . heaven! Of course Marx did not literally believe this. It is a by-product of that particular polemical rhetoric. Yet a more serious question underlies the idiosyncrasy of the particular formulation.

In this way of seeing the problem, and in fact against other emphases by Marx elsewhere, there is a real danger of separating human thought, imagination and concepts from 'men's material life-process', and indeed of separating human consciousness from 'real, active men'. Taken crudely and literally, as indeed it has sometimes been taken, this is, ironically, a familiar position of bourgeois philistinism, of the kind satirized by Brecht as 'eats first, morals after', or more seriously of the kind now regularly propagated by apologists of capitalism, in the argument that we must first 'create wealth' and then, on the proceeds, 'improve the quality of life'.

Marx's central emphasis was so much on the necessary totality of human activity that any reduction of this kind has to be firmly rejected. In the matter of human labour in general it is indeed from him that we can most clearly learn a more adequate conception. Thus:

> We presuppose labour in a form that stamps it as exclusively human. A spider conducts operations that resemble those of a weaver, and a bee puts to shame many an architect in the construction of her cells. But what distinguishes the worst architect from the best of bees is this, that the architect raises his structure in imagination before he erects it in reality. At the end of every labour-process, we get a result that already existed in the imagination of the labourer at its commence-

ment. He not only effects a change of form in the material on which he works, but he also realizes a purpose of his own that gives the law to his *modus operandi*, and to which he must subordinate his will.[12]

This convincing account of the specifically human character of work includes, as will be seen, not only the foreseeing concept of what is being made but ideally integrated concepts of how and why it is being made. This is intended to enforce Marx's conception of what is truly human in labour, and thus to provide a standard from which it is reasonable to describe certain forms of human work – those in which the worker has been deprived, by force or by the possession by others of his means and conditions of production, of the necessary human qualities of foresight, decision, consciousness and control – as degraded or sub-human, in no hyperbolic sense. Thus 'real, active men', in all their activities, are full of consciousness, foresight, concepts of how and why, or to the degree that they are not have been reduced from this fully human status by social and economic conditions which practically diminish their humanity, and which it is then a central human task to change. The revolution of labour, to achieve this fully human status, is of course Marx's central political perspective.

But then it remains very strange that in the early writings, in which he wrote most directly of what we now call 'cultural' activities, Marx worked with so reduced and so vulnerable a definition of consciousness. It can of course be argued that what he then had mainly in mind was not the integrated consciousness of necessary human labour and genuine production, but what he and others could see as the phantasmagoria of religious and metaphysical speculation or the self-justifying systems of law, politics and economic theory which ratified oppression, privilege and exploitation. What he wanted to argue, we can agree, was that any and all of these impressive systems of ideas must be placed or replaced in their true social and material context, and that in that sense we should not first listen to what men 'say, imagine or conceive' – thus limiting

[12] *Capital* (London, 1954), vol. 1, p. 178.

ourselves to these selected and abstracted terms – but should rather look at the whole body of activities and conditions within which these ideas and systems were generated. When we put it like that, we are in fact describing Marx's central and most influential argument.

Yet, with many serious subsequent effects, this was not all that he actually said. His contempt for what some kinds of men 'say, imagine or conceive' – self-justifying, indifferent or fantasy-ridden accounts of a world that was after all open to fuller and more direct examination, and especially that world of necessary labour which underpinned and made possible all such apologia and speculation – rushed him into weakening his own most essential case. This case was that

> the whole previous conception of history has either completely neglected this real basis of history (the real process of production, starting out from the simple material production of life) or else has considered it as a secondary matter without any connexion with the course of history. Consequently, history has always to be written in accordance with an external standard; the real production of life appears as ahistorical, while what is historical appears as separated from ordinary life.[13]

That received and fundamental error was massively corrected, but at the cost, in some formulations, of making intellectual and cultural production, of any kind, appear to be 'immaterial'.

For, of course, even for the historical record of the real processes of production, 'the simple material production of life', it is necessary to attend, critically, to what men have said, imagined and conceived. There is important non-verbal evidence of human material production, as, most notably, in the total absence of verbal evidence, in the essentially material inquiries of prehistoric archaeology. But we have only to move from those illuminating analyses of pots, tools, weapons, work in earth and stone, to analyses which are able also to include verbal records of production, social relations and change, to

[13] MEGA, vol. 1, part 5, pp. 28–9.

realize that Marx's positive emphasis, on the inclusion of material production as historically central, is greatly enriched when we have evidence of what men of the time, in ways that of course need critical interpretation, quite materially 'said, imagined and conceived' – in practice necessarily in material ways, in writing and in work with stone, pigment and metal. The persuasive philosophical presupposition, that we must begin from active human beings, in all their evident social and cultural diversity, rather than from some abstractly imagined and conceived concept of Man, must not be weakened by what would in the end be the philistine dismissal or relegation of what actual people, in definite material conditions and by unarguably material processes – writing, printing, painting, sculpting, building – said, imagined and conceived.

Thus, at the root of the problem of Marx's contribution to a theory of culture, and with critical effect on the subsequent development of a Marxist tradition, we have to restore the practical activities which we now generalize as culture to the full social material process on which he insisted. Against the tone of some of his formulations, and against much influential subsequent interpretation of these activities as merely reflective of and secondary to the then abstracted and specialized 'material production', we have to emphasize cultural practice as from the beginning social and material, in ways with which in fact he might have been among the first to agree.

5

Is it possible to clarify these difficult problems and arguments by making a distinction which obviously comes to mind: between those intellectual and cultural processes which, as we have seen Marx arguing, are necessary elements of any form of truly human labour, and those other forms of intellectual and cultural production which are undertaken in their own terms, not as elements of another more general process but as what

Marx had called in his *Rheinische Zeitung* articles 'ends in themselves'?

The distinction seems to give us some early advantages. We can all see the difference between the exercise of intelligence and foresight in ploughing a field or planting a crop or breeding a certain type of animal and, on the other hand, the processes involved in writing a poem or composing a symphony or making a piece of sculpture. It is true that there are some obviously intermediate cases, such as making and decorating a cooking pot, or building a house with attention not only to its function as shelter but also to its appearance and style, or making clothes which not only cover us but are intended to enhance our appearance or to signify some social position. Yet it might still be possible to distinguish between work which is intended to satisfy a manifest physical need and work which, whatever its other uses, is not directly related to manifest physical need in anything like the same way.

Yet the distinctions being made here have in the end to be submitted to Marx's conception of the totality of the social process, which makes any simple extraction of certain practices as 'ends in themselves' very doubtful. There is some genuine uncertainty here in what Marx meant. The central difficulty is a confusion or slide between a simple and overwhelming assertion of the fact that human beings must eat and ensure the material conditions for their physical survival and reproduction, and the only apparently similar argument that human labour is the production and reproduction of real life in this persuasively restricted sense. It is not only that in modern economies the greater part of human labour is applied for purposes which go far beyond the assurance of food and of the conditions for survival and reproduction. Marx in fact showed very clearly that the satisfaction of basic needs, through a definite mode of production leading to certain definite social relations, *produced* new needs and new definitions of need, which in their turn became, beyond the bare necessities, the forms and objects of further production.

But it is also and more fundamentally, from the historical, anthropological and archaeological records, that even at stages of minimal or subsistence production, though then in highly variable ways, human beings apply energy not only to the isolable physically necessary tasks but, in varying degrees of connection with these, to social and cultural purposes which are from the beginning part of their distinctively human organization. We may now think we can separate their carved 'cult' or 'fertility' objects, their ceremonial practices in initiation and burial, their 'symbolic' presentation or representation of facts of kinship and identity, their dances and masks, their narratives or 'myths' of human and natural origins, as 'magical' activities or, in some of the surviving objects (the famous cave paintings are an obvious example) as 'art'. But it should be clear, if we have taken Marx's sense of the total social process, which is richly justified when any of these practices are seen in living and lived relationships with other practices, that the external categorical distinction between 'necessary material production' and other forms of activity and practice is radically misleading. On the contrary, just because the necessary material production is human and social, it is cast from the beginning in whole human and social forms: indeed precisely in those forms, which are at root forms of the practical organization and distribution of interest and energy, which we now call 'cultures'.

In its central sense, Marx would not only accept but emphasize this position:

The production of ideas, of conceptions, of consciousness, is at first directly interwoven with the material activity and the material intercourse of men, the language of real life. Conceiving, thinking, the mental intercourse of men, appear at this stage as the direct efflux of their material behaviour. The same applies to mental production as expressed in the language of politics, laws, morality, religion, metaphysics, etc., of a people. Men are the producers of their conceptions, ideas, etc., – real, active men, as they are conditioned by a definite development of their productive forces and of the intercourse corresponding to these, up to its furthest forms. Consciousness can never be anything else than conscious existence, and the existence of men is their actual life-process.[14]

Yet there are in fact still several problems, if we are to get this full central sense, and its complex implications, clear.

First, in an area that has already been discussed (for this passage again directly precedes the 'earth to heaven' and 'reflexes and echoes' formulations previously examined), there is the description of conceiving and thinking as 'efflux', which, when read in association with the later formulations, is undoubtedly reductive, not only from the observable record but from the much more acceptable earlier formulation of 'directly interwoven'. It is in the movement from a sense of the simultaneous and fundamentally indissoluble human process of conception and labour, labour and conception, to the narrower polemical sense of what is in effect a two-stage process – associated human labour, but then as its 'efflux' or 'echo', or, worse, 'phantom', the consciousness which might be seen as the very process and condition of association but which can now be virtually a by-product – that all the difficulties of Marx's own and many Marxist conceptions of culture can be seen to begin.

Then, second, there is a very puzzling combination of historical and categorical argument. The historical element is initially very clear: '*at first* directly interwoven'. This connects with one of Marx's most important cultural arguments, that the real relations between culture and society, or between art and labour, have always to be seen in terms of the particular mode of production and social order within which the relations practically occur. Thus the emphasis on 'at first directly interwoven' has to be understood in relation to his arguments about the effects of an historically subsequent *division* of labour, to the point where, very notably in modern class societies, 'mental labour' – intellectual and artistic work – can be both categorically and practically separated from 'manual labour'. This results not only in the degradation of what is marked off, in dominating and exploiting ways, as 'mere

[14] Ibid., pp. 15–17.

manual labour', deprived of its human conditions of conscious
purpose and control, but in the false separation of 'mental
labour', now held to be restricted to a certain class. The effect
is not only the undervaluation of manual labour – in practice of
the millions of manual labourers – on whom in fact the
maintenance of human life still absolutely depends. The effect
is also on the character of 'mental labour' itself. In its
separation from the basic processes of assuring human existence it is inherently more likely to develop false conceptions of
both general and specific human conditions, since it is not as
a matter of necessary practice exposed to and tested by human
activity in general. Even more, since the fact of the division of
labour, in this basic class sense, is not just a matter of different
kinds of work but of social relations which determine greater
rewards and greater respect for 'mental labour', and of these
relations as established in and protected by a specifically
exploiting and unequal social order, the operations of 'mental
labour' cannot be assumed in advance to be exclusively devoted
to 'higher' or 'the highest' human concerns, but are in many or
perhaps all cases likely to be bound up, in greater or lesser
degree, with propagation, ratification, defence, apologia, natu-
ralization of that exploiting and unequal social order itself.

This is one of Marx's most powerful arguments, and we must
return to it. But at this stage it is necessary to notice that what
is already, at least in embryo, an historical formulation of the
variable relations between necessary material production and
'what men say, imagine or conceive', becomes, too quickly, a
categorical assertion of a merely 'reflexive' relation between
what is primary and what is its 'efflux'. This loss of direction
in the argument is, however, in practice less important than the
apparent conceptual scheme which then distances the argument
from real history, by the implicit postulation of two states: 'at
first directly interwoven' and then 'in conditions of the division
of labour'. The contrast is rhetorically striking, as in many
Romantic and Utopian (and as it happens also Christian)
conceptions of a primal integration and a later fragmentation or
fall. But so broad a contrast cannot in fact be substituted for
the more complex and differentiated history of different kinds
of integration and different kinds and degrees of division of

labour, which are not the categorical but the practical and historical forms of the 'activities of real men'.

Marx would not have disagreed with this. In his studies of economic history he continually sought and exemplified the processes of specific development, within his central emphasis.

> This method of approach is not without presuppositions, but it begins with the real presuppositions and does not abandon them for a moment. Its premises are men, not in some imaginary condition of fulfilment or stability, but in their actual, empirically observable process of development under determinate conditions. As soon as this active life-process is delineated, history ceases to be a collection of dead facts as it is with the empiricists (themselves still abstract) or an illusory activity of illusory subjects, as with the idealists. Where speculation ends – in real life – real, positive science, the representation of the practical activity and the practical process of development of men begins.[15]

Yet, because of the directions he gave to his major work, in an understandable choice of emphasis on the crisis of poverty and exploitation, the recommended kind of inquiry is not carried out in relation to art and is only partly carried out in relation to intellectual systems and ideas. It would be absurd to blame Marx for this, in view of the massive achievement of the work to which he gave his primary attention, but the result has been that his occasional relatively general pronouncements in these other areas have frequently been taken in a sense quite contrary to his own emphasis on method: have been taken, that is to say, as general and then abstract presuppositions about the relations between the material process and art and ideas. The worst consequence of this is in fact the neglect of the real social and material history of the *production* of art and ideas: a form of production which, like everything else, has to be studied as 'the practical activity and the practical process of development of men'. Yet, before we can do this, in anything like Marx's terms, we have to look again at his underlying position on the division of labour.

6

It is clear that, at different times, Marx meant rather different things by this crucial concept. His most influential use, in relation to culture, could hardly be more emphatically expressed:

> The division of labour only becomes a real division from the moment when the distinction between material and mental labour appears. From this moment, consciousness *can* really imagine that it is something other than consciousness of existing practice, that it is *really* conceiving something without conceiving something *real*; from now on consciousness is in a position to emancipate itself from the world and to proceed to the formation of 'pure' theory, theology, philosophy, ethics, etc.[16]

It is a powerful emphasis, with important possibilities for analysis, but it is clear that its formulation involves two intellectual operations which actually work against Marx's central emphasis. The first of these is the significant term 'moment': a received concept from schemes of universal history and in this kind of use essentially idealist. The effect of such a term is to flatten or altogether evade the highly variable relations between 'material' and 'mental' labour, in actual history, and to substitute an ideal and ahistorical contrast, of a simple kind. It is then not surprising that, within the language of the same mode of thought, the second operation follows, in which not actual people, in specific social relations, but 'consciousness' – that now ideal category – begins to 'imagine' and to 'conceive' and can even 'emancipate itself from the

[16] Ibid., p. 21.

world'. Even when, as before, we have allowed for the
polemical intention, in an argument against the proponents of
'pure' theory, the effect of this way of thinking, even when it
has reversed the relative valuation of the categories, is to
confirm their prepotence, and then in practice to hide the
continuing determinate and thus variable social and material
conditions of all 'mental labour', including that which is offered
as the most 'pure'.

Indeed we do not have to go beyond Marx to make the point.
In thinking about production in general, he was clear that
historical evidence must prevail over categorical assumptions:

> The organization and division of labour varies according to
> the instruments of labour available. The hand mill implies a
> different division of labour from that of the steam mill. To
> begin with the division of labour in general, in order to arrive
> at a specific instrument of production – machinery – is
> therefore to fly in the face of history.[17]

But then this same point is highly relevant to the actual
processes of 'mental labour'. Even if we retain, at this point,
his categorical distinction between 'material' and 'mental'
labour (overriding, as we shall see, the diverse social and
historical conditions within which this distinction is variably
practised and theorized), it soon becomes clear, from historical
evidence, that the productive forces of 'mental labour' have, in
themselves, an inescapable material and thus social history.
Thus there are obvious differences between 'mental labour'
which is still fundamentally oral in its production and distribution, and 'mental labour' which is produced and distributed
through systems of writing and printing. The most obvious
difference is that in predominantly oral conditions the actual
process of 'mental labour' is at least in principle accessible to
all normal members of a society. The faculty of speaking and
of understanding speech has been a normal function of the most
general socialization. The faculties of writing and reading, on

[17] MEGA, vol. 1, part 6, p. 197.

the other hand, have to be specifically acquired, for the purposes of taking part, in whatever degree, in the social processes of 'mental labour'. It is then no surprise that one of the most common forms of the division between 'manual' and 'mental' labour is socially and materially specified in the capacity or incapacity to write and read. What in general argument may appear to be a categorical division has this precise social and material set of conditions. A history of writing and reading, not in the narrow technical sense but in its full social and material conditions, is then a necessary element of any 'real, positive science, the representation of the practical activity and the practical process of development of men'.

But then the division of labour, though fundamentally influenced by such developments in the forces of production, cannot be reduced to a history of technical means alone. It would, for example, be rash to claim that before the invention of writing there was no 'division between material and mental labour' in the important sense that Marx intends, which is at root a form of class division between those who have practically appropriated the general human faculties of consciousness, intention and control and those who have been made the objects of this appropriation, as the manual instruments – the 'hands' – of these other men's 'mental' decisions and intentions. The whole record of slavery in predominantly 'oral' conditions, to take no further case, argues against this. At the same time it is evident that the invention of a specific technical system, writing, provides obvious conditions in which an increasing part of the historical records, the laws and the ideas of a society, is embodied in a communicative system to which the majority of people have no or no independent access. That is a very practical form of a socially and materially inherent division of labour.

Yet again it would be rash to assert that the results of the long popular struggle for literacy – a struggle which still today is very far from complete – have abolished the underlying division between 'manual' and 'mental' labour. To be able to write and to read is a major advance in the possibility of sharing in the general culture of a literate society, but there are still typically determinate conditions in which the exercise of these faculties is differentially directed. Thus in late eighteenth-century England it was argued that the poor should be taught to read, but not to write. Reading would enable them to read the Bible, and to learn its morality, or later to read instructions and notices. Having anything to write on their own account was seen as a crazy or mischievous idea. Again, in our own time, there is an enforced division of labour, even among literate people, in the organization of modern newspapers, in which there is one class of men – editors, journalists, correspondents – who *write* and another class of men whose proposed sole function is to *print*. Any attempt by the printers to have a say in what is written is denounced as interference with the 'freedom of the press', although it is then obvious that this freedom has been wholly formulated within the enforced division of labour. It is ironic that the possessors of capital, who can buy or hire whole newspapers – the material means of production and the services of journalists and printers alike – are able in practice to intervene and define the conditions of this supposed freedom, enforcing an even more fundamental form of the division of labour, between those who possess or can purchase these means of intellectual production and those who do or can not. It is not 'consciousness' which is in a position to emancipate itself, in the production of 'pure' news or a 'free' press; it is a precise class of men, within conditions which do not at all derive from the sphere of 'mental' labour alone but from the whole social and economic relations between capital and labour of any kind.

Further, that once critical form of an historically specific shift in the division of labour, in the long and varied change from oral or primarily oral to literate and authoritatively literate material and social conditions, is not categorically reversed when, as increasingly through the twentieth century, modern 'oral' forms, in radio and television, become as important as and in the end probably more important than print. One general condition is restored, at a higher level. The capacity to receive and to transmit, through speech, is again a function of normal general socialization; it does not depend, as in the case of writing and reading, on particular forms of instruction which may be differentially distributed or altogether withheld from actual majorities. In this sense the cultural shift is radical. More people can and do express their ideas directly, and more people, with measurable social and political effects, find themselves listening to *other men and women* rather than reading, at first or second hand, written opinions described and prescribed as authoritative.

Yet a fundamental division of labour still exists, at two levels. First, because the ownership and control of these powerful systems of transmitted speech are subject to the general conditions of political and economic organization, and are in practice normally directed by state or capitalist institutions. Second, because, as a form of this, there is an attempted and typically successful distinction between those who have 'something to say', in their own right – leaders, personalities, celebrities, presenters, official performers – and what is then called 'the public' – 'the listening or viewing public' – who if they speak at all speak in that assigned capacity.

Marx would have understood the spectacle of the degeneration of that phrase of the democratic ideal – *vox populi*, the voice of the people – into the resigned or cynical *vox pop* of professional broadcasters: the essentially random selection and collection of voices at a different level of substance and recognition from those who, within the division of labour, have 'something to say'. He would also have understood, very clearly, those negative versions of an undifferentiated public, a 'mass', which find their most memorable expression in the use of 'you' to describe everyone who is not a professional journalist or broadcaster, or the limited group they recognize as individuals. 'You Write', they write, above a selection of letters from some readers, whether 'you', reading it, have written or not. 'Your Reactions', they say, introducing similar selections, whether 'you', listening, have reacted or not. There was an old radical recognition of fundamental social divisions, based in the division of labour, as 'Them' and 'Us'. Within the altered conditions of modern communication systems, there is a profoundly unradical recognition of that division of labour which has persisted even after the generalization of basic communicative skills and the development of new, relatively direct media: 'Us' (writing or speaking); 'You' (reading or listening). This is not a categorical 'moment'; it is a precise social and material form.

7

What then of the relation between the 'division of labour' and the attempted distinction between forms of mental labour which are aspects of more general productive processes and those other forms which were seen, at least by the young Marx, as 'ends in themselves'?

The examples taken thus far belong mainly to an area which is not easily distinguished by a simple contrast between 'general production' and what can be specialized, on the basis of 'ends in themselves', as 'high culture'. Most of them belong, in fact, to an area of quite material production which is yet distinguishable from certain obvious kinds of 'material production' in Marx's most limited sense. We have already looked at the problem this limited sense raises, in its too easily taken implication of 'material labour' as (only) the production of the absolute material necessities of life. In all his practical analyses, Marx was quite exceptionally aware of the profound, prolonged and intricate interaction between these basic productive processes and the social order to which, in his view, they gave rise. His famous or notorious metaphor of 'base' and 'superstructure', to express this fundamental relationship, has the effect, it is true, of underemphasizing or even hiding the forms of interaction which he characteristically recognized. If we take the metaphor literally we find that what we have, ironically, is a classic and memorable assertion of a categorical, as distinct from an historical, division of labour. The material activities all occur in the 'base'; the mental activities all in the 'superstructure'. As a polemical point against the general assumption that all human history was directed by autonomous ideas the metaphor retains its relevance and force. But as a method, or as a set of tools for analysis, it leads us in wholly wrong directions.

What we have seen in the case of general communicative (cultural) institutions is a form of activity which is in its immediate processes indissolubly mental *and* material, and in its central functions directed not only to the production of ideas but to the manifestation or ratification of a social order within which, necessarily, all the most basic material production is in practice carried on. It is possible, as a hypothetical 'moment', to define an initial situation in which human beings can do no more than provide for their absolute physical needs, and then to see all history as dependent from that material necessity. But it was Marx more than anyone else who showed 'man making himself', affecting and eventually transforming both human and natural conditions, by the processes of associated labour. Then in the fact of that association there is the outline of this or that social order, and as one of its central elements – in story, dance, marks of community and identity – a set of cultural processes. If we can begin from this real situation, in all its actual historical variety, we can avoid the pointless play of categorical priorities and begin to examine what is really in question: the process of *determination* within different but always and necessarily connected activities.

This analysis of real determinations is inevitably complex. We should not assume in advance that the basic structural relations between different kinds of activity are themselves ahistorical, yielding regular uniformities and laws which can then be applied to any specific social and historical situation. Marx had already in effect recognized this when he described the 'moment' – which in his perspectives can only be a moment in human history – 'when the distinction between material and mental labour appears'. And it is again in practice unlikely that he would have held to the idea that this is a single moment, a categorical shift, rather than the diverse and complex historical process, illuminated but neither explained nor examined by the categorical distinction, in which the true social relations even between the extremes of 'manual without mental' and 'mental without manual' labour but more significantly between the very variable degrees of 'manual with mental' and 'mental with manual' can alone be discovered.

This argument bears heavily against the most widely known

cultural proposition in Marx, in the formula of 'base and superstructure'. Yet of course it bears just as heavily against the dominant modern proposition that there are forms of 'mental labour' which can be assumed, categorically, to be 'ends in themselves': that proposition which, as we saw, Marx in his earliest writing picked up and repeated. It is then not a matter of trading adversary quotations within Marx's own work. The least useful form of the important argument which these alternative propositions introduce is also, unfortunately, the most common form, in which indiscriminate and absolute, non-historical positions are pitted each against the other. What Marx himself did, to make possible a more discriminating inquiry, was in this area relatively sketchy and unfinished. But we can look in more detail at what he actually did, first in relation to art and then in relation to ideas.

8

Two discussions of art stand out: that on Raphael and others in *The German Ideology*, and that on Greek art in the *General Introduction* (1857) to the *Critique of Political Economy*. First, on Raphael, where he is arguing against Stirner:

> [He] imagines that Raphael produced his pictures independently of the division of labour that existed in Rome at the time. If he were to compare Raphael with Leonardo da Vinci and Titian, he would know how greatly Raphael's works of art depended on the flourishing of Rome at that time, which occurred under Florentine influence, while the works of Leonardo depended on the state of things in Florence, and the works of Titian, at a later period, depended on the totally different development of Venice. Raphael as much as any other artist was determined by the technical advances in art made before him, by the organization of society and the division of labour in all the countries with which his locality had intercourse. Whether an individual like Raphael suc-

ceeds in developing his talent depends wholly on demand,
which in turn depends on the division of labour and the
conditions of human culture resulting from it.[18]

This, as far as it goes, is an identifiable 'sociological' position,
readily translated into a particular kind of 'art history'. It would
be very difficult to deny its most general propositions, which
are now in effect commonplace. It is useful that Marx includes
'technical advances in art' as well as more general social and
historical conditions, but this is not much more than a passing
reference, to what within Marx's general perspective should be
seen as a central fact: the material history of painting itself, of
which the painters themselves were very much aware in its
immediately accessible form as techniques of work (labour).
More emphasis is given to general factors of social environment
and demand, which can certainly be confirmed from this and
similar histories. But there is then an evident gap, between the
briefly mentioned technical dimension (in fact the 'manual
labour' of painting) and a general environment. And in fact it
is in that gap, in that area of actual intersections between a
material process, general social conditions, and the unmen-
tioned assumptions about the purposes and content of art within
those conditions, that the decisive questions about the art itself
are to be found. By including the specific social and historical
conditions Marx has usefully broadened the scope of the
inquiry, but he has not then made it.

In fact, in his argument against Stirner, he passes at once to
a different though related case:

In proclaiming the uniqueness of work in science and art,
Stirner adopts a position far inferior to that of the bourgeoisie. At the present time it has already been found
necessary to organize this 'unique' activity ... In Paris, the
great demand for vaudevilles and novels brought about the
organization of work for their production, organization

[18] *The German Ideology*, in K. Marx, *Selected Writings*, ed. D. McLellan
(Oxford, 1977), p. 189.

which at any rate yields something better than its 'unique' competitors in Germany.[19]

This is a potentially important point, but it is hurriedly and even carelessly made. It is indeed a fact, against simple assertions of all works of art as 'ends in themselves', that a major part of modern cultural production is commercially organized, and that at least some work has from the beginning this commercial intention – the work of art as a saleable commodity – while much other work has a mixture of commercial and other intentions. Moreover this is an historically traceable development, from conditions of state and ecclesiastical patronage to the conditions of a developing capitalist market (I have described these historical conditions and phases in *Culture* [London: Fontana, 1981]).

But then, precisely because these conditions have a real history, with consequently variable relations between artists and their societies, the argument cannot be conducted, positively or negatively, around simple general propositions. Moreover, Marx's persuasive recognition of the extent to which modern cultural production has been 'organized by the market' remains relatively external. What does it mean to say 'the great demand for vaudevilles and novels'? Everything that Marx wrote elsewhere about 'demand', in the complexities of changing modes of production, must prevent us accepting any 'great demand' of this kind as some sort of primary cause. The conditions not only of demand but of production, and these within much more general social conditions, need to be specifically analysed before the argument can be rationally pursued, and the danger of course is that the merely polemical position can become, quite quickly, a reductive account of the making of art, against which, in its turn, a sublimated account, taking little or no notice of conditions which have unquestionably influenced and often determined actual production, is complacently reasserted. This is the more likely in the tone of Marx's remark about 'a position far inferior to that of the bourgeoisie', which gives bourgeois arrangements altogether

[19] Ibid.

too much credit and merely evades the persistent problem: that at least some art, made within determinate social conditions, is not reducible to their most general character but has qualities which attract such descriptions as 'uniqueness' or 'ends in themselves'.

In a later argument, Marx seems well aware of this:

It is well known that certain periods of highest development of art stand in no direct connection with the general development of society, nor with the material basis and the skeleton structure of its organization. Witness the example of the Greeks as compared with modern art or even Shakespeare. As concerns certain forms of art, e.g., the *epos*, it is even acknowledged that as soon as the production of art as such appears they can never be produced in their epoch-making, classical aspect; and accordingly, that in the domain of art certain of its important forms are possible only at an undeveloped stage of art development. If that is true of the mutual relations of different modes of art within the domain of art itself, it is far less surprising that the same is true of the relations of art as a whole to the general development of society. The difficulty lies only in the general formulation of these contradictions. No sooner are they made specific than they are clarified.[20]

This is some of Marx's most developed thinking about art, yet it is obviously still uncertain and unfinished. It has the great merit of recommending specific analysis, and of recognizing the problem which he had defined in an earlier note as 'the unequal relation between the development of material production and, e.g., artistic production'.[21] Yet it is limited by what are really preconceptions rather than ideas of 'progress' and 'development'.

Marx did not want to apply the idea of material progress to the history of art; his attachment to early Greek art was much too strong for that. All he can then fall back on, however, is the

[20] Cit. Baxandall and Morawski, *op. cit.*, p. 134.
[21] Ibid.

extraordinary proposition that 'in the domain of art certain of its important forms are possible only at an undeveloped stage of art development', which, insofar as it means anything, leads straight to an identification of art with naivety, and is then no more than a familiar kind of reactionary Romanticism. In fact he goes on to explain the continuing aesthetic appeal of Greek art in terms of the Greeks as 'normal children', its 'eternal charm' as inseparably connected with 'unripe social conditions'. He even generalizes this as 'the historical childhood of humanity'.

It is difficult to believe that this is the Marx of the major work. His recognition of the problem is important. It belongs to the breadth of interest that we recognized at the beginning. But his offered solution is absurd. It is not only that Classical Athens was not, by any timescale, the 'historical childhood of humanity'; it is altogether too late for that. It is, more crucially, that the forms of Greek art and writing of which we have knowledge are unarguably mature, in their own terms. It is their long prehistory, only sketchily available, that might attract analysis of development, but even then it would be real development, in specific social and material processes, rather than the hazy idealism of an 'undeveloped stage of art development'.

There is indeed need to recognize what Marx called 'unequal relations' of development. But the underlying problem here is the two possible senses of 'unequalness' or, better, 'unevenness'. Thus it can be argued and indeed demonstrated that in particular social orders there is uneven development of various human faculties and practices. Such unevenness is wholly open to Marxist analysis, which can show how particular social orders and particular modes of production select certain faculties and practices for development within determinate general conditions, and by the same token neglect or even repress certain others. Moreover this can also be seen as more than conscious selection, or neglect and repression. In some important cases the character of the basic material production processes makes possible the development and extension of certain kinds of art (steam-machinery, the chemical industry, electronics are obvious examples), and there is almost always some significant relation between material production in general and the material processes in art. In either case, the uneven development of human faculties and practices has a discoverable social and material history.

On the other hand 'unevenness' can be construed, as in fact in Marx's argument about the Greeks, in terms of a generalized world history, where the problem is the evident lack of correlation between *increased* material production and *qualitatively better* art. But it must then be asked why this is seen as a problem at all. It is only from a very crude and undiscriminated idea of progress that it could ever be assumed that there is a regular relation between increased production and the quality of art. Marx was at once attracted to a notion of increased production as an index of general human progress (obviously in some senses a reasonable idea but at times involving ambiguities and even absurdities in the historical judgment of social orders which have increased production through increasing exploitation) and at the same time deeply committed to an idea of the general development of all human faculties and resources. When he took this uncertainty, between what are at times incompatible ideas, into the question of art, he could do little more than restate or evade it, though the necessary way through the problem, in terms of *contradiction*, was elsewhere one of his major methods of analysis.

For it is a fact of historical variation that art in general, and then arts of different kinds, are differentially valued in different social orders and in their own internal phases. It is this historical specificity, rather than a generalizing progress, which is the ground for any history or historical analysis of the arts. There is still the problem of quality, but here Marx simply reverts to the received idealist notion of absolute, indeed 'classical', quality. It is not necessary to deny the effectively permanent value, within traceable historical and cultural continuities, of certain works of art from many historical periods, to be able to argue that *judgment* also, in its real terms of accessibility, recognition, understanding of theme and form, comparison, is itself an historical process. This need not mean that all judgments are relative, though that many of them are, including some of the most confident, is easily proved from the record.

But it does mean, in ways which Marx elsewhere would quickly have recognized, and indeed in some other areas discovered and taught, that the processes of reception and judgment, quite as much as the processes of original production, occur within definite social relations.

Moreover, in the case of art, where simple physical consumption is not in question, no work is in any full practical sense produced until it is also received. The social and material conditions of the original production are indeed stable: the material object (painting, sculpture) or the material notations (music, writing) are there, if they survive, once for all. Yet until a further (and in practice variable) social and material process occurs, necessarily including its own conditions and expectations, the objects and the notations are not fully available for response. Often the varying conditions and expectations of response actually alter the object or the notation as it is *then* perceived and valued. Yet there are also some important continuities, which in Marxist terms do not relate to some unchanging pre-given human nature, nor to notions of the 'childhood' or 'maturity' of humanity, but to a range of human faculties, resources and potentials – some of the most important based in a relatively unchanged human biological constitution; others in persistent experiences of love and parentage and death, qualified but always present in all social conditions; others again in the facts of human presence in a physical world – with which certain works connect, in active and powerful ways, often apparently beyond the limited fixed ideas of any particular society and time.

Thus the question of value, in Marxist terms, while often a matter of direct and immediate social analysis – as in practice Marx exemplified – can be also, in more complex cases, a combination, in varying proportions, of such direct and immediate analysis and a more extensive, more open recognition and analysis of forms of material production – *works* of art – which embody and activate elements of that range of human faculties, resources and potentials which is factually wider than the determinations of any particular social order and which, both as historical evidence and as revolutionary aspiration, is the practical expression of actual and possible human development. This ultimate point of reference, not ideal but practical in those forms of material production which we distinguish as major art, is of course very relevant to Marx, who drew from it, sometimes with explicit reference to art as its evidence, his ideas of the overcoming of human alienation (from its own possible fully human conditions and resources) and his most general ideas of the necessity and object of social revolution.

9

To move from Marx on art to Marx on ideas is to enter a very different and much more authoritative dimension. It is here that his major contribution to cultural theory was made.

> In order to study the connexion between intellectual and material production it is above all essential to conceive the latter in its determined historical form and not as a general category. For example, there corresponds to the capitalist mode of production a type of intellectual production quite different from that which corresponded to the medieval mode of production. Unless material production itself is understood in its specific historical form, it is impossible to grasp the characteristics of the intellectual production which corresponds to it or the reciprocal action between the two.[22]

We have already looked at some of the fundamental difficulties in the *categorical* distinction between, and then separation of, 'intellectual' and 'material' production. Yet, while retaining the necessary emphases that were then made, we can look at this part of Marx's work as a way of understanding his critical concept of *determination*.

It is already, as this passage shows, a matter of historically specific determinations, rather than some categorical law of

[22] *Theorien uber den Mehrwert* (Berlin, 1956), vol 1, p. 381.

regular determination, of the kind indicated by crude application of the 'base-superstructure' metaphor. But then this recognition is relevant to some of his other arguments on this matter. Thus:

> The ideas of the ruling class are, in every age, the ruling ideas: i.e., the class which is the dominant *material* force in society is at the same time its dominant *intellectual* force. The class which has the means of material production at its disposal has control at the same time over the means of mental production, so that in consequence the ideas of those who lack the means of mental production are, in general, subject to it.[23]

This early formulation can be read as a categorical proposition, but it can more usefully be taken as an *historical* proposition, which can then be tested by specific evidence. As such it is in practice of great value. Marx's welcome emphasis, here, on 'the means of mental production', as distinct from other abstract uses of 'mental production' as if it were an unlocated 'consciousness', shows us where to look for certain fundamental conditions of intellectual production and distribution. And then we do find, again and again, that such conditions and controls are practically decisive, indeed determining. It is the point which Marx's enemies can never forgive him for making, and that yet, from repeated practical experience – down to the contemporary controls exercised by corporate capitalism, most notably in the press – has quite relentlessly to be made.

Yet it is necessary even here to recognize socially specific and differential forms of determination. The weakest case is that which Marx actually goes on, in this passage, to make:

> The dominant ideas are nothing more than the ideal expression of the dominant material relationships, the dominant material relationships grasped as ideas, and thus of the

[23] MEGA, vol. 1, part 5, p. 35.

Sumpton / W.D.

071 630 7769.

13. Santa Bend

Jocey. Thomson B.A.[Hons.]

Reluctant 1st4A

Applied

Access course Oppington.

(Goldsmith) Eng. 1yrs

Brickwork, Hum. B.A. (Hons.)

relationships which make one class the ruling one; they are consequently the ideas of its dominance.[24]

The fact that this is often true, especially in systems of law and political constitution, but at times also more generally, should not hurry us into accepting the assertion that such ideas are 'nothing more than' the ideal expression of dominance.

For, first, the argument is too static. It is often the case, as even in law and political theory, to say nothing of natural philosophy and moral argument, that there are historical continuities and effects in certain bodies of thinking which make them more than locally determined by specific and temporary forms of dominance. None of them can ever be put *above* history, but the historical process, in this as in other respects, includes both *residual* and *emergent* forms of thought and belief, which can in practice enter into very complex relations with the more specifically and locally dominant. In any developed social order, we can expect to find not only interaction but also actual conflict between residual, dominant and emergent forms of thought, in general as well as in special areas. Moreover there is often conflict, related to this complexity, between different versions of the dominant, which is by no means always a ready translation of a singular material class interest.

This point connects, second, with the fact that, in class-dominated social orders, there are not only variable relations between different classes, with varied effects in intellectual work (of the kind Marx indeed later recognized in his observation that 'the existence of revolutionary ideas in a particular age presupposes the existence of a revolutionary class'[25]) but also complex relations between *fractions* of the dominant class, which in highly developed orders is more often a coalition or amalgam of particular material interests than a quite singular interest. This internal complexity, within dominance, has to be related to an internal division which Marx himself describes:

[24] Ibid.
[25] Ibid., p. 36.

Within [the ruling] class one part appears as the thinkers of the class (its active conceptualizing ideologists, who make it their chief source of livelihood to develop and perfect the illusions of the class about itself), while the others have a more passive and receptive attitude to these ideas and illusions... This cleavage ... may even develop into a certain hostility and opposition between the two parts, but in the event of a practical collision in which the class itself is endangered, it disappears of its own accord ...[26]

This is suggestive but too simple. The division of labour between ideologists and active members of the ruling class is already subject to the fact of fractional interests. But also, within such a division of labour, specialized intellectual institutions come to develop not only their own local material interests but more crucially their internal intellectual criteria and continuities. These lead often to evident asymmetries and incongruities with more general institutions of the class, and indeed to conflicts, including internal and external intellectual conflicts. Very complex relations then occur, in much more than 'two parts', and these kinds of 'hostility and opposition' do not, on the record, 'disappear of their own accord'. Such relations are much affected by the fact of variable distance, as Engels later noted, between different forms of thought and direct political and material interests. But the complexity is not reducible to the facts of relative distance (as between, say, philosophy and law) alone; this can be seen, for example, in the serious internal divisions within modern capitalist *economic* thought.

Nevertheless, though needing these major qualifications as the means to any veridical analysis, Marx's central insistence on determining pressures, exercised by the material relations of a social order on both the practice and the nature of many if not all kinds of intellectual work, is to be welcomed as a revolutionary advance. Yet it is not only a matter of direct or indirect pressures. It is also, as the other crucial process of determination, a matter of practical and theoretical limits. Marx

[26] Ibid.

expressed this position in a remarkable analysis of mid-nineteenth-century France:

> What makes them representatives of the petty bourgeoisie (though 'according to their education and individual position they may be as far apart as heaven and earth') is the fact that in their minds they do not get beyond the limits which the latter do not get beyond in life, that they are consequently driven, theoretically, to the same problems and solutions to which material interest and social position drive the latter practically. This is, in general, the relationship between the *political* and *literary representatives* of a class and the class they represent.[27]

This can be taken too simply, but it is the source of the important modern Marxist conception of *homology*, or formal correspondence, between certain kinds of art and thought and the social relations within which they are shaped. This conception can reveal determining relations at a quite different level from the bare proposition that 'ideas are nothing more than the ideal expression of the dominant material relationships'; among other reasons in the fact that something more than reflection or representation is then often in question, and art and ideas can be seen as structurally formed, but then also actively formed, in their own terms, within a general social order and its complex internal relations.

Marx's other productive emphasis, which can in general be taken as decisive, is his argument that dominant ideas (and, we might add, dominant artistic *forms*) take on, in the period of their dominance, the appearance of universality: a dominant class employs

> an ideal formula, to give its ideas the form of universality and to represent them as the only rational and universally valid ones.[28]

[27] *The Eighteenth Brumaire of Louis Bonaparte*, in K. Marx and F. Engels, *Selected Works* (Moscow, 1962), vol. 1, p. 275.
[28] MEGA, vol. 1, part 5, p. 36.

The immense pressure of these notions of universal validity has been so major a factor in intellectual history, their deeply graved habits of mind so difficult to escape from, not only in intellectual work but in everyday practice and assumption (the ruling but in fact historically conditioned 'common sense' which Gramsci identified as the central element of *hegemony*, within and beyond direct dominance) that it is in this great challenge by Marx that much of his most general intellectual importance is to be found.

10

To learn from Marx is not to learn formulae or even methods, and this is especially the case, as has been argued, in those parts of his work, on art and ideas, where he was not able to develop or to demonstrate his most interesting suggestions, or was actually still limited by the dominant ideas of his time. The two areas in which this lack of development has been most limiting are, first, the history of the social and material means and conditions of cultural production, which needs to be established in its own terms as a necessary part of any historical materialism; and, second, the nature of language, which Marx recognized, briefly, as material, and defined as 'practical consciousness', but which for just these reasons is a more central and fundamental element of the whole social process than was recognized in the later propositions of 'manual' and 'mental', 'base' and 'superstructure', 'reality' and 'consciousness'. It is only from the most active senses of the material production of culture and of language as a social and material process that it is possible to develop the kind of cultural theory which can now be seen as necessary, and even central, in Marx's most general theory of human production and development. That he did not develop such a cultural theory, and indeed that from some more limited formulations misleading forms of 'Marxist' cultural theory were developed and propagated, in ways that actually blocked the inquiry, must now be acknowledged. Yet it remains true that the thrust of his general work is still, apart from social life itself, the most active inspiration for the making of such a cultural theory, even where we have not only to interpret but to change it.

History

Victor Kiernan

When Engels late in life described the founders of bourgeois philosophy as adventurous minds, not cramped like their successors by specialization and narrowing horizons, and often working out their thoughts amid the noise and heat of contemporary strife,[1] he must have had in mind the founders of socialism as well. At any rate it was very true of Marx and himself. They grew up close to the main highroad of modern events, exposed to the pressure of forces old and new but not yet overpoweringly complex. On one side they had in their ears the whistle of the steam-engine, on the other the snores of an elder Europe whose torpor even the French Revolution seemed to have disturbed only for a moment. They might well have an intuition, not illusory, that humanity was entering an age of ordeal and decision, and must at all costs find the right way.

They plunged into the search for it with an ardour which ensured that their ideas were many and bold, but irregularly thrown off, and left in the end in a form into which diverse meanings could be read. In his funeral speech Engels claimed for his friend, besides many minor discoveries, two vast ones: 'the law of development of human history', and the special law of capitalist development. A century later we are still far from being able to feel that we understand the human record; and Marx was no more than a self-taught and occasional historian. Yet we can say of him, what T.S. Eliot said was the mark of a great poet, that after him no one else can write without having to take account of him.

'I am one that am nourished by my victuals,' the hungry servant in Shakespeare protests to his love-lorn master, feeding on amorous fancies; a stock contrast of plebeian with aristocrat, and an expression of the common sense of mankind. This

[1] F. Engels, *Dialectics of Nature* (English edn: Moscow, 1953), pp. 2–3.

instinctive sense of the primacy of the material, with food in first place, was elaborated by writers of the eighteenth-century Enlightenment into a treatment of history as a succession of epochs each marked by its own type of economy, starting with hunting and fishing and going on to agriculture.[2] Four main stages were recognized, or 'modes of subsistence' as they were called by the brilliant 'Scottish school' of theorists, stimulated by the rapid transformation their country was undergoing as Marx and Engels were by that of Western Europe. A more abrupt scene-changing in 1789 shed lurid light on the dynamics of change. It was clear that the ascendancy of a nobility was being supplanted by that of an upper-middle or business class. That this meant also an economic shift to a more positively capitalist organization was nearly as obvious.

Lenin was to point out that French historians after 1815 were finding the key to history in the tug of war of rival classes.[3] Kautsky declared that by the 1840s 'all the essential elements of the materialist conception of history had been supplied', and were only waiting to be fused together by socialist insight.[4] So much was 'Marxism' in the air by that time, Engels himself remarked some years after Marx's death, that the same conception was discovered independently by an untutored German workingman, Joseph Dietzgen.[5] During the early 1840s circumstances were carrying Marx and Engels out of their somnolent Germany into France with its lively political spirit kindled by the Revolution, and England, well ahead with its machine industry. New surroundings helped to bring together their scattered sources of inspiration, and set them on the track of a way of thinking that would combine them all. It could be most readily looked for in the field of history, with its inexhaustible materials waiting to be classified and arranged, for the elucidation of the present and charting of the future. To them by now this meant a socialist future, and it was the

[2] See R.L. Meek, *Social Science and the Ignoble Savage* (Cambridge, 1976).
[3] V.I. Lenin, 'Marx' (1914), in *Marx, Engels, Marxism* (collection of articles), ed. J. Fineberg (English edn: London, 1936), p. 14.
[4] K. Kautsky, *Ethics and the Materialist Conception of History* (1906), tr. J.B. Askew (fourth edn: Chicago, 1918), p. 14.
[5] F. Engels, *Ludwig Feuerbach and the End of Classical German Philosophy* (Berlin, 1886), section IV.

working class they had in view as the new social force destined to give history its next great push forward.

Germany had no historians worth the name, in their opinion, because it had no national history, whereas France and England had at least made a start at writing history on rational lines, including economic history in which the Germans were most deficient.[6] Neither of the two could think of turning himself into a professional historian, carrying out first-hand research on the principles that were being worked out; their aim from first to last was to get a bird's-eye view of history, from which its broad outline and patterns of change could be mapped. For facts this meant relying on others. How much of their method they borrowed from Hegel and his 'dialectic' has never ceased to be a vexed question. One view is that Marx turned his back on the dialectic as soon as he emancipated himself from Hegelian philosophy, and only sparingly returned to it in later years.[7] A second is that he rejected it, in his reaction against idealism, for a good many years, but thereafter adopted it afresh, so that his theory of history is properly called 'dialectical materialism', even if he did not give it that title himself.[8] A third is that he and Engels never really abandoned it.[9] They seldom wrote history, or even discussed it between themselves, in the set terms of Hegelian logic. Yet it may be safest on the whole to conclude that its main concepts, resorted to more often instinctively than consciously, continued to be part of the way they thought about complex processes and interactions.

In the mid-1840s a number of essays by Marx, some published, others not, show him exploring various angles of history, with sharpening clarity. As a German he was closer to the European past than his French, still more his English, contemporaries. He noticed how obsolescent regimes are apt to undergo a reversal, and gave as an instance that absolutist

[6] K. Marx and F. Engels, *The German Ideology*, English edn of parts 1 and 3, ed. R. Pascal (London, 1938), p. 38.
[7] See for this view, with a wealth of detail, M. Rubel, in *Rubel on Karl Marx: Five Essays*, ed. J. O'Malley and K. Algozin (Cambridge, 1981).
[8] See, e.g., H. Lefebvre, *Dialectical Materialism* (1938; English edn: London, 1968), pp. 81–2, 86. Cf. J. Seigel, *Marx's Fate* (Princeton, 1978), pp. 320ff.
[9] G. Plekhanov, *Fundamental Problems of Marxism* (1908), tr. E. and C. Paul (London, n.d.), pp. 25–6.

government in his day favoured decentralization, instead of as earlier its opposite, the centralism 'wherein consists its proper civilizing activity'; and it was now impeding trade and industry instead of fostering them, and turning for support away from the towns to the countryside.[10]

In the summer of 1843 he was busy studying English history, and the English, French and American revolutions: the New World was having its share in forming his outlook. He was looking on the civil war in seventeenth-century England as what Marxists would learn to call a 'bourgeois revolution', and was dissatisfied with its presentation by Guizot, the French right-wing liberal politician and historian. Guizot thought of the issue between Charles I and parliament in merely political terms, he complained; and the real reason why the revolution, and more still its 1688 pendent, could be praised by Guizot as so admirably moderate was that most of the big landlords originated from the Reformation, and were a class not in conflict but rather in complete harmony with bourgeois life. They were in fact 'not feudal but middle-class'.[11] Intensive research has not altogether confirmed this diagnosis, but its author was a historian making a very promising start.

In 1844 insurrections of weavers in factories in Silesia and Bohemia deeply impressed Marx and Engels as harbingers of revolution of another sort, and a display of class-conscious militancy. These impressionable young men may have derived from them an over-hopeful estimate of the innate revolutionariness of the proletariat; but in 1845, thus heartened, they felt ready to embark on an all-round exposition of their ideas. The result, *The German Ideology*, was a bundle of long essays, some on topics of less permanent interest than others; the first and most momentous, on the post-Hegelian philosopher Feuerbach, was in reality their 'first and most comprehensive statement of historical materialism'.[12] It is brimful of originality, along with the exhilaration of discovery. At the same time, in

---

[10] 'Moralizing Criticism and Critical Morality' (1847), in *Karl Marx: Selected Essays*, tr. H.J. Stenning (London, n.d.), p. 152. (K. Marx and F. Engels, *Werke* [Berlin, 1964], vol. 4, p. 347.)

[11] 'The English Revolution', in H.J. Stenning, *op. cit.*, pp. 202–5.

[12] R. Pascal, Preface to *The German Ideology*, *op. cit.*, p. ix.

their minds their picture of history was a strictly objective one; their business was to set up in place of 'Utopian socialism' a 'scientific socialism' which demanded an equally rigorous study of history as its groundwork, not a propagandist mythology.

They were feeling their way towards a very broad threefold demarcation: an epoch of 'primitive communism', or 'clan society'; a second, relatively brief but dynamic, of class division; then a synthesis of these two, socialism or classless society on a high technological level. About the number and character of stages within the second time-span, their speculations were to take many turns. What were to be known as their 'modes of production' were a more complex version of the stages chalked out by their predecessors. Each was a combination of two pairs, tools and materials making up the 'forces of production', labour power and social organization the 'relations of production'.[13] Each formed an unstable compound, to whose internal disharmonies the current of change could be traced. None could be permanent, for alterations in what we may call in sum the potential of production would affect everything else, and prompt another class to strive for the dominant position.

These salient features were most readily identified close at hand, in European feudalism and capitalism. It was not far-fetched to argue that feudalism was brought to an end by production on new, capitalist lines growing up within it and releasing new ambitions. It has been observed that the notion of productive energy straining at the leash of an antiquated framework could easily be drawn from the condition of Germany in the 1840s; 'this was certainly how things looked to liberals and industrialists at the time'.[14] As a further step, it was open to Marx and Engels to forecast that in a similar though not identical fashion industrial potential would swell to proportions which the capitalist framework would find it impossible to contain – as may well seem to be happening today.

[13] A good exposition will be found in V. Venable, *Human Nature: the Marxian View* (London, 1946), pp. 82ff. Cf. D.R. Gandy, *Marx and History* (University of Texas Press, 1979), pp. 129ff.
[14] J.M. Maguire, *Marx's Theory of Politics* (Cambridge, 1978), p. 53; he draws on T.S. Hamerow's account of Germany.

There was always an ambiguity in the argument between two postulated strains on each system in turn: this inner tension between 'forces of production' and 'relations of production', and an outward, more visible one between ruling and subordinate classes. These two could not coincide with any exactness, and from then on Marx and Engels – and their successors – would try to combine them with emphasis now on one, now on the other. To a man of action like Lenin it would be natural enough to think of class struggle as the Open Sesame to history. To Marx and Engels as philosophers of history it was the other contradiction that was fundamental, and represented their basic hypothesis.

Using their words in a somewhat different sense (as, it cannot be denied, they too frequently did[15]) they tried to bring practical realities home to the German mind by asserting that 'Not criticism but revolution is the driving force of history.'[16] In the shape of revolution, and of class struggle more at large, they were stressing, now as later, the *ultima ratio* of physical force. In the shape of war, on the other hand, their aim was to minimize its significance, reduce it to mere sound and fury. Their interest was in production, not destruction. 'Up till now,' they wrote, 'violence, war, pillage, rape and slaughter, etc., have been accepted as the driving force of history.'[17] They controverted this by maintaining that no martial prowess could override economic limits, and victors have had to adapt themselves to 'the stage of development of the productive forces they find in existence'; hence after the barbarian invasions of the Roman empire 'the conquerors very soon took over language, culture and manners from the conquered.'[18]

But this was very far from being the whole story of the beginnings of medieval Europe. And the further afield they looked, the harder it proved to find situations fitting into their formula. Rome itself, the mighty ancestor with whom every European has to come to terms, offered many puzzles. The empire, and slavery which they assumed to be 'the basis of the

---

[15] Cf. M. Evans, *Karl Marx* (London, 1975), pp. 64, 68, 71.
[16] *The German Ideology*, p. 29.
[17] Ibid., p. 10.
[18] Ibid., p. 62.

whole productive system',[19] had been built on conquest. On their own showing it would appear a counter-productive system, rather than an enlargement of output; for they held that Rome's decline was caused by over-concentration of landowning in Italy, with slaves replacing free farmers ruined by an influx of tribute corn from the provinces.

Imperfect success is not to be wondered at in such an enterprise, an attempt to make sense of history by finding a logic underlying its apparent confusion. In the course of it they were finding novel things to say, though none worked out with any fullness, about incidental problems they came up against, always trying to follow the precept laid down early in the work that the historian must in every case analyse 'the connection of the social and political structure with production'.[20] It was a fruitful idea, capable of many applications, that the state which arose with the cleavage between individual and community was in one way a substitute for the old tribal community, in an illusory form to be sure but with a firm foothold in the surviving sentiment of solidarity.[21] There is an explanation to be found here of why kings, as personifications of state or pseudo-community, continued for so many ages to be revered by the masses whom they took the lead in exploiting.

The thought is carried on into another, that so long as classes are indeterminate, not yet hardened into their modern distinctness, the state retains a considerable measure of independence from them all, because 'no one section of the population can achieve dominance over the others.'[22] This they held was still true of their Germany. In other words, the now habitual Marxist view of every type of state as controlled by a ruling class does not correspond with the conclusion Marx and Engels came to in the formative days of their thinking about history, however true it may be to call governments of our own day executive committees of the capitalists.

Western Europe's transition from medieval to modern may well rank as the greatest new departure in all human history. On

[19] Ibid., pp. 10–11.
[20] Ibid., p. 13.
[21] Ibid., pp. 22–4, 72, 75.
[22] Ibid., pp. 59–60.

the political side it was accompanied by the 'absolute' monarchy, whose bearings can be very variously judged. Marx and Engels referred to it often, and in a style oddly closer to what is now conventional than 'Marxist', as an autonomous power. They could do so because of their concept of the state as substitute community, which could be supposed to act and sometimes believe itself to be acting for the common good against anti-social groups. By the sixteenth century, according to *The German Ideology*, men of business had grown so strong that 'the princes took up their interests in order to overthrow the feudal nobility by means of the bourgeoisie.'[23] A variation on the same theme can be found in a sketch of Spanish history by Marx a decade later. He depicted the Comunero rebels of 1520 (one-sidedly, if we go by some recent interpretations) as defenders of medieval liberties against a ruler endeavouring to turn feudal into absolute monarchy: they failed because of hostility between nobility and townsmen – regarded by Marx as roughly equal in strength – which enabled the crown first to defeat the rebel towns with the help of the nobles, and then to turn on the latter.[24]

Ultimately the hypothesis Marx and Engels were hammering out in 1845–6 ought, if valid, to throw light on how all thought and culture have been related to economic life. This they never fully brought their minds to bear on, though numerous and often striking pointers are scattered through their writings. In this joint work, and later on at times as well, they were laying heavy emphasis on the material substratum of the human record. They themselves were clearly impatient to break out from their native German atmosphere, bulging with nebulous or gaseous abstractions, a monstrous quantity of cerebration to every pennyworth of hard fact. They were both moreover lively young men with strong literary leanings and a taste for mordant satire, quite ready at times to say things startlingly in order *épater les bourgeois*.

'Ideology' in their title stood for a special sort of mental activity, or social psychology, set forth in their opening

[23] Ibid., p. 60.
[24] K. Marx and F. Engels, *Revolution in Spain* (collected articles; New York, 1939), pp. 22–4.

statement: 'Hitherto men have constantly made up for themselves false conceptions about themselves,' and they were now in need of liberation from 'phantoms of their brains' which imprisoned them.[25] Every society, that is, exhales from its collective life accepted but largely bogus notions about the way it lives. Many are purveyed by professional ideologues; this has been furthered by the separation, always emphasized by Marx and Engels, of mental from physical as division of labour advanced.[26] Ideas thus hatched, they also warned, have been taken too much at face value by later minds of similar cast. Historians have imagined the illusions of past epochs about themselves to be true – a reminder still pertinent, and followed by a sardonic comparison between the gullible scholar and the plain shopkeeper, 'very well able to distinguish between what somebody professes to be and what he really is'.[27]

Bent on brushing away all such cobwebs, Marx and Engels could dismiss 'ideology' as no more than a mechanical reflection of social life, with no vitality of its own, 'no history, no development'; they used the simile of a camera obscura, reproducing images faithfully, but upside down.[28] Even of ideology with their restricted meaning this was an inadequate account, if only because ideas with no energy of their own could not acquire the sway attributed to them. Sometimes, too, Marx and Engels, and some of their later followers much more, were tempted to see all ideas, including far more complex or subtle ones, as no more than shadows of material life, instead of looking for reciprocal interactions.

No publisher was forthcoming, and with magnificent prodigality the manuscript was abandoned, as its authors said, to the gnawing criticism of the mice. Re-reading it forty years later Engels recalled that the vital first section was unfinished. It is understandable that they may have come to feel that they were getting out of their depth; but his verdict that the work only proved 'how incomplete at that time was our knowledge of

[25] *The German Ideology*, p. 1.
[26] Ibid., pp. 20–1.
[27] Ibid., pp. 30, 43.
[28] Ibid., p. 14.

economic history'[29] did it vastly less than justice. Mere fragment though it might be, it was a milestone in the evolution of historical thinking, even if scarcely any of its propositions would be repeated exactly by any Marxist today. It seems extraordinary, and is certainly lamentable, that they never found time to take it up again together. Most of their work was very haphazardly done, and this is exceptionally true of their theory of history, despite the importance they unmistakably attached to it.

Distractions followed, and in 1848 they were plunged into the maelstrom of the European revolutions; another hindrance to quiet study, but their experiences inspired several writings on the events of 1848–9 and their sequel. In all of these, history as the backcloth of politics was in evidence, and the fact that Marx and Engels owed part of their understanding of it to their share, however modest, in making it, lends point to their comments on the contemporary scene. They could find confirmation of some of their theorems in what had been happening. Austria between 1815 and 1848 had been insulated from Europe by its ultra-conservative Hapsburg government, which nevertheless was powerless to hinder 'a slow underground movement' of growth in trade and industry and the commercial classes, and this 'came everywhere into collision with the old feudal institutions'.[30]

Two pamphlets by Marx were an ambitious attempt to interpret events in France from the February revolution of 1848 to the *coup d'état* by Louis-Napoleon in December 1851. In *The Class Struggles in France 1848–50* he tried for the first time, as Engels said in a foreword to a later edition, to explain a series of contemporary events in terms of his economic conception of history. It was followed in 1852 by *The Eighteenth Brumaire of Louis Bonaparte*, a title referring to the coup that brought the first Napoleon to power in 1799. These two works display exceptional brilliance both of insight and of style; they are an intricate counterpoint of class interests and party passions, depicted with all Marx's peculiar sardonic humour and more

---

[29] Preface to *Ludwig Feuerbach*.
[30] F. Engels, *Germany: Revolution and Counter-Revolution* (1851; London edn, 1933), pp. 36–7.

than his usual wealth of literary allusions. *Brumaire* opens with words which have become famous: men make their own history, but not by their own free choice, because they are always clogged by the legacy of the past. 'The tradition of all the dead generations weighs like a nightmare on the minds of the living.' To Marx's eyes mankind stumbles onward half conscious, half sleepwalking or hypnotized.

Individual figures are not neglected, especially Bonaparte, always flitting through the background shades. Marx sets himself a hard task in undertaking to account for the rise of a man whom he never ceased to regard as a mediocrity, a mere political trickster. He gave great prominence to the rhythm of economic activity, as an immediate as well as long-term influence on politics; its improvement from the middle of 1848 seemed to him the reason for the recovery of conservatism in France and Europe, while renewed depression in the spring of 1851 unsettled things again and helped to give Bonaparte his chance. He was repeating a maxim of *The German Ideology* when he wrote that as in private life the historian must distinguish between romantic phrases and the real interests behind them; and in analysing the 'party of order' he made much of the cleavage that weakened it between the two royalist factions, the Legitimist representing large landed property and the Orleanist standing for big business, with high finance in the lead. Marx was strongly impressed by the gulf between town and country as revealed in these years. Bonaparte was elected President by the votes of the peasantry, the class embodying, in Marx's words, barbarism within civilization, which however he counted on, thanks to its deepening impoverishment, to become in the future an indispensable ally for the working class. Above all the classes towered a state whose vast multitude of employees gave it a semi-autonomous life, and whose hypertrophy he traced back to the days of absolute monarchy.

Meanwhile Engels was turning his attention further afield. One of several echoes of 1848–9 in his book on the Peasant War of 1524–5, which he wrote in 1850, is an allusion to the use of Czech and Croat soldiers against the German-speaking peasant rebels in Austria.[31] In a way he could think of history repeating itself. Germany's retarded development left sundry evils of 1520 still in being in 1848, like the feudal dues weighing on the countryside. He was writing 'the first Marxist work of *history*', as distinct from historical theory, and the model for much Marxist historiography of days to come.[32] It went beyond *The German Ideology* in having necessarily to reckon with ideas as active influence instead of passive reflection. Engels must have been helped by his own firmly religious upbringing; he could feel emotionally with Thomas Münzer, moving as he himself had done from religion to social involvement.[33] He could contemplate the Reformation as an early exercise in bourgeois revolution (thus providing later Marxists with another tough morsel to chew over), abortive because of the failure of the anti-feudal outbreak of 1524, failure for which he laid part of the blame on Luther.

Engels had done some fighting as well as writing in 1849, and he was to become a recognized expert on army matters. Military considerations have a prominent place in the book. He saw the levies of the nobles triumphing through their strength in cavalry, ready to charge and rout insurgents shaken by cannon-fire.[34] But above all the rising failed, in his opinion, because of the same narrow-minded localism, and the same hesitancy and willingness to compromise, as the German middle classes and their spokesmen showed in 1848–9. Here was fresh reason to think of the proletariat as the destined maker of revolution, because of its far greater concentration and the unity of action this made possible. Peasant revolt led by a disciplined party, such as Asia has given birth to in our century, was still far out of sight.

These compositions of 1850–2 were followed by a copious stream of articles on things taking place in arenas in and out of

[31] F. Engels, *The Peasant War in Germany* (English edn: Moscow, 1956), p. 149. For some recent comments on this work see B. Scribner and G. Benecke, eds., *The German Peasant War 1525: New Viewpoints* (London, 1979). Cf. D. McLellan, *Engels* (London, 1977), p. 27: 'It was in writing history that Engels' talents found their fullest expression.'
[32] T. Carver, *Engels* (Oxford, 1981), pp. 33–4.
[33] *The Peasant War*, pp. 67ff.
[34] Ibid., p. 130.

Europe. They kept for the most part to a straightforward political approach. Marx must have felt that day by day or year by year episodes are affected by too many contingencies and unpredictables to be amenable to long-range calculation: history has to be studied by two time-charts, neither of them without its importance. Pressing need for journalistic earnings prompted the articles. Still, their themes stirred his interest in historical antecedents afresh, and suggested further speculations.

In 1854 a Liberal revolution took place in Spain, with the small working class taking a hand for the first time, and, after two troubled years, a counter-revolution. Marx had already made some study of the Spanish resistance to Napoleon and of the Liberal years 1820–3, he told Engels, and he was now trying to fill in the gaps, not finding it easy to hit on the key – but, he added characteristically, with his favourite *Don Quixote* a good starting point.[35] In his prefatory sketches he dwelt on jarring class interests in the resistance, the divergence between progressives and conservatives. He shows no great enthusiasm for it as a patriotic struggle; at its first outbreak, he writes, it looked less revolutionary than anti-revolutionary, and popular sentiment, rabidly Catholic and enraged against everything modern and enlightened that France represented, had throughout a strongly reactionary flavour.[36] The rapturous welcome given to the restored King Ferdinand, bringing back with him despotism and Inquisition, elicits the comment: 'A more humiliating spectacle has seldom been witnessed by the world.'[37] No one was further from identifying *vox populi* with *vox Dei*.

1854–6 was also the time of the Crimean War, to which he devoted, with assistance from Engels on military affairs, far the bulkiest of his series of commentaries. Here we see him studying international relations, through the medium of the first grand conflict since 1815. For him the worst obstacle to European progress was tsarism, against which in 1848 he and Engels had longed for a 'revolutionary war'. Now that Britain

[35] Letter of 2 September 1854.
[36] *Revolution in Spain*, pp. 31, 33.
[37] Ibid., p. 71.

with France as ally was at war with Russia, he was feverishly
eager to see a conventional trial of arms turning into a resolute
drive that would liberate both Europe and Russia from the dead
weight of tsarism. It cannot be gainsaid that the relegation of
war to a minor place in *The German Ideology* seems to be
directly contradicted by the hopes now rested on this 'revolutionary war'. Marx grew more and more disgusted with what
in his eyes was a very half-hearted effort by the Allies, a
'phoney war' likely to peter out with nothing accomplished. He
was indignant at the Western bourgeoisie for shirking, like the
German in 1848, a duty laid on it by the 'historical mission' he
attributed to each class in turn in furtherance of the great
historical process. Some of his most vitriolic language was
bestowed on Cobden and the Manchester School, as basely
money-grubbing and pacific.[38]

Marx's serious interest in India was set alight by the debate
on renewal of the East India Company charter in 1853, and then
in 1857 was fanned by the Mutiny. As always, he could not help
delving into the past. In Europe he had been searching for the
secret of change, in Asia he was confronted by a seeming
absence of that elixir of life: history's 'laws of motion' were
paralysed. This strange and unwelcome phenomenon drew him
to the bedrock of things, the manner of existence of the masses.
He and Engels were struck at the outset by the report, first set
afloat by the seventeenth-century French traveller Bernier, that
there was no private landowning in India, that all land belonged
to the state.[39] Immobility might be a natural consequence, they
thought. Later on, with the Mutiny priming a fresh flow of
information and public discussion, Marx had doubts about the
alleged dearth of private property in land.[40] Land tenure in India
has proved an immensely complicated subject, still being
painfully disentangled.

[38] *The Eastern Question*, ed. E.M. and E. Aveling (London, 1897), e.g., pp. 62,
231–6. See generally on Marx's views about right and wrong wars Dona Torr,
ed., *Marxism, Nationality and War* (London, 1940).
[39] Marx to Engels, 2 June 1853, and Engels to Marx, 6 June 1853. The letters
will be found in the selected *Correspondence 1846–1895*, tr. Dona Torr
(London, 1934), pp. 64ff.
[40] K. Marx and F. Engels, *The First Indian War of Independence 1857–1859*
(collected articles; Moscow, 1959), pp. 150–1.

Marx's picture in any case was of a small self-contained village, finding its own food and its own simple craft wares, a brotherhood of poverty and ignorance. The reality was less egalitarian than he supposed; but the Indian village might well be, as he surmised, a convenient footstool for autocracy. Economic and political were thus fitted together. If the state, there or in the rest of Asia, was responsible for anything useful, it might be water-control and irrigation. This was a supposition frequently considered by him and Engels, and they came near at times to endorsing what has been called the 'hydraulic theory' of the oriental state. It is most plausible when applied to China, surprisingly not mentioned in an early article on India in a list of countries whose climate might make large-scale irrigation a necessity.[41] This too remains a point of controversy; it seems likely that in most kingdoms less was done by governments, more by local enterprise, private or collective, than Marx was led to think.

His estimate of the British conquest was another weighty concession to the efficacy of war and conquest, so much pushed into the background in *The German Ideology*. If German medieval expansion had been a civilizing force in Eastern Europe, as Engels maintained,[42] British expansion in Asia might be so likewise. Marx denounced the brutality and rapacity of the subjugation of India, most angrily of all during the reconquest in 1857-8 – in his journalism he had no inhibitions against confronting history as a moralist – but it did at least open the way to change. He was thinking of India being liberated by it not from bad rulers, but from old fixed grooves of social habit. This would come about at first destructively, through machine competition crippling handicrafts, then more constructively by bringing in new technology and a new mentality.

From 1856 to 1860 England was fighting its second Opium War with China. To Marx China seemed even more stationary than India, and he thought he had found the root cause in a self-sufficiency, in both food and clothing, not merely within every village but within every household. He looked forward

[41] Ibid., pp. 16–17.
[42] *Germany: Revolution and Counter-Revolution*, pp. 55–6, 86.

to the equilibrium being upset by manufactured imports, forced into the country along with opium by Western military power; he was greatly over-estimating the rate at which this could happen. With a keen dramatic sense, he loved to see History seizing its cue, doing things with well-timed effect like a *pièce bien faite* in the theatre. Naval attack on Canton would cause commercial collapse there, he wrote, which would rebound on Europe, lead to unemployment, and spread revolution over the continent.[43] We need not take all his pronouncements in this vein literally, but it was in line with his expectation of working-class revolt as offspring of capitalist crisis.

In a more sober tone Engels was speaking for both men when in an article of 1857 he condemned British barbarities in China and poured scorn on their perpetrators' objections to unorthodox Chinese methods of self-defence, but wound up with a hopeful prediction of 'the death struggle of the oldest empire in the world, and the opening of a new day for all Asia'.[44] His and Marx's historical vision was optimistic about the future, tragic when it turned to the past, as a record so dreadfully bad that any sacrifice was worth while to get away from it. Bolshevism in the years after 1917 may be said to have acted on the same conviction.

In 1857–8, with a full-scale economic crisis in prospect, Marx was busy with a voluminous outline of his long-planned *magnum opus* on economics, and it included a lengthy section on *Pre-capitalist Economic Formations*. Evidently he felt that a thorough analysis of capitalism, the latest mode of production, required as prelude a survey of earlier modes and the relation in which they stood to one another; nothing less than a sort of X-ray photograph of world history. This task was being undertaken near the end of a decade of watchful observation of history on the march, leading further and further outwards from Western Europe to the Far East. In the course of it Marx had amassed knowledge of the past whose essence he was now trying to distil. Still committed to the modes of production, he was setting himself to reckon them up and arrange them into an

[43] *Marx on China 1853–1860* (collected articles), ed. Dona Torr (London, 1851), p. 7 (June 1853).
[44] Ibid., pp. 50–1 (June 1857).

evolutionary pattern. One may feel that an insatiable curiosity, and the passion inherited from German philosophy for universal understanding, were carrying him too far afield; and that more might have been achieved by concentration on European history, or those phases of it well enough known to make a fairly detailed scrutiny of it practicable.

His only published statement arising from these speculations was the often-quoted one of 1859 about a sequence of four modes of production: Asiatic (or primitive), slave, feudal, capitalist.[45] As it stands it can only be called, as an editor of the *Pre-capitalist Economic Formations* says, disconcertingly 'brief, unsupported and unexplained'.[46] Eighteen years later Marx was indignant with a Russian commentator who wanted to elevate his 'sketch of the genesis of capitalism in Western Europe into an historico-philosophic theory of the *marche générale* imposed by fate upon every people'.[47] In 1857–8 he saw a common beginning in what he termed, sociologically rather than geographically, an 'Asiatic mode of production'; from this primal base, however, Western Europe, but not Asia, had broken away.

The next discernible stage appeared to be slavery. This can grow within societies, through debt, crime and so on, but only on a limited scale. No inner law of mutation seems to have been responsible for it, unless it was a law of population. Marx did indeed conjecture, in orthodox enough style, that pressure of population in early Rome led to wars of expansion, reduction of opponents to slavery, and consequent landlord ascendancy, ending in expropriation of the peasantry. He might have been expected to think of the patrician beneficiaries as instigating the wars, in which peasants were often conscripted to fight unwillingly. But in his view the Mediterranean city-state was organized primarily for land-grabbing: war was 'the great all-embracing task, the great communal labour'.[48] He was

---

[45] Preface to *A Contribution to the Critique of Political Economy*.
[46] E.J. Hobsbawm, Introduction to K. Marx, *Pre-capitalist Economic Formations* (London, 1964), p. 11.
[47] *Correspondence* (Dona Torr), p. 354. Cf. M. Evans, *op. cit.*, p. 73.
[48] *Pre-capitalist Economic Formations*, pp. 71–2.

virtually construing war as part of a mode of production; realistically, perhaps, but leaving less originality to the concept than it had claimed at the outset. He had been coming to think of serfdom as well as slavery as ordinarily brought about by conquest: in a letter of 1856 he wrote of its growth within Polish society as an exceptional happening.[49]

He never abandoned the mode of production as the building-block of history; he and Engels went on in later years thinking tentatively of miscellaneous classifications and sub-species, 'Ancient', 'German', 'Slavonic', but the idea was less precise now than when they first hit on it, and enveloped in many obscurities. It may be deemed valuable for the epochs they were least unfamiliar with; further back in history, or further away from Western Europe, its relevance is more dubious. An essential of the capitalist economy from which their inquiry set out is that the possessing class takes the lead in the relations of production; capitalists manage it themselves. A parallel might be drawn with the demesne farming practised at times in medieval Europe, and its recrudescence in Eastern Europe in the early modern era; also with slavery, because it too drew the owners, the master-class, into the organization of production; and with the Asiatic (or the Inca) state, or landlords, when they directed water-control. But whereas capitalism has been the most dynamic system, water-control in China was part and parcel of the most immobile of all larger structures.

Altogether the list of these cases is not long. Within the Indian village, relations of production were limited to barter exchange of food for craft wares, while above it stood the state, or its deputies, skimming off a good part of the surplus. In far the greater number of societies there has been the same parasitism, with no functional link between production and consumption. What confronts us is a limited number of economies surmounted by an endless array of modes of appropriation, methods by which the stronger have levied tribute from the weaker.

An uneasy feeling of something missing may have lent insistence to another thought in the *Pre-capitalist Economic*

[49] To Engels, 30 October 1856.

Formations, the significance of individual energy and initiative. Man himself after all is the chief force of production, and Marx was after all a man of the Romantic age with its cult of the demonic personality, who found a congenial symbol in Prometheus. Asiatic society is the most unchanging, he writes at one point, because in it 'the individual does not become independent of the community'.[50] In the birth of the individual the city, in its European guise as a political entity, not a mere agglomeration, had a crucial part to play. Marx allowed for this by recognizing, if he did not explain, the distance between urban life in Asia and that of classical Europe with its citizenship and its freedom of self-development.[51]

Lenin correctly ascribed to Marx not invention of the 'materialist conception of history' but 'consistent continuation and extension of materialism into the domain of social phenomena'.[52] If Marx performed much less of this than might have been expected from him, it was because he became so deeply engrossed with the intricate workings of the capitalist economy, and really used himself up on the task. In undertaking it he had no intention of abandoning history, the subject which has convincingly been called his 'true intellectual passion' or vocation,[53] and the only field where all his many talents could be combined. As the grand accelerator of change, capitalism was itself a historical problem, and he would have made this clearer had his strength allowed him to carry out the many-sided investigation that he projected. It was to the advent of capitalism in England that the *Formations* led up, by way of a salutary reminder that a new economic order could not be self-created, but that political authority had much to do with it, like conquest at earlier stages. Vagrants, the debris of a crumbling feudal society, had to be driven into a labour market by penal legislation; in this way, Marx wrote, Tudor monarchy was among the necessary conditions for the establishment of capitalism.[54] From this point of view Henry VIII and Elizabeth

[50] *Pre-capitalist Economic Formations*, p. 83; cf. pp. 91–2.
[51] Ibid., p. 71.
[52] *Marx, Engels, Marxism*, p. 12.
[53] *Rubel on Karl Marx*, pp. 96–8.
[54] *Pre-capitalist Economic Formations*, p. 111.

can be said to have participated in the relations of production. In the historical summary in *Capital* the picture changes to an even darker, and perhaps less accurate one, of peasants uprooted from their holdings so as to be compelled to work for the new masters. It had the advantage of justifying the formula of *The Communist Manifesto* – reiterated in *Capital*[55] – of capitalist expropriators being in their turn expropriated by the working class, to make way for socialism.

Altogether Marx left nothing like a systematic doctrine, and responsibility fell to Engels for pulling together the ideas of both of them; a heavy as well as exacting one, because he had also to take over the mass of unfinished work on economics under which Marx had succumbed, on top of the role of adviser to the socialist movements now stirring everywhere. Considering this, what Engels accomplished in historical theory is very remarkable indeed. It is to be found in his *Anti-Dühring*, in 1878; in the study of Feuerbach in 1886 where a section of the 1845–6 joint design was worked out afresh; in the essay of 1892 'On Historical Materialism',[56] mainly concerned in a more factual way with aspects of modern European development; and in a wonderful set of letters written very late, between 1890 and 1894.

'The materialist interpretation of history is the main item in the intellectual legacy left us by Engels,' it has been said lately by a friendly critic; his comments on or continuations of Marx made him its real originator. The same critic is inclined to tax him with going too far, making the theory sound too much like a rounded whole. Still, as he notices,[57] Engels had begun long before, by coining the title 'materialist conception of history' in a review of Marx in 1859, so that there had been a quarter of a century for Marx to object if he wished. And if Marx's ideas were to survive and exert influence, it was indispensable for

[55] Conclusion to *Capital*, vol. I, ch. 32.
[56] This essay, published as such in 1892–3, formed the chief part of Engels' introduction to the English edition (1892) of his *Socialism: Utopian and Scientific*, a section published separately in 1880 of his *Anti-Dühring* (full title: *Herr Eugen Dühring's Revolution in Science*) of 1878. In his letter of 21 September 1890 to J. Bloch, Engels refers him for light on the theory and practice of history to Marx's *The Eighteenth Brumaire of Louis Bonaparte* (1852), parts of *Capital*, and his own *Anti-Dühring* and *Ludwig Feuerbach*.
[57] T. Carver, *op. cit.*, pp. 62–3.

them to be given a somewhat more regular form, which he himself, with his perpetual dubitations and notebook-fillings and second, third, fourth thoughts on everything, would in all probability never have been able to give. Without Engels the needed systematizing would have been far worse done.

It has been rightly pointed out besides that in the handling of historic fact he was the superior:[58] his practical judgment was sounder, and he never fell into fantasies like Marx's about Palmerston and Moscow and secret agents mysteriously burrowing. It is not without relevance that Engels' life was that of a man of affairs, most of Marx's of a recluse. Engels might see less deeply or comprehensively, but also more realistically. It was characteristic of him to advise Marx to supply *Capital* with more historical illustrations. It is highly regrettable that, having to devote his limited time to the theory, he was not able to undertake further pieces of history-writing like his pioneer work on the Peasant War. Not much of his projected history of Ireland got done. More employment of this kind would have benefited him as a theoretician too, and so enriched posterity doubly.

One item among his many duties was to popularize his friend's ideas, as well as interpret them; for this he was obliged to simplify, and sometimes over-simplified. In an encomium written in June 1877 he summarized the 'new conception of history' in the words: 'Marx has proved that the whole of previous history is a history of class frictions.' He gave the familiar example of bourgeoisie supplanting noblesse in 1789, and added sweepingly: 'From this point of view all the historical phenomena are explicable in the simplest possible way – with sufficient knowledge of the particular economic conditions';[59] a proviso that a hundred years of diligent research since then have only inadequately satisfied.

If he was sometimes simplifying unduly, he has also been charged with the opposite fault of over-elaborating, wrapping up a historical approach too much in Hegelian formulae, under the rubric of 'dialectical materialism'. In these later years he

58 Ibid., p. 38.
59 'Marx', in *Werke* (Berlin, 1962), vol. 19, pp. 96–106; English version in *Reminiscences of Marx and Engels* (Moscow, n.d.).

does seem to have returned, more whole-heartedly than Marx, to Hegelian procedures, as an aid to his formidable task of gathering scattered conjectures together. Later on, if not in his own work, this did have an unfortunate effect by tying Marx too closely to Hegel, and investing Marx's method with too much of a pretentiously esoteric flavour, likely to lead to long words being mistaken for deep ideas. A very superfluous addition to Hegel came into vogue with the foisting on him of the 'dialectical triad', squeezing the flow of history into the tight corset of thesis, antithesis and synthesis. Non-Marxists not surprisingly found it hard to envisage history in so geometrical a style, as a pyramid or procession of isosceles triangles, but it had entered into Marxist orthodoxy by the time this began to percolate into countries like England.

Reliance on Hegelian aids to thinking might sometimes seem to lead Engels himself towards trust in a necessity of history of which human beings were not much more than puppets. If Machiavelli allowed too much room to Fortune, Marxism has often been found fault with for trying to impose on history a rationality foreign to it. This is of course a charge that any attempt at interpretation on any lines must expose itself to. As a counter to it the Enlightenment devised a so-called 'law of unintended consequences', with Vico for one of its proponents, according to which historical events result from men's actions, but do not fulfil men's conscious designs.[60] Such a conclusion may be native to any epoch when people are impelled to consider their situation and wonder how to remedy it, but feel that much in it is beyond their limited strength.

Both Marx and Engels were quite alive to the problem, and their answers were not very dissimilar to Vico's. World history would be 'very mystical', Marx wrote in 1871, if accidents had nothing to do with it, but they were causes of 'acceleration and delay' rather than of radical changes of course.[61] In the same vein Engels wrote: 'where on the surface accident holds sway,

[60] See R.L. Meek, *op. cit.*, pp. 1, 31.
[61] Letter to L. Kugelmann, 17 April 1871. Cf. the objection advanced by G. Leff: 'History is concerned with the contingent'; 'the absence of uniformity from human affairs' is central to it. (*History and Social Theory* [London, 1969], p. 3.)

actually it is always governed by inner, hidden laws and it is only a matter of discovering those laws';[62] and again: 'amid all the endless *host* of accidents ... the economic movement finally asserts itself as necessary.'[63] These propositions may be cavilled at as taking for granted what requires to be proved, namely that there is a single final determinant, that this is the expanding energy of production, and that it carries mankind in one ultimate direction. Any invoking of 'hidden laws', shepherding us towards socialism willy-nilly, must arouse some uneasiness; and it is hard to adopt even a 'guiding thread' to history, as Marx modestly called his method,[64] without drifting into thinking of it as a 'law'. In the end judgment can only rest on a weighing up of probability, in the light of collective experience.

As regards Engels, uneasiness must gain something from his attitude to physical science. Over many years he was collecting materials for a never completed work, published long after his death as *Dialectics of Nature*. There he invites scepticism about the dialectical principle by placing the entire universe as well as human existence under the sway of its 'laws'. He had an old soldier's liking for order and precision, and his mind might well turn with relief at times to Nature as a realm where chance could be left behind. Knowing so much both of science and of history, he could have done praiseworthy service by writing on scientific history. This is touched on here and there in *Dialectics of Nature*, but it was a generalization too many later students were to make do with that 'From the very beginning the origin and development of the sciences has been determined by production.'[65] The instances adduced, from ancient Egypt, are the needs of irrigation, town-planning and war, only one of which belongs to the sphere of production.

Engels wrote odd pieces on topics of military history, for which also he was excellently qualified, but it is a great pity that he did not undertake some extended study of it, or of the 'sociology of war'. There is a prophetic ring in his remark that

[62] *Ludwig Feuerbach*, section IV.
[63] Letter to J. Bloch, 21 September 1890.
[64] Preface to *A Critique of Political Economy*.
[65] *Dialectics of Nature*, p. 214.

in modern times the effects of war have been altering, 'at least among great nations: in the long run the defeated power often gains more economically, politically and morally than the victor.'[66] But the only substantial work bearing on war that he embarked on in his later years was a study in 1887–8 of *The Role of Force in History*. This was left unfinished, as if he lost confidence in his argument, a restatement in the light of recent events of a leading thought of *The German Ideology*. It is concerned with the question, so pregnant for the growing socialist movement in Germany, of Bismarck's unification of the country by blood and iron. Engels contended that his achievement could only be temporary, because resting on bayonets instead of on economic development. Yet he held that unification was a precondition of German economic progress.[67] What he had better warrant to think insecure was the preservation, which was Bismarck's true aim, of the obsolete Prussian monarchy and social structure. Yet German industry accommodated itself to them contentedly enough.[68] When the throne collapsed it was through no revolt either of bourgeoisie or of working class, but defeat in a European war, in other words through a fresh intervention of force.

It was a penalty Marx and Engels had to pay for their failure to work out their method more comprehensively, and the fact that most of their joint or several meditations on it had never seen the light, that there was a gap between them and the next generation, a stretch of time when their thinking, so far as it was known, was largely misunderstood. It is clear that towards the end Engels was very conscious of this danger, and did his best to guard against it. He fully understood that tracing historical interconnections required detailed research in every particular case; in 1880 he was regretting that very little had yet been done. Instead vulgarizers, young intellectuals of the socialist mass movement and its fringes, were treating Marxism as a short cut,

---

[66] Letter to C. Schmidt, 27 October 1890.
[67] F. Engels, *The Role of Force in History*, tr. J. Cohen, ed. E. Wangermann (London, 1968), pp. 46ff.
[68] As Wangermann emphasizes in his introduction to *The Role of Force*, p. 27.

a substitute for patient investigation.[69] The main burden of his parting admonitions was a warning against crude, one-sided use of the materialist explanations which he and Marx in youth had enjoyed rubbing their readers' noses in as a means of driving out old, ingrained illusions. Ultimately the determining factor, he wrote now in a letter of 1890, is the economic, but it is not the sole force at work; and he went on to blame himself and Marx for having obscured this truth.[70]

A long letter of a few weeks later is a miniature treatise in which full allowance is made for the ability of, for instance, a legal system, which grows, if not in every detail, out of society's material operations, to react on them: it has done so very markedly by helping to shape property and inheritance, so different in France and England since the French Revolution. Due place is also given to the fact that remoter branches of thinking, like philosophy and religion, are not born exclusively from the actual condition of society, but 'have a prehistoric stock, found already in existence and taken over in the historic period'.[71] A good illustration of the shuttling to and fro of ideas is the saying in *Dialectics of Nature* that after Darwin the old notion of natural harmony was suddenly exchanged for an equally lopsided myth of universal strife: this derived from the Hobbesian war of all against all, compounded by capitalist competition, and was now being illegitimately transferred back again from biology into sociology.[72]

By the late nineteenth century history was gaining a secure place in the universities of Europe, with economic history more and more vigorous. It was long before Marxist theory could have any influence on academic practice. At Oxbridge it was virtually unknown before the 1930s. For long it remained closely tied to the political movement, a link which brought it into greater prominence, or notoriety, than it would have had otherwise, but also subjected it to some cramping, the fate of

---

[69] Engels to C. Schmidt, 5 August 1890. He writes here that 'the materialist conception of history also has a lot of friends nowadays to whom it serves as an excuse for *not* studying history.'
[70] To J. Bloch, 21 September 1890.
[71] To C. Schmidt, 27 October 1890.
[72] *Dialectics of Nature*, pp. 208–9.

all official doctrines. It continued to owe most of its development to individuals who were also active political workers, mostly by those with a bent for study like Kautsky, one of the direct successors of Marx and Engels, rather than the true men of action like Lenin. Another distinction can be drawn between those who wrote about specific historical topics, and those drawn to historical theory. The latter were often party leaders, who felt it their responsibility to give the movement sound guidance on theory as well as on current tactics. As Kautsky said, the materialist conception should enable socialists not only to understand history better, but to make history better.[73]

Kautsky wrote about a wide variety of eras, ancient and modern; men like him were legitimate heirs of Marx and Engels in taking all history for their province, before the specialists who were coming on the scene could cut it up into private enclosures. His concern was far from exclusively with economic foundations: religion was one of his fields, and his work on Thomas More displayed an interest in the outstanding individual, as well as in the earliest socialism which had been part of Engels' theme in his *Peasant War*. Regrettably his work as a historian came under a cloud after 1917 and his collision with Lenin and lapse from grace.

In a work published in 1906 he attempted to restate and add to Marxist historical theory on a broader moral basis. It was an indigestible feature of the theory as left by its founders that it seemed to care little about ethical impulses. Marx might be deeply a moralist, but in his scheme the duties or 'missions' of progressive classes were ambiguously interwoven with pressure of blind forces. Kautsky set himself to trace the evolution of the moral feelings, and show how they flowered from men's social life, from the earliest times. Marx and Engels had been drawn to prehistory in their later years, under the spell of the American anthropologist Lewis Morgan whose findings they took as confirmation of their own tenets; and Kautsky held that study of it, working on the ordinary stuff of human life, brought out more patently than the record of historical times an

[73] K. Kautsky, *op. cit.*, p. 7.

evolutionary process within which technology interacted with religion and all the rest.[74]

He tackled a frequent misunderstanding of Marxist theory, that technology by itself determined social structures; and an objection founded on it that heterogeneous societies could be supported by the same techniques of production. His solution is not altogether clear, but he saw diversity as arising in the first place from geographical settings, 'differences in the natural and social surroundings'.[75] Morality, he allowed, like 'the rest of the complicated social superstructure', might drift some distance from its social foundations, but then it would wither before long into mere formal observance. Meanwhile the struggling masses confronted the old order with a new ethic of their own, which with their successful rise would become the moral code of a whole society.[76]

In the diffusion of Marxism from its West European cradle into other climes, one of its attractions was often its historical theory, promising revelations of their past to peoples trying to understand how it was that they found themselves where they were. In Russia there was already among historians an interest in the principles of their craft, one manifestation it has been shrewdly suggested of 'the familiar self-consciousness of Russian culture'.[77] Marxism was carried forward most notably by Plekhanov, who resembled Kautsky in being better suited to scholarship than to political storm and stress, and in being exceedingly well read over a very wide range. He too was attracted to the new science of anthropology, and he found much to discuss in primitive religion and arts.

His *Defence of Materialism* came out in 1895. Much of it was an inquiry into the ancestry of Marxist theory, starting with the French materialists of the Enlightenment and going on to French historiography after the Revolution and Napoleon, and thence by way of Utopian socialism and German idealism to

---

[74] Ibid., pp. 110–11.
[75] Ibid., pp. 164ff.
[76] Ibid., pp. 184–5.
[77] G.M. Enteen, *The Soviet Scholar-Bureaucrat: M.N. Pokrovskii and the Society of Marxist Historians* (Pennsylvania State University, 1978), p. 7.

'modern materialism'. This was for him very definitely 'dialectical materialism', sharply distinguished in another work of the same time from the simply 'economic' version, which he associated with figures as oddly assorted as Thorold Rogers and Blanqui, with Guizot and Tocqueville for forerunners. What they did, in his view, was to pick out and make much of an 'economic factor' which, attuned to their estimate of human nature, was really only a disguised idealism. Its place was with a 'theory of factors', to which every specialist added his own – religion, law, etc. – all together forming a bundle of independent variables whose orbits were impossible to chart.[78] Marxism was able to chart them by virtue of its monistic approach, its reduction of everything to a single process with one basic determinant and multiple internal exchanges.

Plekhanov felt acutely, as Engels had done, that Marx's historical teaching was in urgent need of clarification because it was being misused by 'those who utter so many follies in his name'.[79] Hence the large space devoted to it in his last work, *Fundamental Problems of Marxism*, published in 1908. He, like Kautsky, put much weight on geographical environment as governing 'the development of economic forces and, therefore, the development of all the other social relations'. This accounted for the bifurcation of the Western and Asian lines of evolution, 'the classical and the oriental', from their common antecedent, 'the clan type of social organization'.[80] But as soon as specific relations of production formed, they in turn affected the further unfolding of the forces of production; so also did external relations, intercourse with other communities. It was not therefore a matter of unmediated control of social evolution, except at the most primitive level, by climate and other physical elements, as supposed by Buckle and his disciples.[81] Earlier Plekhanov had observed that the rise of the state in Western Europe did not appear to be directly moulded by the system of production,[82] and now he was widening the 'decisive

---

[78] G. Plekhanov, *The Materialist Conception of History* (1895; English edn: London, 1940), pp. 12ff.
[79] *Fundamental Problems*, p. 25.
[80] Ibid., pp. 33–4, 51.
[81] Ibid., pp. 36, 40–1.
[82] *The Materialist Conception*, p. 32.

influence' of the political, legal, miscellaneous relations engendered by economic life on 'the whole psychology of man as a social being'.[83]

After the Revolution it was Bukharin who became the accredited spokesman of Marxism at Moscow, including historical theory though he himself was more economist or philosopher. He wrote in a very sanguine tone, with a confidence inspired by the triumph of 1917; in his estimation very little thought was required to make 'the full wealth of the Marxian method absolutely clear in comparison with all other schools and tendencies'.[84] His appeals to the 'laws' of history were loud and frequent, and he seemed disposed to equate them with those of natural science.[85] He drew no line between 'historical', 'economic' or 'dialectical' materialism; and his exposition has a somewhat pedestrian march, as though intended for elementary reading. Of historical events he says little; his illustrations are few and obvious.

Lenin found time amid the tempests of 1920 to read and warmly praise Pokrovsky's outline history of Russia,[86] one of the earliest works of Marxist history to become known in the West and to set a standard for budding historians there. Pokrovsky had been in the thick of party activity before the Revolution, and after it was the first organizer of historical studies in the Soviet Union. He held that 'the Russian proletariat must have its own interpretation of the Russian past,'[87] and in the *Brief History*, which grew out of lectures given during the civil war, he too may have been in a measure writing down to his audience. However, he had already before 1917 traced the main lines of his approach. In this, class struggle played the same part as in the West, instead of Russia following a path of its own as Slavophil patriots had wanted to believe. What came to be most controversial was the place he assigned to merchant capital, which he thought powerful enough as early

---

[83] *Fundamental Problems*, p. 42.
[84] N.I. Bukharin, 'Marx's Teaching and its Historical Importance', in Bukharin *et al.*, *Marxism and Modern Thought*, tr. Ralph Fox (London, 1935), p. 33.
[85] Ibid., pp. 43, 44; cf. his *Historical Materialism* (English edn: London, 1925), p. xiii, etc.
[86] *The Letters of Lenin*, tr. E. Hill and D. Mudie (London, 1937), p. 463.
[87] G.M. Enteen, *op. cit.*, p. 21.

as the sixteenth century to use the tsars as its instruments for conquering trade outlets. This was certainly an exaggeration, and in his late years – he died in 1932 – he had perforce to yield much ground to Soviet critics, and to contemplate old Russia more as one form of feudalism. The debate had repercussions abroad, making it a subject of dispute whether state power could ever be wielded by merchant capital – only loosely linked with the means of production – as distinct from industrial capitalism.

In Russia the issue was less purely theoretical, because Pokrovsky's elevation of the trading class implied a demotion of the tsars from their proud eminence, and among them Peter, whom Stalin's admirers were holding up as his great precursor in the modernizing of Russia. A standard allegation against Marxism was turned against Plekhanov: by failing to do justice to the impact of exceptional individuals, it could be said, he was falling into economic determinism and compressing all events into economic grooves. This led to the further charge of making all history lead by smooth progression towards the present day; of giving it, one critic, Gorochov, declared, 'a mystical appearance', a purpose from the outset to arrange the stage for *us*.[88]

Stalin in power made it part of his duty to supply an official summing up of the principles of historical Marxism. This could only make it look more complete and solid than it really was, heedless of Lenin's caution that Marx left no finished doctrine but simply 'laid the cornerstone of the science which socialists *must* advance in all directions.'[89] Stalin's 1938 treatise has a lumpish and schematic character: it admits no doubts or difficulties, and discusses few specific points of history. It was typical of its author's mechanical or bureaucratic turn of mind to choose quotations often from Engels' experiment of applying dialectics to nature, and to conclude that the study of history could be made as exact as a science like biology.[90]

---

[88] F. Gorochov, 'An Anti-Marxist Theory of History', in *International Literature*, no. 9, 1937.
[89] *Marx, Engels, Marxism*, p. 64.
[90] *Dialectical and Historical Materialism* (English edn: Moscow, 1951), p. 23. This was originally (1938) a chapter of the history of the Bolshevik party.

A good deal worse than Stalin's formulation of history, it must be added, was his falsification of it, of recent events at least, his own way of acting on the maxim that theory can show how to make history as well as to write it. 'History is becoming clay in the hands of the potter,' Trotsky commented as he watched the Bolshevik annals undergoing their stealthy transformations.[91] But theory as well as fact suffered; Stalin, as Lukács said, was standing Marxism on its head by making it teach whatever suited his tactics of the moment.[92]

Part of the purpose of the new orthodoxy was to discredit anyone who had been Stalin's rival. Bukharin was found fault with in an authoritative textbook, in darkly scholastic language, on the ground that he made too much of external collisions and environmental influences, whereas the essence of dialectics was the unfolding of inner contradictions.[93] Another manual, published as recently as 1960, took a firm stand on the assertion, which Marx had firmly (though not in print) disclaimed, that in spite of every variation of local detail 'all peoples travel what is basically the same path', because all history depends on 'the development of the productive forces, which obey the same internal laws'.[94] So far as it treads any terrestrial ground, this survey is almost confined to Europe, for all its pose of universality. It lays down that 'The masses are the makers of history' (not much of a compliment, considering what human history has been), with scant definition of what is meant.[95] Respect is paid to ideas and their influence,[96] but so few examples are given, here as throughout, that the statement lacks meaning. It seems on the whole that Marxist theory has made little progress in the USSR, and brought little inspiration to historians in countries in its sphere. Soviet scholars have produced a great deal of good work in numerous fields, but for the most part on the simpler levels of political and economic

[91] L. Trotsky, *Stalin* (London, 1969), vol. 1, p. 207.
[92] Reported by the *Observer*, 1 February 1970.
[93] *A Textbook of Marxist Philosophy*, ed. M. Shirokov; English edn, ed. John Lewis (London, 1937). See section II, chs. 3, 6.
[94] *Fundamentals of Marxism-Leninism*, ed. O. Kuusinen (1960; English edn: London, 1961), p. 153.
[95] Ibid., p. 216.
[96] Ibid., pp. 167–8.

history, not requiring many of the new ideas wanted to illumine more exacting problems.

Marxism in power, in a single embattled state, gave more importance to the state in history than Marx and Engels with their more cosmopolitan outlook had done. It was as ready to admire Richelieu as a paladin of the French nation as Peter of the Russian.[97] In a very different way something similar can be said of Gramsci, writing in the shadow of defeat as Bukharin wrote in the glow of victory, and preoccupied with the fate of his own country. In Mussolini's prisons he was not in a position to write history, but he had leisure to think about it, and he can be seen as one of the firstlings of 'Western Marxism'. He was looking beyond the defeat of his young communist party to Italy's shortcomings during the Risorgimento or national revival of the nineteenth century, and further back to its failure to unite in the sixteenth. In both those periods the foreign presence was the most tangible obstacle. He was curiously fascinated by Machiavelli, took seriously the concluding appeal of *The Prince* for Italy to be freed from the barbarians, and believed that 'a unitary absolute monarchy' was a possibility of that age, in Italy as in France or Spain[98] – where he may have overlooked that there were already national foundations to build on.

For Marxism he made very lofty claims, as a doctrine qualified 'to explain and justify all the past', in a completely historical spirit.[99] On the other hand he was aware that at present it was still only an inchoate body of thought. Non-Marxist efforts to construct a historical sociology he dismissed as 'vulgar evolutionism';[100] Bukharin's presentation he thought not much better. It failed in his opinion to grapple with the fundamental question: 'how does the historical movement arise on the structural base?' What, in other words, is the prime

---

[97] See A.D. Lublinskaya, *French Absolutism: the Crucial Phase 1620–1629*, tr. B. Pearce (Cambridge, 1968).
[98] *Selections from the Prison Notebooks of Antonio Gramsci*, ed. Q. Hoare and G.N. Smith (London, 1971), p. 173.
[99] Ibid., p. 399.
[100] A. Gramsci, *The Modern Prince and Other Writings*, tr. L. Marks (London, 1957), p. 93.

driving force? He considered Bukharin too cavalier in dismissing all previous philosophers as twaddlers, and poor in his aesthetic judgments.[101] More surprisingly Gramsci had equally hard words for Plekhanov, as prone to relapses into 'vulgar materialism' and positivism, and gifted with little historical insight.[102] One puzzle he wrestled with lay in the domain of chance: the effect of errors that leaders might commit – and had lately committed in Italy – in spite of the mechanistic notion that 'every political act is determined, immediately, by the structure.'[103] This runs counter to the axiom that every situation throws up the right man, and suggests a fruitful line of inquiry.

Marxism, which had migrated to central and eastern Europe, was returning to its western birthplace, where it might still be tied to a party but was not under the surveillance of a Marxist government. In France the Revolution, which counted for so much with Marx, had always been in the forefront of historical studies, and provided a point of entry where Marxist ideas could show themselves at their most relevant. A succession of leading scholars carried them more and more into the ascendant, though they have never gone unchallenged. More generally, Marxist thinking has done much, as a stimulus, to raise French history-writing to its present eminence. From the 1930s the English revolution was being rediscovered by Marxists, and became one of the chief nourishers of a flourishing school.[104] Marx and Engels were firm believers in national character, as a deposit of national experience, and it is noteworthy that Marxists in Britain have turned much more to history than, as over much of the continent, to philosophy; while as historians they have been drawn more to specific times and issues than to theory in the abstract.

Meanwhile Marxism was finding its way into Asia, rooting

---

[101] *Selections from the Prison Notebooks*, pp. 431, 470–1.
[102] Ibid., pp. 377–8. Gramsci speaks much more favourably here of Labriola, the pioneer of Marxist thinking in Italy.
[103] Ibid., p. 408.
[104] Cf. P. Anderson, *Considerations on Western Marxism* (London, 1976), p. 102: in England 'the calibre of Marxist *historiography* has probably been superior to that of any other country.' On theory and the British labour movement, see S. Macintyre, *A Proletarian Science: Marxism in Britain 1917–1933* (Cambridge, 1980), ch. 5: 'Historical Materialism'.

itself in lands that Karl Marx strained his eyes to see from distant London, as Sherlock Holmes's mind hovered over his map of Dartmoor in Baker Street. After the post-1918 split the Second and Third Internationals both continued officially Marxist, but it was the Third that took Marxism seriously, and also made strenuous efforts to enlarge a European into a worldwide movement. India was one of its first targets; but a vigilant police made it hard for Marxist literature to enter the country, and for long after 1918 communists were only small, scattered, fractured groups. A critical concern with Marxism and history made its appearance only after Independence. In China there had earlier been a disposition to look to Russian history, especially to times of reform like Peter's, as a lesson to a backward country anxious to catch up with the times;[105] the prompt reception of Marxism in the 1920s was in a way a sequel. But civil war, White terror and Japanese invasion soon interrupted theorizing, and its application to the perplexities of China's past could only be taken up in earnest after the revolution. In another far-off quarter, Latin America, historical Marxism was arousing interest among intellectuals frustrated by a morbid inheritance. Of late years Marxism, or at any rate 'Marxology', has been gaining entry even into what for long was the dark continent of North America; today it abounds in young historians full of their discovery of it as a dazzling novelty.

Both the swelling current of history written under Marxist inspiration, and the volume of writing in defence of or attack on historical Marxism, testify to its vitality. Yet this theory, left so rudimentary by Marx himself, after a century both of debate and of history unrolling itself, still leaves room for manifold disagreements among adherents. All its main concepts still await more precise definition, beginning with the mode of production. Classification of societies has attained clarity only with respect to the two latest modes, capitalist and socialist. In Europe and still more outside, all earlier ones remain questionable.

Slavery, a case in point, was a common feature of ancient

[105] See D.C. Price, *Russia and the Roots of the Chinese Revolution, 1896–1911* (Harvard University Press, 1974), especially ch. 2.

empires; whether Marx and Engels were right in supposing that it ever formed the basis of an entire productive system is open to doubt. Slave labour on the land, as in late republican and imperial Italy, must usually have been devoted to raising of cash crops for markets at a distance. In a debate twenty years ago on the modes and their sequence one suggestion was that if branches of production resting on slavery are the most profitable in an economy, even though forming only a minor part of the total, they entitle it to rank as a slave economy.[106] But it may be needful to draw a line between methods adapted to support of a dominant class, as slavery was in Rome, and those by which the bulk of a population lives.

In Western Europe chronic change and something like an understandable succession of epochs do seem to catch the eye, with a fairly continuous tendency towards a higher level both of organization and of output. Even here, the formation of feudalism from a synthesis of Roman and barbarian has the obvious drawback that it does not show one mode arising logically from another.[107] What it does perhaps indicate is that internal stresses within a single homogeneous system (China may be the best example) have been less fruitful than the double process represented by change within both West-Roman and barbarian society during a long period of neighbourhood, ending in their creeping fusion rather than conquest of one by the other, and resulting in a structure or civilization uniquely complex and correspondingly liable to instability. But the mechanics of the all-important transition from medieval Europe to modern, or feudal to capitalist, are still among the most eagerly debated of all problems of Marxism – in Japan too, on account of analogies with its own passage to modernity in the last century.

In most or all other regions no such progression as Europe's, no onward-leading road, seems visible, only a maze of tracks losing themselves here and there. Radical alteration is very much the exception; the blessing or curse of immobility, or a

[106] R. Browning, in discussion on 'Stages of Social Development', *Marxism Today*, October 1961. Cf. M.I. Finley, *Ancient Slavery and Modern Ideology* (London, 1980), pp. 40ff, 57–8.
[107] Cf. W.H. Shaw, *Marx's Theory of History* (London, 1978), p. 138.

perpetual *da capo*, is far more the rule. Societies have been hard to categorize in Marxist language, since they form a medley not following one after the other but scattered higgledy-piggledy. They have been loosely bundled together as 'feudal'. This rag-bag procedure can be censured with good reason, not only as clashing with the familiar usage of the term to denote the institutional structure of medieval Europe, but also as obscuring the very exceptional and mutable complex that medieval Europe was. When Charlemagne and Akbar, Genjiz Khan and Montezuma, are all herded together like stray animals in a village pound, we do not really learn anything about them.

We are brought back again to the fact that what most societies have had in common is the exploitation of a majority for the benefit of a minority, by dint of armed force, or force softened into use and wont, or sanction of superstition. This is far from representing a 'mode of production' as originally conceived, since in most cases the ruling group takes no more part in production than a protection-racket in Chicago, but merely appropriates; and (as Plekhanov saw) methods of appropriation may, as in India, come and go or evolve while the productive system stands still for ages. Over the greater part of the world the dogma that the 'main historical issues' always 'relate to the development of forces of production'[108] practically reduces history to a blank.

What gives rise to change remains an equally challenging question. Marxists have usually disclaimed a 'technological' explanation, with new tools the prime mover of history, but they have often been very near to it, and they have not offered a clear alternative. Some recent writers have indeed defended the technological view, with the help of more sophisticated reasoning.[109] Marx replaced God with technology, one concludes, as 'the ultimate arbiter of history'.[110] But new tools will only transform a society if it is ready to welcome them; so that we are left to ask how this readiness has come about. A tool may

---

[108] M. Cornforth, *The Open Philosophy and the Open Society* (London, 1968), pp. 138–9.
[109] See, e.g., W.H. Shaw, *op. cit.*, p. 81 etc.
[110] J. McMurtry, *The Structure of Marx's World-View* (Princeton, 1978), p. 219; cf. pp. 157, 214. For an opposite view see V. Venable, *op. cit.*, pp. 89–91.

turn up, it has been shown, in response to changed environmental requirement, as when in Africa the hoe replaces the digging-stick. Then the tool is 'the result and no longer the cause'.[111] But new equipment has not always in the past, or not even often, been forthcoming when needed, and this cannot be explained on technical grounds alone.

The starting point seems as hard to find as the end of a tangled ball of string. Now that runaway multiplication of human beings is threatening to become humanity's worst of all perils, it is inevitable that some Marxists as well as others should look to population pressure as the arch-disturber of equilibrium. Marx's view of early Roman expansion might be quoted in their favour; but they are criticized for giving too little attention to the social and economic contexts within which numbers grow, or do not grow, and thus yielding to a sort of 'demographic determinism'.[112]

Much change has come about through intercourse between different communities, most abruptly through war and conquest, with no more logic than that armed force has flowed to wherever resistance was weak and booty cheap, as spontaneously as today capital flows towards the most tempting profits. By this means arts and crafts, weapons and techniques, have been carried from region to region as capriciously as seeds borne on the wind, while Turks ruled Bulgaria, Spaniards ruled Peru, Afghans Bengal. Conquest brought into being most of that swarm of 'feudal' or parasitical societies that occupy most of history. Each has had its own intrinsic quality, its local contacts and antagonisms and culture, to which Marxist scrutiny can properly be applied; but these societies have nearly always been incapable of sustained growth, sterile like hybrid plants or animals, and therefore intractable to the wider Marxist scheme of evolution.

Revolution, one of the points of departure of Marx's own study of history, has aroused the stiffest disagreements

---

[111] F. Braudel, *Capitalism and Material Life 1400–1800* (1967; English edn: London, 1973), p. 116.
[112] See R. Brenner, 'Agrarian Class Structure and Economic Development in Pre-industrial Europe', in *Past and Present*, no. 70, February 1976, and the debate arising from this in nos. 78, 79, 80, 85.

between Marxists and others. Much light has been thrown on it, but – as happens in natural science – each step forward has thrown up fresh dilemmas. One hindrance is that there have been very few revolutions, either 'bourgeois' or socialist, to compare, and scarcely any pre-modern ones that seem at home in any Marxist category. Students of the English revolution set out by bracketing it with 1789, and explaining both in terms of productive forces bursting the integuments of an old order. But it has been hard to demonstrate this, and also, in England on the political plane, to identify the combatants as champions of older and newer classes. A 'revolutionary bourgeoisie' is far from easy to pin down even in the French case, or at any time before the nineteenth century, and then it was invariably a failure. Without it we seem to have *Hamlet* without the prince of Denmark. Marxists have had to reconsider their analysis of revolution as the overthrow of an obsolete regime by a dynamic class bent on establishing a new mode of production on its ruins. No one willed modern capitalism; it was, so far as the men of 1642 or 1789 were concerned, a by-product. There were already capitalists, and they came out of the turmoil with power in their hands to build a capitalist order; but this is no proof that the revolution was therefore made and managed by them.

It may be necessary to think of these upheavals as semi-accidental, in their timing being due to things like Charles I's quarrel with the Scots, or the bad harvests before 1789; and confused, because of discordance between the two vibrations shaking an old society: growth of productive forces, and friction between classes, the two things connected but each following a rhythm of its own. An obtrusive complication was the intervention of other social strata – English yeomen and petty bourgeois, French peasants and artisans – with interests and mentality distinct from those of both the major combatants. The two tremors may not merely fail to synchronize, or reinforce each other, but may positively collide; if, for example, peasants rebel against being expropriated and turned into labourers to expedite the growth of capitalism. In such a case the class struggle which Bukharin called 'the motive force of history'[113] is a brake on it instead. We may even have to ask whether in China chronic peasant revolt was one of the reasons why history stuck fast.

Clearly one of the factors of human change is man himself, whom Marxists are often arraigned for taking too little notice of. They deny the charge, but it is true that they have thought most commonly of mankind in the mass; though it was to Winwood Reade, not any Marxist, that Sherlock Holmes owed his axiom that 'while the individual man is an insoluble puzzle, in the aggregate he is a mathematical certainty.'[114] Their bent has been towards rationalizing behaviour overmuch. Neither man nor his history is in any strict sense rational, though both may come by degrees to be rationally comprehended. But this requires more knowledge of the puzzling individual, or elite group, as an indispensable part-cause of historical change. Marx evidently had this in mind when he spoke of the absence of the individual from Asia.

All this borders on the enigma of human freedom. Marx, it is said, 'could not allow free will to those whose activity was to be explained and predicted by his theory.'[115] Marx the moralist would not have pleaded guilty to this, Marx the scientific socialist might often be constrained to. Without diving too deep into opaque waters, note may be taken of the most contentious aspect of the human dimension, the status to be assigned to 'great men'. Indifference to them, and to biography, is one reason why Marxist history-writing has sometimes been called dull. Really it has wavered between under- and over-valuation, in a way that betrays uncertainty. In its early optimistic conviction of having found the clue, its sensation of being borne on by an irresistible tide, the rise of a unique new class, Marxism felt no more need of aid from exceptional individuals than from Providence. Later on, when socialism had to come to grips with practical difficulties that often seemed insuperable, a nostalgia for great men revived.

[113] *Historical Materialism*, p. 78.
[114] A. Conan Doyle, *The Sign of Four* (London, 1890), ch. 9. Cf. V. Gordon Childe's remark that to turn statistical laws describing masses of particles into historical laws is too mechanistic: *History* (London, 1947), p. 82.
[115] A. Walker, *Marx: His Theory and its Context* (London, 1978), p. 107; cf. G. Leff, *The Tyranny of Concepts* (London, 1961), pp. 153ff.

Lenin and Stalin in Russia, Mao in China – both countries where a new economy had to be built by an exertion of will, against the grain of history – loomed up larger than life as personifications of heroic effort. Marx himself, it may be added, has always been looked up to by Marxists from Engels on as a very great man.

Marxism has strengthened a willingness among most historians, which would have grown in any case, to think of all compartments of history as opening on to each other. Engels defined dialectics as 'the science of interconnections', in contrast with metaphysics;[116] but he admitted that he and Marx had not given sufficient thought to the obscure processes by which ideas come to birth.[117] Marxism has thought of successive tiers rising above the economic foundations of society: political institutions and laws, as Plekhanov said, directly governed by it, art or philosophy only indirectly, with the mediation of levels in between.[118] This has not protected it against charges like Mannheim's of '*directly* associating even the most esoteric and spiritual products of the mind with the economic and power interests of a certain class'.[119] All sorts of irregularities complicate the working model. While the 'base' may be stationary for long periods the 'superstructure' may be blown about by winds of change. Or economy may alter while ideology lags. Civilizations, Braudel has written, are 'strange collections of commodities, symbols, illusions, phantasms', all churning together.[120]

Comprehension of all this is improving, thanks to numerous explorations of the history of ideas, of the arts, of religion, of science. It is on this side, it has been noticed, that 'Western Marxism' is most proficient, and can be said to have compiled a body of writing 'far richer and subtler than anything within the classical heritage of historical materialism'.[121] The reason may well be that it has found itself cut off from any realistic

---

[116] Letter to C. Schmidt, 27 October 1890.
[117] Letter to F. Mehring, 14 July 1893.
[118] *The Materialist Conception of History*, p. 28.
[119] K. Mannheim, *Essays on the Sociology of Knowledge* (London, 1952), p. 184.
[120] F. Braudel, *op. cit.*, p. 243.
[121] P. Anderson, *op. cit.*, p. 78.

prospect of socialism in power in any near future, and hence has been less taken up with practical concerns. 'Base and superstructure' is an image that goes back to Marx himself, but one that he used only a handful of times.[122] It is being felt now to be too static and rigid. A biological image, of some kind of symbiotic relationship, may be more appropriate. There is not one plane of existence on which Homo Sapiens acts, another on which he thinks; he is a thinking creature in all his doings, and only animal behaviour can be exclusively regulated by material causes.

Not many years ago Marxist and 'bourgeois' history-writing could look as different as chalk from cheese; today they often differ much less obviously. For one thing Marxism has shed most of the old vocabulary borrowed from Hegel, though how much, if any, of his logic is still to be considered valid has not been frankly faced. The formal framework is omitted, rather than repudiated; thereby Marxism may have grown more reasonable, but less readily recognizable. It is far less closely tied to party considerations than it used to be. In Japanese universities, where Marxist historians are legion, many of them are not socialists, and some are conservatives, who simply find Marxism a useful tool.[123] It is in short no longer easy to say who is entitled to call himself – if he chooses – a Marxist.

It may be nearly as hard to say who is *not*, in some measure, so widely has the influence of Marx's more general ideas spread. Among historians nowadays only the most unlettered are ignorant of him, only the dullest have failed to learn something from him. Fairly typically, an English historian some years ago expressing his distrust of single-cause interpretations deprecated, nevertheless, 'any partisan approach that would dismiss Marxism offhand; Marx was a great thinker.'[124] More lately a Dutch historian commenced a chapter of a biography by saying: 'we are all familiar with the teachings of Marx', and know that account has to be taken of the big objective forces.[125]

[122] D.R. Gandy, *op. cit.*, p. 153. M. Evans. *op. cit.*, p. 62, calls it 'an unfortunate metaphor from the language of constructional engineering.'
[123] Information from Ian Gow, of Sheffield University.
[124] V. Purcell, *The Boxer Uprising* (Cambridge, 1963), pp. 270–1.
[125] J. den Tex, *Oldenbarnevelt* (Cambridge, 1973), vol. 1, ch. 6.

There was a time when Marxists were resentful of outsiders taking over some of their ideas and, as they felt, denaturing them; the fashionable 'Sociology of Knowledge' looked to them like historical materialism minus class struggle, a bowdlerizing on a par with Tate's *King Lear*. Since the embitterments of Cold War years there has been a freer interchange of opinions and criticisms. It is to a great extent through the controversies Marxism has stirred up, ever since it became impossible to ignore it, that history as a science has advanced.

By and large Marxist writing has grown plainer, less esoteric, but in some directions it has been proliferating into scholastic abstruseness, or running to academic seed, through increasing detachment from practical politics. These divagations are often the more baffling because couched – like so much contemporary sociology – in a worse than Hegelian jargon, as arcane as Marx's handwriting, a language that as Lord Dundreary would say 'no feller can understand'. Recent 'structuralist' glosses of Marx seem, a critic remarks, to lose all contact with his materialism.[126] Any historical school needs fresh air from outside, but Marxist history may be in some danger of too much encroachment by theorists lacking in factual acquaintance with history. A case where the merits of an intrusion are hard to gauge is that of Althusser, with his insistence on a genuine Marxist philosophy of history, to be gathered together from elements latent in Marx's work, and his dismissal of history-writing without this as mere 'historicism' or humanism, and of Gramsci as one of the chief delinquents.[127]

Another development, to be welcomed with some caution, has taken the form of a number of ambitious attempts at wide-arching hypotheses intended to embrace whole epochs and their ramifying problems. Marx and Engels indulged in such speculation, though as a rule tentatively; and it is valuable as an antidote to the specialization forced on scholarship now, confinement to narrow areas where there may be little scope for

[126] A. Brewer, *Marxist Theories of Imperialism* (London, 1980), p. 12.
[127] L. Althusser, 'Philosophy as a Revolutionary Weapon' (interview, 1968), translation in *New Left Review*, no. 64, 1970. For a useful critique see N. Geras, 'Althusser's Marxism', in *New Left Review*, no. 71, 1972. Cf. P. Anderson, *op. cit.*, p. 84.

a Marxist approach to stand out from others. Wallerstein's thesis of a 'world market' as the indispensable setting of the advance to capitalism[128] is impressive, but not always easy to square with humdrum detail. Frank's portrayal, with Latin American poverty for its backcloth, of the rise of capitalism in Europe as a cannibalistic preying on other continents, cutting short their development,[129] suffers much more from a lack of congruence with history as known to the textbook.

It may often seem that to try to interpret non-European histories on Marxist lines is as misconceived as to classify non-Aryan languages by the rules of English or Latin grammar. But this can be debated less one-sidedly and more fruitfully now that there are Marxists everywhere. Communism in the Third World has had close links with colonial nationalism and liberation movements, and this is bound to be reflected in Marxist theory; as with Christianity, new peoples taking up Marxism are making it their own, not something to be expounded to them from Europe. It was in this spirit that Cabral, the revolutionary leader in Portuguese Guinea and a pioneer of African Marxism, rejected any postulate of history beginning with class struggle, and the implication that great tracts of Africa, Asia, America had no history worth the name until they were turned into colonies: 'This we refuse to accept.'[130] It is undeniable, after all, that history in the sense of migrations, inventions, cults, adaptations to environment, was going on for millennia before true classes and class conflict began.

India was the country outside Europe that Marx gave most thought to, and his articles on it, collected and republished in the 1930s, did much to rouse interest among Indian socialists in their national history. Marxists there have been less intent than in some other countries on claiming an evolution running through the same sequence of stages as Europe's, by way of a

[128] I. Wallerstein, *The Modern World-System* (New York, 1974).
[129] A.G. Frank, *Capitalism and Underdevelopment in Latin America* (New York, 1967). In both this and Wallerstein's work, A. Brewer (*op. cit.*, p. 264), while recognizing their value, complains of a lack of thorough analysis 'to back up their sloganistic generalizations'.
[130] *Revolution in Guinea. An African People's Struggle*, selected texts by Amilcar Cabral (London, 1969), p. 77.

denial of European uniqueness. But many have been increasingly concerned to maintain that India was moving on its own towards capitalism, the gateway to socialism, before it succumbed to British imperialism.

Against Marx's forecast of beneficial results in the long run from this interruption or disruption of Indian history, or lack of history, it is urged that the real shortage was of enough information to allow him to discover an economic life in old India with an energy and forward movement of its own. Even so, it may be urged that foreign intervention was needed to release energy from obstructions that were holding it up, as it did, all can agree, in the case of Japan. But many Indian Marxists are not prepared to admit that their country had come to a standstill, and had to be painfully dragged back on to the narrow causeway of progress by imperialism. Their picture of pre-colonial India is one of trade and finance blooming, agriculture improving, political conditions in the wake of the Mughal empire far less chaotic than British propagandists gave them out to be. On this showing Britain, so far from jerking India forward, was thrusting it back, by cutting short its progress, destroying its manufactures, condemning it to the underdevelopment of the entire colonial world.

If the contention can be substantiated it will turn a fresh page of historical Marxism, at the expense of some of its older notions. At present no more can be said than that sufficient evidence of an indigenous Indian advance is not yet forthcoming. Meanwhile the polemics have at least thrown up novel ideas; among them, that of a special 'colonial mode of production', an economy and society combining capitalist with pre-capitalist structures, is advocated by a number of Marxists both Western and Indian.[131] Quite apart from controversial issues of the recent past, Marxist historians have been taking a very active hand in the investigation at many points of India's often enigmatic annals, and its prehistory.[132]

In China much fruitless effort was expended, as a Western

---

[131] E.g., Lucien Rey; Hamza Alavi. Cf. A. Brewer, *op. cit.*, pp. 186–7.
[132] A good many of them are represented in the large volume of *Essays in Honour of Professor S.C. Sarkar* (People's Publishing House, New Delhi, 1976).

scholar respectfully critical of Marxism writes, in the endeavour to categorize the national story without distorting either it, or historical materialism, or both; the great stumbling-block being the dogma of 'a universally applicable model of progress'.[133] It seems perverse to insist on an epoch of slavery in ancient China because Marx believed there was one in ancient Europe; socialism can regard all men and peoples as equals without any myth of equal pedigrees. By this insistence Chinese Marxism only landed itself in difficulties, like Cinderella's sisters trying to get their feet into her slipper; a new sort of Chinese foot-binding. An embarrassment early encountered was that feudalism, in the sense of rule by feudal lords and princes, broke up exceptionally early, and yet for another couple of thousand years China failed to move on to capitalism.[134]

Early on, Marx and Engels too summarily wrote off agrarian risings in medieval Europe as 'totally ineffective because of the isolation and consequent crudity of the peasants'.[135] Chinese historians can scarcely endorse such a view of the peasant rebellions that were so striking a feature of China's past. Yet it is a puzzle how to think of them as progressive if the touchstone of progress is to be economic expansion. A promising if not conclusive answer has been found in the dictum that despite failure 'the class struggle nonetheless affected the deeper undercurrents of history.'[136] Another facet of the Chinese approach which has been noted is the greater weight given to the force of ideas and of human will than in classical Marxism. For the Chinese revolution, with its very weak urban and working-class base, there has been little choice but to rely on faith to move mountains.

A generation ago a young Marxist historian could feel like a Columbus boldly crossing seas and oceans while timider navigators hugged their shores. Since then it has sometimes appeared to the onlooker that in order to keep afloat, historical

---

[133] A. Dirlik, *Revolution and History. The Origins of Marxist Historiography in China 1919–1937* (University of California Press, 1978), pp. 229–31.
[134] Ibid., p. 116; cf. ch. 6, on problems of periodizing.
[135] *The German Ideology*, p. 46.
[136] J.P. Harrison, *The Communists and Chinese Peasant Rebellions. A Study in the Rewriting of Chinese History* (London edn: 1970), p. 20; cf. pp. 190–1.

Marxism has had to introduce so many qualifications and refinements, admit so many exceptions, that it resembles the Ptolemaic system in decline, tacking on more and more epicycles to explain celestial anomalies.[137] Nevertheless a hundred years have gone by since Marx, and no Copernicus has come forward with a better scheme. Whatever objections it is open to, all other ways either of interpreting history or of writing it without benefit of any philosophy are open to far more. Opponents have found it easier to criticize Marxism than to defend themselves against its criticism. Fallible as they may often be, Marx's outlines, even his guesses, belong to the world of reality; his map has no fabulous continents or Mountains of the Moon, no 'seas of butter and seas of treacle'.

History has moved towards some at least of the destinations he expected, but by more roundabout routes. The time may be at hand when the economic and political spheres of his thinking, to which in his day he had to give priority, will be less helpful to our much-altered planet, at least to societies entering a 'post-industrial' era, than his illumination of the past, the conjectures comprised within his historical theory about how man's workaday life has been married to the arts, sciences, religions. It may be regrettable that a corpus of ideas still in the making, the work of many minds, goes under one man's name. But in Marx's centenary year it is proper to make all the acknowledgment due to an unforgettable genius.

[137] A criticism made in a New Left Club discussion at Edinburgh in March 1961.

Sociology

Tom Bottomore

1. The early reception of Marxist ideas

Sociologists were among the first social scientists to recognize the importance of Marx's thought for their own discipline. Ferdinand Tönnies, in the preface to his influential book *Gemeinschaft und Gesellschaft* (1887), acknowledged his indebtedness to Marx, whom he described as a 'most remarkable and most profound social philosopher', as the discoverer of the capitalist mode of production and a thinker who had attempted to formulate the same idea that Tönnies himself was seeking to express in new concepts.[1] At the very first international congress of sociology, in 1894, scholars from several countries (including Tönnies, Kovalevsky and Ferri)[2] contributed papers which discussed Marx's theory, and a subsequent congress (1900) was devoted entirely to a discussion of 'historical materialism'.[3] During the 1890s Marxism also began to be taught in a few universities, notably by Carl Grünberg[4] at the

---

[1] Tönnies, *op. cit.*, tr. *Community and Society* (London: Routledge and Kegan Paul, 1955). In 1921 Tönnies published a study of Marx (English edn: *Karl Marx: His Life and Work* [East Lansing: Michigan State University Press, 1974]) in which he reiterated the importance of Marx's work, and in the second part of the book examined some of the theoretical problems – both economic and sociological – which it poses.

[2] See *Annales de l'Institut International de Sociologie*, ed. René Worms, vol. I (Paris, 1895). Kovalevsky, in his paper on the early forms of society in Russia, referred also to the sociological studies of P. Lavrov, whom Marx had known and esteemed. E. Ferri, an Italian criminologist, developed his ideas in *Socialisme et science positive: Darwin, Spencer, Marx* (1896; English edn: *Socialism and Positive Science*, 1905), where he argued that 'scientific socialism is simply the logical application of the postulates of Darwin and Spencer in the field of political economy and sociology.'

[3] See *Annales de l'Institut International de Sociologie* (Paris, 1901).

[4] Carl Grünberg (1861–1940) became professor of political economy in Vienna, where he taught mainly on economic history, agrarian questions and the history of the labour movement, from 1894 to 1924; then moved to Frankfurt to become the first director of the newly established Institute for Social Research. He is probably best known for the journal which he founded (1910) and edited, the *Archiv für die Geschichte des Sozialismus und der Arbeiterbewegung*.

University of Vienna and by Antonio Labriola[5] at the University of Rome, and was more widely expounded and debated in scholarly publications as well as in socialist journals such as *Die Neue Zeit* (edited by Karl Kautsky) and *Le Devenir social* (edited by Georges Sorel). In the latter journal Sorel wrote a noteworthy critical study of Durkheim's *Rules of Sociological Method*.[6]

Meanwhile, from the other side, critical assessments or refutations of Marxist theory began to appear, not only in political economy (often including an important sociological element),[7] but also in the field of sociology as it began to establish itself in the universities as a general social science. One of the first major criticisms was R. Stammler's *Wirtschaft und Recht nach der materialistischen Geschichtsauffassung* (1896) which argued that the social relations of production cannot exist outside a definite system of legal rules, and hence that juridical norms are actually the indispensable premise of economic activity, rather than vice versa.[8] During this decade Max Weber also began his long, but oblique and episodic, encounter with Marxism, in the course of which he expressed

---

[5] Antonio Labriola (1843–1904) taught philosophy at the University of Rome from 1874 to 1904, published the first Italian translation of *The Communist Manifesto* in 1890, and a collection of essays, which made him widely known, *The Materialist Conception of History*, in 1900 (English edn: Chicago, 1908).

[6] Georges Sorel, 'Les théories de M. Durkheim', *Le Devenir social*, I, nos. 1 and 2 (1895), pp. 1–26, 148–80 (English tr. of part in Tom Bottomore and Patrick Goode, eds., *Readings in Marxist Sociology*, 1983).

[7] Two major contributions, occasioned by the publication of the third volume of *Capital* in 1894, were the long essays by Werner Sombart, 'Zur Kritik des ökonomischen Systems von Karl Marx', *Archiv für soziale Gesetzgebung und Statistik*, VII (1894), pp. 555–94; and by Eugen von Böhm-Bawerk, *Zum Abschluss des Marxschen System* (1896), translated as *Karl Marx and the Close of his System* (1898). The latter work attracted a counter criticism from Rudolf Hilferding, *Böhm-Bawerks Marx-Kritik*, which remains one of the best expositions of a sociological conception of the economy. The texts by Böhm-Bawerk and Hilferding have been published together, in English, in a volume edited with an introduction by Paul M. Sweezy (New York: Augustus M. Kelley, 1949).

[8] In due course the second edition of Stammler's book was critically examined by Max Weber, in an essay (1907; English edn, *Critique of Stammler*, New York: The Free Press, 1977) in which he made clear his opposition to *any* attempt to discover an 'ultimately determining factor' (whether material or ideal) in social and cultural history. Subsequently, Stammler's book was criticized from a Marxist standpoint by Max Adler, 'R. Stammlers Kritik der materialistischen Geschichtsauffassung', in *Marxistische Probleme* (1913).

two principal objections to the Marxist theory: first, that the 'economic interpretation of history', like any other attempt to formulate a total conception of social and cultural phenomena, could only be a one-sided interpretation from a particular value standpoint, not a universally valid science;[9] and second, that the Marxist idea of socialism, derived from this theory of history, was erroneous, for socialism would greatly strengthen the trend towards an ever-increasing bureaucratization of social life and its outcome was more likely to be the 'dictatorship of the official' than the 'dictatorship of the proletariat'.[10]

In France, similarly, the spread of Marxist thought evoked a response from Durkheim, whose first implicit reference to it was in his discussion of class conflict in the concluding part of *The Division of Labour in Society* (1894) on the 'abnormal forms of the division of labour'. Then, in 1895–6, he began a course of lectures on socialism, the third year of which he intended to devote to Marx and German socialism, but the course was abandoned after the first year. Under Durkheim's direction *L'Année Sociologique* reviewed several Marxist works and French translations of Marx, between 1898 and 1901; and Durkheim himself wrote two reviews, one of Labriola's *Essays on the Materialist Conception of History*,[11] in which he recognized some merit in Marx's attempt to construct a social science, finding 'extremely fruitful this idea that social life should be explained, not by the notions of those who participate in it, but by more profound causes ... to be sought mainly in the manner according to which the associated individuals are grouped', the second of Ernest Grosse's *Die Formen der Familie und die Formen der Wirtschaft*,[12] where he observed, however, that the inadequacy of the 'economic materialist' conception was most evident in the study of the family.

[9] See the preceding note, and also Weber's remarks at the end of *The Protestant Ethic and the Spirit of Capitalism* (1904; English edn, London: Allen and Unwin, 1976).
[10] See his lecture on socialism (1918, published in *Gesammelte Aufsätze zur Soziologie und Sozialpolitik*, 1924; English tr. in W.G. Runciman, ed., *Max Weber: Selections in Translation*, Cambridge: Cambridge University Press, 1978), and also his various comments on socialism in *Economy and Society* (1922; English edn, 3 vols., New York: Bedminster Press, 1968).
[11] *Revue Philosophique*, XLIV, pp. 645–51.
[12] *L'Année Sociologique*, I, pp. 319–32.

Elsewhere in Europe, too, Marxist ideas were spreading rapidly. In Italy, as I have mentioned, Labriola began to expound the materialist conception of history, and his writings, along with Stammler's book, were the starting point for several studies of historical materialism by Croce, who described it as 'a fashionable subject' which 'has rapidly attained great fame'.[13] In Croce's view (and here he agreed with Labriola) Marx's theory was not a new philosophy of history; but nor was it simply a new method (as Engels and Labriola seemed to assert): 'It is properly this: a mass of new data, of new experiences, of which the historian becomes conscious.' This, however, was largely compatible with Labriola's general conception of history as 'nothing more than the history of society'; or in other words, a sociological history or historical sociology. In Russia, Marx's theory had a considerable influence; the first translation of *Capital*, vol. I, was published there in 1872, in an edition of 3000 copies, and later in the same year a substantial and largely favourable review appeared in the St Petersburg journal *Vestnik Europy*.[14] This diffusion of Marx's work led eventually to the emergence of a Russian 'school' of Marxism, in which the leading figure was G.V. Plekhanov. In his principal theoretical work, *In Defence of Materialism. The Development of the Monist View of History* (1895),[15] Plekhanov argued that Marxism is a comprehensive world-view or philosophy ('dialectical materialism', a term which he invented), which is applied, in 'historical materialism', to the study of social phenomena. In discussing the latter sphere, Plekhanov was mainly concerned to uphold the conception of 'productive forces' as the ultimately determining factor in social development, while recognizing (as did Engels

---

[13] Benedetto Croce, 'Concerning the Scientific Form of Historical Materialism'. This essay, along with several others, all dating from the period 1895 to 1899, is published in English in Benedetto Croce, *Historical Materialism and the Economics of Karl Marx* (London: Howard Latimer, 1913).
[14] Marx quoted this review at length in his postscript to the second German edition of *Capital* (1873), and commented that the writer 'describes so aptly and ... so generously, the method I have actually used', in an attempt 'to demonstrate, by means of exact scientific study, the necessity of definite and orderly successions in social relations ...'
[15] English edn, London: Lawrence and Wishart, 1947.

at this time[16]) that there is interaction between the economic base and the cultural and political superstructure, and to provide a more thorough analysis of what is meant by the economic or technological determination of social life 'in the last resort', within the framework of a single unitary historical process.[17] Plekhanov also contributed to the development of a Marxist sociology of art,[18] and together with Mehring he was a pioneer in this field.

The extensive discussion of Marx's theory in the last decade of the nineteenth century was to a great extent the consequence of the rapid growth of the socialist movement in Europe, especially in Germany, and the adoption of a Marxist view of society by large sections of that movement. This was true for both the advocates and the opponents of Marxism. As Löwith wrote much later: 'Like our actual society, which it studies, social science is not unified but divided in two: bourgeois sociology and Marxism.'[19] Marxist social science, although it had, as I have indicated, a few representatives in the universities, was expounded and developed for the most part through the institutions of the socialist movement – party schools and conferences, socialist publishing houses – by scholars who were also engaged, for much of the time, in party politics.[20] On the other side, academic sociology, as it developed particularly in Germany and France, could be seen in part at least as a response by bourgeois society to the danger represented by the Marxist theory of society as an intellectual arm of the socialist movement.

Over the next few decades academic sociology and Marxist

[16] See his letters to J. Bloch (21 September 1890), C. Schmidt (27 October 1890), F. Mehring (14 July 1893) and W. Borgius (25 January 1894).
[17] See, on Plekhanov's work and its background, S.H. Baron, *Plekhanov: The Father of Russian Marxism* (Stanford, 1963).
[18] See especially, *Art and Social Life* (1912; English edn, London: Lawrence and Wishart, 1953).
[19] Karl Löwith, *Max Weber and Karl Marx* (1932; English edn, London: Allen and Unwin, 1982).
[20] Hilferding, in the preface to *Finance Capital* (1910; English edn, London: Routledge and Kegan Paul, 1981), replied quite reasonably to reproaches that Marxism had failed to advance economic theory: 'The Marxist finds himself in a peculiar situation; excluded from the universities, which afford the time required for scientific research, he is obliged to defer his scientific work to those leisure hours which his political struggles may spare him.'

social science continued to develop along these separate paths. In Germany Kautsky contributed particularly to the historical study of social classes and class struggles in such works as *The Class Antagonisms of 1789* (1889) and *The Foundations of Christianity* (1908), and founded (in 1883) the journal *Die Neue Zeit*, which became the principal forum for the discussion of Marxist theory. Also in this period Mehring laid the foundations of a Marxist sociology of art and literature, and of the history of ideas, with *Die Lessing-Legende* (1893) and numerous studies of modern writers. Elsewhere in Europe, aside from the work of Labriola and Plekhanov already mentioned, there were important contributions to a Marxist sociology by Sorel, in his critical essay on Durkheim's sociology (see above), and in the essays written from 1898 onwards which were subsequently collected in *Matériaux d'une théorie du prolétariat* (1908); and in the writings of Pannekoek on science (though most of these belong to a somewhat later period).[21]

By the end of the century, however, some major theoretical disagreements, largely influenced by sociological considerations, had emerged within Marxism itself, in the 'revisionist controversy'. Bernstein's articles published in *Die Neue Zeit* from the end of 1896 and subsequently as a book,[22] which were the focal point of the controversy, formulated two main theses. First, if Marxism is a science then its results must ultimately be testable by empirical evidence, and from this standpoint some parts of the theory now needed to be revised, because the course of development in the capitalist societies was diverging from that foreseen by Marx; the class structure was becoming more complex, the middle classes were not disappearing, a polarization of classes was not taking place, misery was not increasing, and economic crises were becoming less rather than more severe. Second, he argued (though very briefly) that Marxism as a positive science needs to be complemented by an

[21] See below, p. 114.
[22] Eduard Bernstein, *Die Voraussetzungen des Sozialismus und die Aufgaben der Sozialdemokratie* (1899; tr. under the title *Evolutionary Socialism*, 1909, reprinted New York: Schocken Books, 1961).

ethical theory.[23] Other Marxists replied to Bernstein's critique in a variety of ways. Thus Kautsky reasserted the orthodox view of the 'inevitable' economic breakdown of capitalism and presented the whole issue largely in terms of upholding the Marxist revolutionary idea against reformism, as did Rosa Luxemburg in *Sozialreform oder Revolution?* (1899; second, revised edition 1908). Other substantial criticisms of Bernstein's views came from Labriola, and especially from the Austro-Marxists who conceived their own version of Marxist theory as being directed against diverse forms of revisionism, including the influence of the marginalist economic theory (which was quite considerable in the case of Bernstein himself). Finally, Lenin asserted – and this view became part of Leninist and Stalinist orthodoxy – that revisionism was simply the ideology of the 'labour aristocracy' in the working-class movement.

Nevertheless, in spite of the criticisms levelled against Bernstein, many of the issues which he raised have remained at the centre of scientific discussion, as well as political controversy, among Marxist thinkers. Not only in the following decade, when the outlines of a Marxist sociology were more clearly drawn, but right up to the present day, the main features of the development of modern capitalism – the nature of its crises, the changing class structure (and especially the changes in the situation of the working class), the meaning of class conflict in a democratic political system, the growth of state intervention, and the effects of cultural change – have been the material of numerous Marxist studies, which in turn have given rise to reformulations of the theoretical scheme as a whole.

[23] For a fuller account of Bernstein's ideas and their context, and in particular the influence of neo-Kantianism on his 'positivism' and his ethical views, see Peter Gay, *The Dilemma of Democratic Socialism* (New York: Columbia University Press, 1952).

2. The 'Golden Age' of Marxist sociology[24]

In the period from the end of the nineteenth century to 1914 Marxist sociology made a significant advance. Not only did many of the thinkers mentioned previously continue and extend their work, but more important, the first recognizable 'school' of sociology appeared within Marxism in the shape of Austro-Marxism. The leading Austro-Marxist thinkers – Max Adler, Otto Bauer, Rudolf Hilferding and Karl Renner – all regarded Marxism as a sociological theory, and saw their own studies as contributions to various fields of sociology. Otto Bauer later described the general character of the school as follows:

> What united them was not a specific political orientation, but the particular character of their intellectual work. They had all grown up in a period when men such as Stammler, Windelband and Rickert were attacking Marxism with philosophical arguments; hence they were obliged to engage in controversy with the representatives of modern philosophical trends. If Marx and Engels began from Hegel, and the later Marxists from materialism, the more recent 'Austro-Marxists' had as their point of departure Kant and Mach. On the other side these 'Austro-Marxists' had to engage in controversy with the so-called Austrian school of political economy, and this debate too influenced the method and structure of their thought. Finally, they all had to learn, in the old Austria rent by national struggles, how to apply the Marxist conception of history to very complicated phenomena which defied analysis by any superficial or schematic use of the Marxist method.[25]

[24] It was the American Marxist Louis Boudin who first referred to this period as 'our Golden Age, the unforgettable period of the first decade of this century' (in a letter to Friedrich Adler, 28 February 1951). Boudin was intellectually close to the Austro-Marxists and originated the term 'Austro-Marxism'.
[25] Otto Bauer, 'What is Austro-Marxism?', tr. in Tom Bottomore and Patrick Goode, eds., *Austro-Marxism* (Oxford: Oxford University Press, 1978), pp. 45–8.

I have given an account elsewhere of the origins and development of the school,[26] and here I will confine myself to discussing a few of its major contributions to sociological thought and research. In the first place, the Austro-Marxists, and notably Max Adler, set out to establish the foundations of Marxism as an empirical science of society, and they were profoundly influenced, as Bauer indicated, by a philosophy of science inspired by neo-Kantianism and the positivism of Ernst Mach.[27] The greater part of Max Adler's work was devoted to clarifying the distinctive nature of the 'social' and formulating a conception of social association (or 'socialized humanity') as a transcendental condition of experience in Kant's sense. Thus in his essay on 'The Sociology in Marxism'[28] after declaring that 'Marxism is identical with sociology', he continued:

> ... theoretical reflection on social life does not begin either with the concept of society ... or with the isolated individual ... but with the individual as he *really* is; an individual who is always necessarily connected with other human beings in his thought and existence, since he must logically assume the existence of other beings of the same kind as himself. As soon as human beings appear they already have necessary relations of thought and action to each other.

Adler employed this idea of a transcendental condition of social knowledge not only in explicating and vindicating Marx's conception of 'socialized humanity', but also in criticizing other

[26] In my introduction to *Austro-Marxism, op. cit.*, pp. 8–15.
[27] Thus they followed a course parallel to that of the philosophers of science who later constituted the Vienna Circle, and there was indeed a direct link between these two intellectual currents in the person of Otto Neurath (see *Austro-Marxism, op. cit.*, p. 5). In one of his essays, Max Adler observed that he saw in Marx's work 'only a form of natural science positivism, more or less in the manner of Ernst Mach' (*Marxistische Probleme*, 1913, p. 62). This general conception of Marxism as a science was also derived in part from Carl Grünberg who was the teacher of many of the Austro-Marxists, and who later summed up his own view, in his inaugural address as the first director of the Frankfurt Institute for Social Research (*Festrede*, 1924), as being that 'the materialist conception of history neither is, nor aims to be, a philosophical system ... its object is not abstractions, but the given concrete world in its process of development and change.'
[28] 'Die Soziologie im Marxismus' (1924; tr. in Bottomore and Goode, eds., *Readings in Marxist Sociology, op. cit.*).

theoretical schemes and philosophies of science. From this critical aspect his thought was directed against a superficial positivism and simple-minded empiricism (as was much neo-Kantian thought), but also against the excessive formalism of some kinds of neo-Kantianism itself, which led to a preoccupation with the construction of abstract models divorced from empirical investigation, and finally, against various forms of social teleology which were being advanced as alternatives to causal explanation.[29] Undoubtedly, Adler made a major contribution, comparable with that of Max Weber, to the 'Methodenstreit' in the social sciences at the turn of the century, and it has not yet received the attention which it deserves.[30]

But Adler was not exclusively concerned with the philosophy of science. In *Die Staatsauffassung des Marxismus* (1922) he examined the differences between a sociological (Marxist) and a formal theory of law, and discussed critically Kelsen's 'pure theory of law'; he made an important contribution to Marxist analyses of ideology and culture;[31] and he wrote extensively on democracy and on the working-class movement.[32] The other Austro-Marxist thinkers produced major studies in a variety of fields. Otto Bauer published in 1907 *Die Nationalitätenfrage und die Sozialdemokratie* (second, enlarged edition 1924), which was the first substantial Marxist analysis of nation states and nationalism in relation to socialism, and remains unrivalled to the present day. Among many other works he also undertook

[29] On the last point, see especially *Kausalität und Teleologie im Streite um die Wissenschaft* (1904). It is important to emphasize here, since some later commentators have confused the issue, that the neo-Kantianism of Adler, and of the other Austro-Marxists, was confined to the philosophy of science and had little to do with the idea of complementing Marxist social science with a Kantian ethic, which they explicitly rejected. Nevertheless, their conception of Marxism as a positive science did raise questions about the normative aims of the socialist movement, which Adler attempted to resolve in various ways (see Bottomore and Goode, eds., *Austro-Marxism*, pp. 20–1).

[30] Recently, however, there has been a growth of interest, provoked in part, no doubt, by the revival of the 'Methodenstreit' in the past two decades. See, for example, the discussion of Adler in Leszek Kolakowski, *Main Currents of Marxism* (Oxford: Clarendon Press, 1978), vol. II, pp. 258–73.

[31] See especially *Der Sozialismus und die Intellektuellen* (1910), *Georg Simmels Bedeutung für die Geistesgeschichte* (1919), and the chapter (ch. 11) on ideology in *Lehrbuch der materialistischen Geschichtsauffassung* (1930).

[32] See *Politische oder soziale Demokratie* (1926), and 'Wandlung der Arbeiterklasse?' (1933; tr. of part in Bottomore and Goode, eds., *Austro-Marxism*, pp. 217–48).

a sociological and historical study of the Austrian revolution,[33] and an analysis of the 'rationalization' of production as an element in the postwar development of capitalism.[34]

Karl Renner, too, published some early studies on the problem of nationalities in the Austro-Hungarian Empire, but he is best known for his pioneering contribution to a Marxist sociology of law, *The Institutions of Private Law and their Social Functions* (1904),[35] in which he investigated the changing functions of legal norms in response to changes in the economic structure. A particularly interesting aspect of Renner's study is that he attributed an active role to law in maintaining or modifying social relationships, and did not regard it as a mere reflection of economic conditions. In this respect he shared the general view of the Austro-Marxists concerning the relation between 'base' and 'superstructure'; a view which emphasized 'interaction' rather than a strict economic determinism, even 'in the last resort', and attributed great importance to the ideologies of nationalism and imperialism, and to the growing role of the state in the organization of economic and social life. Indeed, Renner published in 1916 a series of essays on 'Problems of Marxism'[36] in which he concentrated largely on the consequences of state intervention, and observed that 'capitalist society, as Marx experienced and described it, no longer exists ... one might say that *laissez-faire* capitalism has changed into state capitalism... Socialism can no longer be related to the *laissez-faire* economic order; we face entirely new and different problems.' Much later, in a general study of the changes in modern society,[37] he returned to this subject, but also examined in detail the changes in class structure – in particular, the expansion of the new middle class, which he called the 'service class' – and its political consequences.

Lastly, Rudolf Hilferding, in *Finance Capital* and in later

[33] *Die Österreichische Revolution* (1923; abridged English version New York: Burt Franklin, 1925).
[34] *Kapitalismus und Sozialismus nach dem Weltkrieg*, vol. I, *Rationalisierung oder Fehlrationalisierung?* (1931).
[35] Revised ed, 1929; English edn, London: Routledge and Kegan Paul, 1949.
[36] In *Der Kampf*, IX (1916; English tr. of part in Bottomore and Goode, eds., *Austro-Marxism*, pp. 91–101).
[37] *Wandlungen der modernen Gesellschaft* (posthumously published, Vienna: Verlag der Wiener Volksbuchhandlung, 1953).

essays (1915, 1924, 1927),[38] elaborated his conception of 'organized capitalism', which was characterized by the economic dominance of the large corporations and the banks, in close association with a strongly interventionist state. As a result of this development, in Hilferding's view, the socialization of the economy, which was now to an increasing extent planned and centrally managed, had greatly advanced and constituted the basis for a transition to socialism. In his last writings, however, Hilferding became more aware of the dangers inherent in the growing power of the state, and this is a question to which I shall return.

Alongside this creation of a Marxist school of sociology there was a continued development of sociological inquiry by other European Marxists. Thus Pannekoek published a study, *Marxism and Darwinism* (1909),[39] in which, having outlined a distinction between the spheres of natural science and social science, he argued that the attempts to transfer theories directly from one sphere to the other – as in the case of the 'social Darwinists' – produced false and misleading conceptions. He then went on to examine the ways in which theories in both spheres were connected with class struggles, as scientific expressions of the world views of different classes. Here, and in his later writings, Pannekoek provided some of the elements for a Marxist sociology and history of science, which began to be more fully developed in the 1930s.[40]

In the same field of Marxist studies of the cultural 'superstructure', Mehring and Plekhanov continued their work in literary criticism, while Sorel, from a highly idiosyncratic position, presented Marxism under two aspects, as a realistic theory of history and as the ideology of class struggle, and expounded in *Reflections on Violence* (1908 and later enlarged

---

[38] See *Finance Capital* (1910; English tr. London: Routledge and Kegan Paul, 1981); 'Arbeitsgemeinschaft der Klassen?', *Der Kampf*, VIII (1915); 'Probleme der Zeit', *Die Gesellschaft*, I, 1 (1924); 'Die Aufgaben der Sozialdemokratie in der Republik' (Berlin, 1927; English tr. of part of the 1927 essay in Bottomore and Goode, eds., *Readings in Marxist Sociology*, *op. cit.*).

[39] English edn, Chicago: Charles H. Kerr, 1912.

[40] For an account of Pannekoek's life and work see Serge Bricianer, *Pannekoek and the Workers' Councils* (St Louis, Mo.: Telos Press, 1978), Introduction, pp. 31–55.

editions)[41] his conception of myth as a 'body of images' which inspires and organizes a social group – the myth of the proletariat being the general strike.[42] Mention should also be made here of the Polish sociologist Ludwick Krzywicki, whose general view of historical materialism seems to have been very similar to the neo-Kantian conception of the Austro-Marxists, and who treated the independent influence of ideas, in particular of legal systems, in much the same manner as did Renner.[43]

During this period of just over a decade, therefore, the elements of a Marxist sociology were firmly established in Europe;[44] and while its base remained in the socialist movement rather than in the universities, it nevertheless came to be widely debated and increasingly influential among academic scholars and students as its intellectual force and practical significance was gradually recognized. But this intellectual and political advance was brought to an abrupt end by the First World War, which shattered the unity of the socialist movement and created new divisions in Marxist thought.

[41] English edn, Glencoe, Ill.: Free Press, 1950.

[42] Sorel had already made this distinction in his critical essay on Durkheim's sociology (1895) where he observed that 'what we can ask of a social science is that it should make us aware of the development and the importance of revolutionary forces, but whereas formerly the future was grasped by means of a hypothesis accorded all the deference shown to a scientific theory, we can now only have *indeterminate* views about the future, expressible only in the language of of the artistic imagination.' It would be extremely interesting to re-examine Sorel's conception of myth in the light of recent structuralist studies of myth and ideology.

[43] On Krzywicki's work, see Kolakowski, *Main Currents of Marxism*, vol. II, pp. 193–207.

[44] But not in Britain, where neither sociology nor Marxism had much intellectual influence until quite recently. In the USA, the impact upon the social sciences was somewhat greater, notably in the case of Thorstein Veblen, but there was no substantial development of indigenous Marxist social theory, in part, no doubt, because of the weakness of the American socialist movement. E.R.A. Seligman published a short critical study, *The Economic Interpretation of History* in 1902, while the only major Marxist work was Louis Boudin's *The Theoretical System of Karl Marx* (1907), which provided a lucid exposition of the materialist conception of history, and a response to various critics, including particularly Bernstein. But Boudin's work was much better known, and more appreciated, in Europe than in the USA.

3. *Communist orthodoxy and Western Marxism*

With the collapse of the Second International in 1914, the subsequent victory of the Russian Revolution, and the failure of the postwar revolutions in Central Europe, Marxism underwent a profound change. Now not only bourgeois society, but the socialist movement itself, was divided in two. The centre of gravity of Marxist thought shifted to Eastern Europe, and the 'orthodox' or 'official' Marxism which soon became institutionalized in the USSR differed greatly from that of the preceding period. Dialectical materialism was enthroned as an incontrovertible world view, historical materialism as the application of its basic principles to social and historical questions. Marxism ceased to be a science of society, and became instead the ideology of a political regime. Indeed, it had already begun to acquire this character in the writings of Lenin and Trotsky – both of whom were political pamphleteers and activists rather than thinkers – before the Revolution, and the transmutation was finally accomplished by Stalin, who imposed by force, under the name of Marxism-Leninism, an intellectually impoverished doctrine which bolstered his own power and policies.[45]

In such conditions a Marxist sociology could not exist. Two Russian sociologists who afterwards became well known in the West – Pitirim Sorokin and Georges Gurvitch – left the USSR in the early 1920s. The last major attempt to sustain the character of Marxism as a science of society, engaged in scientific controversy with other sociological theories, was Bukharin's textbook, *Historical Materialism: a System of Sociology* (1921).[46] By the late 1920s, with the growing ascendancy of Stalin, serious theoretical debate, or Marxist

[45] And notably the policy of 'socialism in one country', or forced industrialization. On the relation between Stalinist ideology and practice see H. Marcuse, *Soviet Marxism* (London: Routledge and Kegan Paul, 1958). See also F. Claudin, *The Communist Movement: from Comintern to Cominform* (Harmondsworth: Penguin Books, 1975).

[46] English edn, 1925.

scholarship as Riazanov,[47] for example, practised it, had become impossible. Dispassionately considered, it is an astonishing phenomenon that in the sixty-five years of existence of the 'first workers' state' not a single original work of Marxist social theory has been produced there, and that the further development of Marxist thought has taken place almost entirely in Western Europe.

In one sense, of course, this is not surprising. Marxism is, after all, a Western body of thought, originally formed in the context of Western intellectual traditions in philosophy and the social sciences, and directed upon the structure of European societies and their historical transformations from the ancient world of Greece and Rome to nineteenth-century capitalism. Western Marxism, from this point of view, is simply the mainstream of Marxist thought; communist orthodoxy a deviation, if not an aberration, engendered in peculiar social and historical conditions. Nevertheless, what has come to be discussed as 'Western Marxism' in recent years[48] possesses some distinctive features, which define it as a new phase in the development of Marxist social theory. It had, in fact, a dual character: on one side it was a response to the impact of Soviet Marxism, taking the form, in many cases, of a critical rejection of communist orthodoxy and of the kind of society which was being constructed in the USSR; on the other, an attempt to comprehend and analyse the new phenomena which were emerging in the Western capitalist societies.

But Western Marxism, in this sense, was far from being a homogeneous body of thought. In the first place, some of the thinkers who were associated with it also had close, if sometimes uneasy and temporary, relations with communist orthodoxy, while others were from the outset fierce critics of that orthodoxy and of the Leninist (and still more the Stalinist)

[47] David Riazanov was the founder and first director of the Marx-Engels Institute in Moscow, and editor of the only complete critical edition of the writings of Marx and Engels ever undertaken (*Karl Marx/Friedrich Engels: Historisch-Kritische Gesamtausgabe*), which remained unfinished, with only the first twelve volumes published, when he 'disappeared' in 1931 as one of the early victims of Stalin.
[48] See Perry Anderson, *Considerations on Western Marxism* (London: New Left Books, 1976); Andrew Arato and Paul Breines, *The Young Lukács and the Origins of Western Marxism* (London: Pluto Press, 1979).

regime. Second, much Western Marxist thought, from 1917 onwards, was characterized by a rejection of the idea of Marxism as a sociological theory, and the adoption of a view which saw it rather as a 'critical philosophy'; but at the same time Marxist sociology continued to be developed, notably by the Austro-Marxists, and to have a wider influence, as for example in Karl Mannheim's sociology of knowledge. Finally, there were very considerable differences among the Western Marxists in their interpretations of the new features, and the dominant tendencies of development, in the capitalist societies.

Three thinkers whose work has often been regarded as expressing most clearly the distinctive nature of Western Marxism – Korsch, Lukács and Gramsci – exemplify one strand, with its own diversity, within this current of thought. In the early 1920s Korsch and Lukács both arrived independently at a reinterpretation of Marxism which emphasized its close relation to Hegel's philosophy and conceived it rather as the philosophical world view of the proletariat than as any kind of science of society.[49] Similarly, Gramsci described Marxism as a 'philosophy of praxis' which 'contains in itself all the fundamental elements needed to construct a total and integral conception of the world . . . everything that is needed to give life to an integral civilization.'[50] At the same time all three thinkers specifically criticized the attempts to develop Marxism as a positive science of society (or general sociology),[51] and Korsch and Lukács saw these attempts as the intellectual counterpart of the spread of revisionism and reformism in the labour

[49] See Karl Korsch, *Marxism and Philosophy* (1923; English edn, London: New Left Books, 1970); Georg Lukács, *History and Class Consciousness* (1923; English edn, London: The Merlin Press, 1971). Korsch referred to the 'essential and necessary connection between German idealism and Marxism', and to the 'materialist philosophy' of Marx as the 'theoretical expression of the revolutionary movement of the proletariat' (*op. cit.*, pp. 41–2); similarly, Lukács defined Marxist theory as 'essentially the intellectual expression of the revolutionary process itself' (*op. cit.*, p. 3).

[50] Antonio Gramsci, *Selections from the Prison Notebooks* (London: Lawrence and Wishart, 1971), p. 462.

[51] Korsch, *op. cit.*, pp. 54–8; Lukács, 'Technology and Social Relations' (1925; English tr. in *New Left Review*, XXXIX, 1966); Gramsci, *op. cit.*, pp. 425–30.

movement.[52] The most important element in this version of Marxist thought is its emphasis upon class consciousness and political activism, especially as these are embodied in a revolutionary party – that is to say, upon intellectual and cultural factors as they are manifested in the development of 'world views' or ideologies – and concomitantly a marked indifference to any systematic analysis of the objective development of the capitalist economy and social structure.

This particular reorientation of Marxist theory was undoubtedly influenced by the revolutionary movements after the First World War, and by Lenin's idea of a 'vanguard party', but it was also profoundly affected by what has been described as a more general 'revolt against positivism' in European social thought.[53] Hence, in this respect too, Marxism was not entirely cut off from the general development of sociology; and the evolution of Lukács' thought, in particular, shows the influence of Simmel and Max Weber – of their cultural criticism, their rejection of positivism (and above all its central tenets concerning the unity of science and the pre-eminence of scientific knowledge), and their assertion of the importance, and possible effectiveness, of subjective consciousness in face of the objective world, including that of culture.[54] But the debate about Marxism as a positive science or a critical philosophy did not cease, even within this particular stream of thought. Korsch gradually modified his view, and in the volume on Marx which he contributed to a series on 'Modern Sociologists' in 1938 he described the conception of Marxism

[52] See especially Korsch's comment that 'the fluid methodology of Marx's materialist dialectic freezes into a number of theoretical formulations about the causal interconnection of historical phenomena in different areas of society ... All these deformations ... can be summed up in one all-inclusive formulation: a unified general theory of social revolution was changed into criticisms of the bourgeois economic order, of the bourgeois state, of the bourgeois system of education, of bourgeois religion, art, science and culture. These criticisms no longer develop by their very nature into revolutionary practice; they can equally well develop into all kinds of attemps at *reform*, which fundamentally remain within the limits of bourgeois society and the bourgeois state ...' (*op. cit.*, pp. 56–7).
[53] See H. Stuart Hughes, *Consciousness and Society* (London: MacGibbon and Kee, 1958), especially ch. 2.
[54] See the discussion of the relationship between Lukács and Simmel in Arato and Breines, *op. cit.*, part I, and also the account of Max Weber's relation to Marxism in Karl Löwith, *op. cit.*

as a general philosophical interpretation of the universe as a distortion of its strongly empirical and critical sense, and concluded that 'The main tendency of historical materialism is no longer "philosophical" but is that of an empirical scientific method.'[55] Lukács too, at the very end of his life abandoned the idea of the proletariat as the identical subject/object of history, and asserted the need for an objective analysis of present-day capitalism.[56]

Moreover, in Western Marxism as a whole a strongly positivist approach continued to flourish, especially in the work of the Austro-Marxists. Here it is worth noting that the 'revolt against positivism' at the end of the nineteenth century was very far from achieving a resounding victory; on the contrary, positivism subsequently had a vigorous revival, largely through the work of the Vienna Circle, and positivist views (in a broad sense) came to be more influential than ever among philosophers of science, and as the tacitly accepted outlook of many social scientists. The fact that the Austro-Marxists (and some others) also followed this path makes it quite misleading to suggest that there was a general opposition between Western Marxism and sociology conceived as a positive, empirical science, as some recent accounts of the intellectual history of Marxism have been inclined to do.[57] Indeed the Austro-Marxists made substantial contributions to the development of sociology in the interwar period, in numerous fields. Max Adler continued to expound and elaborate the conceptual framework of a Marxist sociology,[58] but he also published studies of ideology and revolution, and a notable essay analysing the changes in the

[55] Karl Korsch, *Karl Marx* (London: Chapman and Hall, 1938; revised German edn, Frankfurt: Europäische Verlagsanstalt, 1967), pp. 145, 203.
[56] In his preface to the new edition of *History and Class Consciousness* (1967). See also p. 132 below.
[57] For example, in Arato and Breines, *op. cit.*, to some extent in Perry Anderson, *op. cit.*, and in some studies of the 'critical theory' of the Frankfurt School. There is still a great need for a more comprehensive history of Marxist social theory which would examine its development in relation to the broader movement of ideas in the social sciences.
[58] See especially his *Lehrbuch der materialistischen Geschichtsauffassung*, 2 vols. (Berlin: E. Laubsche Verlagsbuchhandlung, 1930, 1932), republished with a previously unpublished third volume under the general title *Soziologie des Marxismus*, 3 vols. (Vienna: Europa Verlag, 1964); and *Das Rätsel der Gesellschaft* (Vienna: Saturn-Verlag, 1936).

working class in Western capitalism.[59] Otto Bauer published major studies of revolution,[60] as well as one of the best Marxist analyses of fascism.[61] Among the major preoccupations of the Austro-Marxists at this time were the changing character and increasing power of the state, which foreshadowed the possibility of a totalitarian state (already taking shape not only in the fascist regimes, but also in the Stalinist dictatorship), and the consequences of changes in the class structure for the socialist movement. Both Renner and Hilferding published important studies of the 'interventionist state', the latter particularly in his writings on the 'organized capitalism'[62] of the postwar period, and in his last, unfinished monograph on the Marxist theory of the state, in relation to economic development and class struggles.[63] Similarly, both thinkers devoted attention to the new elements in the class structure, and in particular the growth of the 'new middle class', or the 'service class' as Renner called it.[64] The questions which the Austro-Marxists raised – about the nature of twentieth-century capitalism, the changing functions of the state, class relations, the meaning of a socialist revolution, and the character of Soviet society – are still central issues for Marxist sociology (and indeed for sociology in general); and the studies which they devoted to these phenomena still provide an indispensable starting point for the analysis of subsequent developments.

But the Austro-Marxist contribution to Western Marxism has been overshadowed until quite recently by versions of Marxist thought stemming not only from Korsch, Lukács and Gramsci but perhaps even more importantly from the thinkers of the Frankfurt Institute for Social Research. Their 'critical theory',

[59] 'Wandlung der Arbeiterklasse', *Der Kampf*, XXVI (1933), pp. 367–82, 406–14.
[60] In *Die Österreichische Revolution* (Vienna: Wiener Volksbuchhandlung, 1923), and *Zwischen zwei Weltkriegen?* (Bratislava: Eugen Prager Verlag, 1936).
[61] 'Der Faschismus', *Der Sozialistische Kampf*, 16 July 1938, pp. 75–83.
[62] See especially 'Probleme der Zeit', *Die Gesellschaft*, I, 1, 1924, and 'Die Aufgaben der Sozialdemokratie in der Republik' (Berlin, 1927).
[63] *Das historische Problem*. Manuscript (1941) first published in *Zeitschrift für Politik* (New Series), I, 1954.
[64] See especially his posthumously published work, *Wandlungen der modernen Gesellschaft* (Vienna: Wiener Volksbuchhandlung, 1953).

as it has come to be called, is a complex body of thought which has developed in varied forms over a period of more than fifty years, and its relation to sociology can only be very briefly sketched here. What is evident, though, is that from the beginning it was strongly marked by a philosophical conception of Marxism, inspired in part by the work of Korsch and Lukács,[65] which encouraged a critical attitude towards sociology (including any form of Marxist sociology) insofar as this sought to represent social life in terms of law-governed regularities. In the early years of the Institute, under its first director Carl Grünberg, who was himself closely associated with Austro-Marxism,[66] this philosophical orientation was less prominent than it became after Max Horkheimer succeeded him as director in 1930. Horkheimer indeed was the crucial figure in the development of critical theory as the distinctive and pre-eminent intellectual orientation within the Institute (some of whose members continued nevertheless to undertake sociological, historical and economic research of a more 'positivist' and empirical kind);[67] and his essays of the mid-1930s,[68] like the somewhat later work by Herbert Marcuse, *Reason and Revolution*,[69] show the increasing preoccupation with a philosophically grounded cultural criticism, and the strenuous opposition to the positivism of the social sciences (merging later into a more general hostility to science and technology), which became characteristic features of the

[65] Both Korsch and Lukács participated in the 'First Marxist Work Week', held in 1922, which led to the creation of the Frankfurt Institute for Social Research (the institutional basis of the Frankfurt School) in 1923; and much of the discussion at this week-long seminar was devoted to a discussion of Korsch's forthcoming book, *Marxism and Philosophy*. For an account of the creation of the Institute see Martin Jay, *The Dialectical Imagination* (Boston: Little, Brown and Co., 1973), ch. 1. David Held, in his *Introduction to Critical Theory* (London: Hutchinson, 1980), also notes the influence of Korsch and Lukács, saying that 'their writings set an important precedent for the critical theorists.'

[66] See Tom Bottomore and Patrick Goode, eds., *Austro-Marxism,* Introduction, pp. 9–10.

[67] Among them Friedrich Pollock, Franz Neumann and Henryk Grossmann. David Held, *op. cit.*, p. 15, also makes this necessary distinction.

[68] Reprinted in *Kritische Theorie*, 2 vols. (Frankfurt: S. Fischer Verlag, 1968).

[69] *Reason and Revolution: Hegel and the Rise of Social Theory* (New York: Oxford University Press, 1941).

school. However, if the main tendency of critical theory was to reject sociology as bourgeois ideology, it nevertheless contains elements which can be, and to some extent have been, incorporated into a Marxist sociology; at the very least as problematic conceptions of the relation of culture or ideology to the economic system, classes and the state. In the past two decades, moreover, as will be shown in the next section, critical theory as reformulated particularly by Jürgen Habermas has begun to assume a more sociological character.

The influence which Marxism had in the formative stage of sociology before 1914 seems to have diminished in the interwar period. One principal reason for this was the fragmentation and disorientation of Marxist thought itself. On one side it developed in the scientifically unfruitful form of communist orthodoxy, which was rejected as mere dogma by many social scientists (and as the years passed, by increasing numbers of the formerly orthodox themselves), and had a stultifying effect upon those creative thinkers who, out of loyalty to the original vision of the 'workers' state', compromised with it.[70] On the other side it assumed diverse, often antithetical, forms in the work of distinct schools of thought and individual thinkers.[71] There was no longer a common framework, or ground of debate, such as had existed in the previous period. This great diversity certainly resulted in part from the extreme difficulty of analysing and interpreting the changes that were taking place in many different spheres of capitalist society; and in some respects the diverse conceptions prolonged the original 're-visionist' debate in circumstances of much greater complexity and uncertainty. But still it should be said that Marxist theory was in no worse condition than other kinds of sociological thought during this period. There was no major development of the ideas of Durkheim and Weber, and these ideas themselves

[70] Victor Serge wrote percipiently of Lukács that 'he could have endowed communism with a true intellectual greatness if it had developed as a social movement instead of degenerating into a movement in solidarity with an authoritarian power' (*Memoirs of a Revolutionary*, London, 1963). Gramsci escaped having to make such compromises because he was more or less isolated in prison during the worst period of Stalin's dictatorship and died in 1937.
[71] And even within one so-called 'school' if we accept Held's argument in defence of critical theory against some of its critics (*op. cit.*, pp. 356–7).

did not seem to provide much guidance in studying the new social situation created by the war and the postwar revolutionary movements. In France, particularly, the influence of academic sociology was significantly diminished by Marxist criticism.[72] And it is noteworthy that the one body of sociological thought which was recognized as making a major original contribution in Germany, that of Karl Mannheim, was greatly influenced by Marxism, and at the same time dealt directly with the problem of divergent conceptions of the social world[73] which was (as I have indicated) a central issue within sociological theory itself, as well as in Marxist thought.

4. *The revival of Marxist sociology*

The 'dark ages' for Marxist sociology were the two decades between the mid-1930s and the mid-1950s. The rise of fascism in Europe dispersed or destroyed the principal schools of Marxist thought, and sent many individual scholars into exile or prison. After 1945 the Cold War divided the sociological world in two; paraphrasing Marx we might say that at that time the ruling ideas were the ideas of the ruling superpowers. On one side sociology was rejected as 'bourgeois ideology' and its place was taken by the dogmatic scheme of thought known as historical materialism; on the other, Marxism was rejected as 'communist ideology' and Western sociology was largely dominated by American conceptions of the discipline, embodying either a narrow empiricism or theoretical models (functionalism or action theory) which totally ignored Marxism –

[72] See, for example, Paul Nizan, *Les chiens de garde* (Paris: Rieder, 1932). Between 1929 and 1934 a group of Marxist philosophers, including Paul Nizan, emerged in France, and two of its members – Georges Friedmann and Henri Lefebvre – later made important contributions to sociology. Both of them, at different times, broke with communist orthodoxy, and Friedmann eventually abandoned Marxism, though his work remained influenced by Marxist ideas. See George Lichtheim, *Marxism in Modern France* (New York: Columbia University Press, 1966), pp. 86–7.
[73] Especially, of course, in *Ideology and Utopia* (1929; English edn, London: Routledge and Kegan Paul, 1936). The most important Marxist influence on this work came from Lukács' *History and Class Consciousness*.

conceptions that Mills later characterized, in a powerful critique, as 'abstracted empiricism' and 'grand theory'.[74]

But a profound change began in the mid-1950s. The revelations about the Stalinist regime and the process of deStalinization, the intellectual and political revolts in Eastern Europe, and the reappearance of radical movements in the West, ended the communist dominance over Marxist thought and reawakened interest in the rich and varied contribution that Marxism had made to the social sciences. Many thinkers whose work had been neglected or consigned to oblivion during the Stalinist epoch were rediscovered and critically discussed, and at the same time important manuscripts of Marx which had previously been little known – notably the *Economic and Philosophical Manuscripts* (1844) and the *Grundrisse* (1857–8) – were published, translated, and widely diffused.

Marxist ideas have now regained, or acquired for the first time, an important place in all the social sciences. In sociology, they have given rise to two major, and very different, orientations of thought and research, which can be conveniently described as 'critical theory' and 'structuralist Marxism'. The former is a prolongation and development of the ideas of those Marxists associated with the Frankfurt Institute, which was re-established in Germany by 1953. For the next decade and a half, under the direction of Horkheimer and Adorno, its interests remained primarily philosophical and methodological: to criticize and combat positivist conceptions in the social sciences,[75] to extend this criticism to the role of science in social life as a whole, and hence to engage in a critical evaluation of modern culture, from a standpoint which conceives the 'instrumentalist' aim of science to dominate nature as leading

---

[74] C. Wright Mills, *The Sociological Imagination* (New York: Oxford University Press, 1959).
[75] See Theodor W. Adorno *et al.*, *The Positivist Dispute in German Sociology* (London, 1976); also the works of the younger generation of critical theorists, especially Jürgen Habermas, *Knowledge and Human Interests* (London: Heinemann, 1972), and Albrecht Wellmer, *Critical Theory of Society* (New York: Herder and Herder, 1971). For a sharp and succinct criticism of critical theory as expounded by Horkheimer see Kolakowski, *Main Currents of Marxism*, *op. cit.*, vol. III, pp. 352–7.

necessarily, via the social sciences, to a bureaucratic and technocratic domination of human beings.[76]

The preoccupation with methodological questions does not, however, separate critical theory sharply from the concerns of recent sociology. On the contrary, much of its intellectual influence comes from the fact that it is one major element in the 'second revolt against positivism' which has developed over the past two decades, taking diverse forms in phenomenological and interpretive sociology, and in voluntaristic theories of action.[77] What seems more controversial is the relation of critical theory to a specifically Marxist sociology. Many thinkers have questioned how far its concentration upon cultural analysis (or 'ideology-critique'), which tends to promote a view of culture or ideology as being the *principal* factor in sustaining domination,[78] and the marked neglect of economic and political analysis, as well as the diminished significance attributed to classes and class relations in interpreting the nature of modern capitalism, are compatible with any kind of Marxist theory.[79] The question as to how far the Marxist theory of society can and should be revised in the light of sociological research and analysis without ceasing to be Marxist at all is difficult and complicated, and it will be considered more fully in the next part of this essay. As to the particular objections brought against critical theory it should be noted that

---

[76] See Max Horkheimer and Theodor W. Adorno, *Dialectic of Enlightenment* (New York, 1972); Max Horkheimer, *Zur Kritik der instrumentellen Vernunft* (Frankfurt: Suhrkamp, 1967); Jürgen Habermas, 'Science and Technology as Ideology', in *Toward a Rational Society* (Boston: Beacon Press, 1970); Herbert Marcuse, *One-Dimensional Man*, (London: Routledge and Kegan Paul, 1964).

[77] See Anthony Giddens, 'Positivism and its Critics', in Tom Bottomore and Robert Nisbet, eds., *A History of Sociological Analysis* (New York: Basic Books, 1978).

[78] For a critical discussion of this question see Nicholas Abercrombie, Stephen Hill and Bryan Turner, *The Dominant Ideology Thesis* (London: Allen and Unwin, 1981).

[79] Kolakowski, *op. cit.*, vol. III, p. 357, describes it as 'a partial form of Marxism', 'an inconsistent attempt to preserve Marxism without accepting its identification with the proletariat.' Held, while defending critical theory against some of the more extreme attacks by other Marxists, concedes that there is something in the charge that critical theory 'failed to integrate studies of the individual and social consciousness with political economy and institutional analysis', and that it neglected detailed historical inquiry (*op. cit.*, pp. 373–4).

in the recent work of those who belong to the school, or are in some way associated with it, there has been considerably more emphasis on economic and political analysis. This is evident, for example, in Habermas' study of the 'crisis tendencies in advanced capitalism'[80] and in his essay 'Toward a Reconstruction of Historical Materialism';[81] but especially in the work of Claus Offe on political authority and the interventionist state in late capitalist society.[82] No doubt, in all these studies very great importance is still assigned to the ideological regulation of social life, but it can scarcely be claimed that the analysis disregards the economic and political framework in which ideologies are produced; and on the other side it is undeniable that critical theory has played an important part in reawakening sociological interest in ideology[83] and has contributed substantially (together with the work of Lukács, to which it is closely related through the concept of 'reification') to cultural studies, and especially the study of 'mass culture' and the 'culture industry'.[84]

The problem of classes raises a number of important issues which will be discussed further in the next section; here it must suffice to remark that critical theorists are by no means the only thinkers to have questioned the traditional Marxist conception. Marxist sociologists of many different persuasions, from the Austro-Marxists to Poulantzas,[85] have recognized that the class structure of capitalist societies as Marx, Engels and the first generation of Marxists studied it, in its emergent form, has changed in significant ways which make necessary a fundamental reassessment.

[80] *Legitimation Crisis* (London: Heinemann, 1976), part II.
[81] *Communication and the Evolution of Society* (London: Heinemann, 1979), ch. 4.
[82] See especially, 'Political Authority and Class Structures: an Analysis of Late Capitalist Societies', *International Journal of Sociology*, II, 1 (1972).
[83] See *The Dominant Ideology Thesis, op. cit.*
[84] For one kind of study inspired by critical theory, see Claus Offe, *Industry and Inequality: the Achievement Principle in Work and Social Status* (London: Edward Arnold, 1976); for another, which played a part in shaping the 'counter-culture' of the radical movements in the 1960s, Marcuse, *One-Dimensional Man, op. cit.*
[85] See the earlier references to the Austro-Marxist studies of class (pp. 113, 121 above); and Nicos Poulantzas, *Classes in Contemporary Capitalism* (London: New Left Books, 1975).

The second prominent tendency in recent Marxist theory – 'structuralist Marxism' – stands opposed to critical theory on almost every major issue. Its distinctive features derive from two sources: from the methodological studies of Louis Althusser, shaped in turn by French rationalism, especially that of Bachelard; and from the structural anthropology of Lévi-Strauss, itself strongly influenced by structural linguistics. Like the critical theorists, Althusser's principal interests are methodological, but his aim is precisely the opposite of theirs; namely, to establish the 'scientificity' of Marx's theory in contrast with 'ideological' thought (which is held to include diverse forms of historicism, humanism, positivism and empiricism). This is not the place to undertake a thorough critique of Althusser's philosophy of science, which has as one of its curious features that it seems to establish at one and the same time, and in a dogmatic way, not only the 'scientificity' of Marxist theory but also its truth. What is most important, in relation to sociology, is the 'structuralism' of this version of Marxism, which has been most clearly expounded by Maurice Godelier. In his *Perspectives in Marxist Anthropology*[86] he distinguishes between functionalist, structuralist (in the work of Lévi-Strauss) and Marxist approaches, and presents Marxism as a particular type of structuralism, guided by two main principles: first, that the starting point of a social science is not to be found in appearances but in the inner logic of a structure which exists behind the visible relations between human beings; second, that Marxism 'cannot consist merely of a lengthy inquiry into the networks of structural causality without eventually seeking to evaluate the particular and unequal effect that these different structures may have on the functioning . . . of an economic and social formation,' and that we must take 'seriously Marx's fundamental hypothesis on the determining causality "in the final analysis" . . . of the mode or modes of production . . .'[87] To these two principles we must add, I think, a third; namely, that Marxist theory conceives social structures (socio-economic formations) as containing a contradiction or contradictions

---

[86] Cambridge: Cambridge University Press, 1977.
[87] Godelier, *op. cit.*, p. 4.

which provide the dynamic element that brings about change from one historical form of society to another.[88]

The principal consequence of this Marxist structuralist approach in sociology (and equally in social anthropology)[89] has been to concentrate attention on the analysis of modes of production – which again runs counter to the main focus of interest of the critical theorists, though as will be seen later structuralism has also come to have a major influence in cultural studies – while at the same time substituting for the idea of a one-sided determination of the 'superstructure' by the economic 'base' a more complex notion of 'structural causality', in which the different elements or levels in a total structure (the socio-economic formation) are seen as interconnected, and it is the structure as a whole which produces 'effects'. Nevertheless, this attempt to qualify the strict determinism of the base/superstructure model still has recourse to the idea of determination 'in the last resort' by the economy (an idea already propounded by Engels in the 1890s), and it does not seem that the structuralist Marxists have advanced very far in constructing an adequate theoretical model of structural causality or in demonstrating empirically how it operates.[90] In fact, a general conception of the ultimately determinant influence of the mode of production (that is, of technological innovation and of changes in the organization and control of the social labour process, for example, through the growth of multinational corporations) has prevailed, and with the recognition of the greatly enhanced role of the state in the management of the

[88] See on this point Godelier, 'Structure and Contradiction in *Capital*', in Robin Blackburn, ed., *Ideology in Social Science* (London: Fontana, 1972).
[89] It is worth noting that it is since the development of a structuralist approach that Marxism has had its greatest impact upon social anthropology. See the discussion in Raymond Firth, *The Sceptical Anthropologist? Social Anthropology and Marxist Views on Society*, from the Proceedings of the British Academy (London: Oxford University Press, 1972).
[90] In the strict Althusserian version, of course, empirical tests are excluded, since a theoretical 'discourse' is sufficient unto itself. Thus in a work such as Poulantzas' *Classes in Contemporary Capitalism, op. cit.*, what is offered is a conceptual analysis of class, and in particular of the petty bourgeoisie, without any attempt to study empirically, or to explain, the historical growth of the petty bourgeoisie (or 'new middle classes') and the social and political consequences of this important change in the class structure of advanced capitalist societies.

economy has led to a revival and development of the notions of 'organized capitalism' and 'state monopoly capitalism'. This means, of course, that sociology, under the influence of this type of recent Marxist theory, has moved much closer to political economy (and large areas of the two disciplines now overlap), so that Korsch's pertinent criticism of an earlier style of sociology which, he argued, treated the system of social relations as an autonomous sphere of inquiry, quite independent of the material interchange with nature, is now less relevant.[91]

But the structuralist movement as a whole is diverse,[92] and there are other forms of Marxist structuralism than those deriving from Lévi-Strauss or Althusser. One of the most interesting, and sociologically fruitful, is the 'genetic structuralism' of Lucien Goldmann, which was influenced primarily by the work of Lukács and Piaget. Its principal characteristics are that it is concerned with 'structures of meaning' – hence primarily with cultural phenomena – and that it attempts to combine structural and historical analysis. It is not surprising that a structuralist approach should prove useful in the sociological study of culture, for it first showed its value in closely related fields, in the study of language and of literary texts.[93] Goldmann's own method is formulated, and then demonstrated at work, in his major publication *The Hidden God* (1964),[94] where he sets out to study cultural creations as 'significant structures' which are produced not by individuals but by 'collective subjects', and above all by social classes. The task of the Marxist sociologist is both to understand and to explain any cultural phenomenon by first describing precisely its immanent structure and then inserting it 'as a constitutive

[91] He concluded, on this ground, that 'Marx's materialistic science of society is not sociology, but political economy'. Korsch, *Karl Marx* (revised German edn, 1967), p. 277.
[92] For a good general account see Jean Piaget, *Structuralism* (New York: Basic Books, 1970).
[93] See the essays in David Robey, ed., *Structuralism: an Introduction* (Oxford: Oxford University Press, 1973), and C. Lévi-Strauss, *Structural Anthropology* (New York: Basic Books, 1963), ch. II, 'Structural analysis in linguistics and anthropology'.
[94] London: Routledge and Kegan Paul, 1964.

and functional element, in a more comprehensive structure'.[95] But whereas some structuralist studies confine themselves to constructing models of timeless structures, Goldmann, influenced by Piaget's 'constructivism', seeks to incorporate structures in a historical process: 'The structures which constitute human behaviour,' he says, 'are not in reality, from my point of view, universal givens, but specific phenomena resulting from a past genesis and undergoing transformations which presage a future evolution.'[96]

The two broad orientations in recent Marxist thought which I have outlined here, however prominent they may have been, do not by any means encompass all the present-day forms of Marxist sociology. Much of it has remained, in a broad sense, positivist, and those who follow this path can defend their methodology, if necessary, with the help of other philosophies of science, such as the 'new realism',[97] or some versions of neo-Kantianism (which may be related in various ways to realism).[98] In this regard it is worth noting the considerable revival of interest in Austro-Marxism (not only in Austria and Germany, but in the English-speaking countries), which was characterized specifically, as I noted earlier, by a strong commitment to Marxism as an empirical social science. There has now been established, in my view, after the intense methodological (and ideological) debates of the past two decades, the basis for an extensive development of Marxist empirical research, the main features of which will be considered in the following section.

[95] Lucien Goldmann, *Marxisme et sciences humaines* (Paris: Gallimard, 1970), 'La sociologie de la littérature: statut et problèmes de méthode', p. 66.
[96] Ibid., 'Genèse et structure', p. 21. See also Goldmann's discussion of the methods of genetic structuralism in *Cultural Creation* (Oxford: Basil Blackwell, 1977) and *Method in the Sociology of Literature* (Oxford: Basil Blackwell, 1981).
[97] See, in particular, the books by Roy Bhaskar, *A Realist Theory of Science* (Brighton: Harvester Press, second edn, 1978) and *The Possibility of Naturalism: a Philosophical Critique of the Contemporary Human Sciences* (Brighton: Harvester Press, 1979).
[98] See the excellent short discussion of positivism, empiricism and realism in relation to critical theory in Russell Keat, *The Politics of Social Theory* (Oxford: Basil Blackwell, 1981), ch. 1.

5. *Current studies and problems*

It has to be asked of every sociological theory what light it can shed, in particular, upon the major issues and trends of development in contemporary societies. In the case of Marxist sociology this now means that we have to assess its fruitfulness in three principal areas of inquiry. The first is what Lukács referred to in 1970 as 'a *real* analysis of the inherent nature of present-day capitalism'.[99] Here the main problems concern the development of the capitalist economy, the nature of the modern state and especially its role in economic management, and the political significance of classes and other social groups. There seems now to be a fairly widespread agreement among Marxists on the character of the economy in 'late capitalism' or 'advanced capitalism'; namely, the dominance of large corporations (many of them multinational corporations which not only dominate national economies but have a determining influence on the 'world capitalist system') and the greatly enhanced role of the nation state (and to some extent of wider political associations) in economic affairs – in production, the provision of essential services, demand management, and a considerable degree of economic planning.[100] But this general agreement conceals many differences of interpretation. Present-day capitalism may, for instance, be described as 'organized capitalism', using the term Hilferding employed in the 1920s, but Hilferding's theory also involved a specific view of political development, in which the high degree of 'socialization' of the economy under capitalism constitutes the basis for a gradual transition to socialism.[101] An alternative conception, elaborated mainly by East German theorists, is that of 'state

[99] Prefatory note in István Mészáros, ed., *Aspects of History and Class Consciousness* (London: Routledge and Kegan Paul, 1971). Lukács went on to say that this is 'a task Marxism has failed to realize so far'.
[100] In the major Western capitalist societies the proportion of gross national product (GNP) which is expended by public authorities (i.e., not allocated through the market) ranges from 40 per cent to 55 per cent.
[101] See especially his two essays 'Probleme der Zeit', *Die Gesellschaft*, I, 1 (1924), and 'Die Aufgaben der Sozialdemokratie in der Republik' (printed as a pamphlet, Berlin, 1927). Part of the latter essay is translated in Tom Bottomore and Patrick Goode, eds., *Readings in Marxist Sociology, op. cit.*

monopoly capitalism', which has many affinities with Hilferding's ideas but is set in an orthodox communist political context which still sees a radical and abrupt break between capitalism and socialism.[102] Recent analyses of the capitalist economy thus leave the fundamental question of the transition from capitalism to socialism unresolved and controversial.

The problem of the modern state has two main aspects. First, in what sense can it be claimed that the state, in a democratic regime, is simply or primarily an instrument of the economically dominant class? Marx and Engels wrote at a time when democracy existed only in an embryonic form in Europe. The first generation of Marxists were deeply engaged in the political struggle for universal suffrage, and many of them (like Marx himself in his observations on Chartism) saw the suffrage as bringing about 'the political supremacy of the working class'. But democratic regimes were created only slowly and painfully, and some, like the Weimar Republic, were fragile; correspondingly, it has taken a long time for the implications of political democracy to be taken seriously into account in Marxist theory (and the process was greatly hampered by the dominance of communist orthodoxy). Only in the last decade or so has the view come to prevail widely that, in the words of Santiago Carillo, 'the political system established in Western Europe, based on representative political institutions . . . is in essentials valid'.[103] But this is to recognize that the state – a particular form of the state – *is* independent, and is accessible to various classes and social groups as an instrument to promote or defend their interests. And in Western Europe since 1945 it is evident that the state has not been accessible only to the economically dominant class, but has sometimes – and in some cases for relatively long periods – been controlled and used by the working class. This has not resulted anywhere in a transition

[102] This conception has been relatively little discussed in English, but there is a comprehensive account in Paul Wenlock, 'The Theory of State Monopoly Capitalism' (unpublished Ph.D. thesis, University of Leeds, 1981). See also the brief analysis of various theories of modern capitalism in Gerd Hardach and Dieter Karras, *A Short History of Socialist Economic Thought* (London: Edward Arnold, 1978), ch. 4.
[103] Santiago Carillo, *Eurocommunism and the State* (London: Lawrence and Wishart, 1977), p. 105.

from capitalism to socialism; on the contrary, what seems to be characteristic of the period is an oscillation between a trend towards socialism and a counter-trend back towards capitalism. But an explanation of this phenomenon is precisely one of the major difficulties which now confronts any sociological analysis (including a Marxist analysis) of modern Western societies.

Another aspect of this independence is also important; namely, the great increase in the power of the modern state resulting from the extension of its control over the general conditions of economic and social life, the associated growth in numbers of its personnel, and the concentration in its hands of far more effective means of persuasion and coercion. This growing power may lead to a degree of bureaucratic regulation which severely curtails individual liberty – the 'dictatorship of the official' as Weber called it[104] – or in a more extreme case to the emergence of a 'totalitarian state'. The last possibility, realized in practice in some European states in the 1930s, has led Marxist thinkers, notably Hilferding in his last writings,[105] to reconsider the whole theory of the state. What is now needed is a more thorough and systematic analysis of bureaucracy (which Marxist sociologists have not yet provided),[106] and especially of modern political parties, considering that totalitarian regimes have been the creation of mass parties which, although they initially needed the support of various other social groups, were eventually able to acquire a monopoly of

[104] He used this expression particularly in referring to an outcome of socialism (i.e., of a planned economy) which he saw as much more likely than the 'dictatorship of the proletariat'. See his lecture on socialism (1918) translated in W.G. Runciman, ed., *Max Weber: Selections in Translation* (Cambridge: Cambridge University Press, 1978).

[105] Hilferding, *Das historische Problem, op. cit.*

[106] Probably the most useful earlier reflections on the subject of parties, though very tentative and abstract, are those of Gramsci; see *Selections from the Prison Notebooks, op. cit.*, pp. 147–57, 210–18. Bukharin, in *Historical Materialism, op. cit.*, replied briefly to the argument by Robert Michels, *Political Parties* (1911; English edn, New York: Free Press, 1966), that an oligarchy necessarily emerges in any mass party, however democratic its initial orientation; but there has been no comprehensive Marxist critique of this kind of analysis (which is also to be found in Max Weber) as a whole. More recently, however, Marxist studies of bureaucracy have begun to appear, partly as an outcome of experience in the socialist countries; see, for example, András Hegedüs, *Socialism and Bureaucracy* (London: Allison and Busby, 1976).

power by suppressing all autonomous organizations and social movements, and to establish virtually complete control over all spheres of social activity.

A neo-Marxist theory of the state and politics would also need to reassess the relation between class and politics, and in particular to examine the question whether the main contending groups in present-day capitalist societies are indeed the bourgeoisie and the proletariat.[107] Is the dominant group in these societies any longer a bourgeoisie in a strict sense, or must we conclude with Alain Touraine that: 'If property was the criterion of membership in the former dominant classes, the new dominant class is defined by knowledge and a certain level of education'?[108] On the other side, can the proletariat still be conceived as a revolutionary class, the bearer of a new civilization, capable of effecting a radical transformation of society, or has it now been assimilated into welfare capitalism, become reformist, abandoned the socialist goal, been replaced as a radical force by other social groups? And what of the 'new middle classes' or petty bourgeoisie? Like many other Marxists since Bernstein's day, Poulantzas in *Classes in Contemporary Capitalism*[109] attacks the problem of defining this social group in relation to the bourgeoisie and the proletariat, but he has little to say about the political consequences of its acknowledged growth in numbers and social influence. Whether, and under what conditions, its main orientation is conservative, reforming or radical, whether indeed it is a homogeneous group with a consistent political outlook at all, remains a problem for Marxist analysis. If, further, we observe directly the political movements of the past two decades it becomes evident that many of them, especially in the radical period of the 1960s, have

---

[107] I have discussed this question at greater length in 'The Decline of Capitalism, Sociologically Considered', in Arnold Heertje, ed., *Schumpeter's Vision: Capitalism, Socialism and Democracy after 40 Years* (Eastbourne: Praeger, 1981).

[108] Alain Touraine, *The Post-Industrial Society* (London: Wildwood House, 1971). It is interesting that similar conceptions of a 'new dominant class' have been elaborated in the context of the present-day socialist societies, as will be discussed more fully below; see especially, George Konrád and Ivan Szelényi, *The Intellectuals on the Road to Class Power* (Brighton: Harvester Press, 1979).

[109] London: New Left Books, 1975.

not been class movements at all, but that major political struggles have been animated by ethnic groups, students, or women.[110]

The foregoing account indicates the need for an extensive research programme if Marxist sociology is to achieve 'a real analysis' of present-day capitalism. The need is no less great in a second major field of inquiry, which concerns, to adapt Lukács' phrase, 'the inherent nature of present-day socialism'. Marx, as is well known, dismissed the idea of writing 'recipes for the cookshops of the future' – that is to say, producing a detailed plan for a socialist society – but his general conception of such a society is unmistakably clear: it would be a 'society of associated producers' in which human beings would collectively control and direct the social labour process, and thereby create the conditions for an unprecedented growth of personal freedom and self-realization. By these criteria the existing socialist societies are not socialist; some of them much less so than others.

The questions then posed for a Marxist sociology – first, what social forces have produced these societies in their actual form, and second, is their structure such that they have, nevertheless, a capacity to develop into socialist societies of the kind that Marx envisaged? – are not only extremely complex in themselves but raise the further question of whether they can be adequately treated at all within a Marxist conceptual framework. Thus, in attempting to answer the first question we have to deal with some general conditions of social life – such as the impossibility of a genuine collective control of the economy in any large-scale society, and the propensity of the representative bodies which are the necessary alternative to create new hierarchies – for which Marxism does not provide an analytical model; and with particular historical circumstances – the fact that the major attempts to construct a socialist society have

---

[110] Such movements have provoked many controversies, for example about possible Marxist conceptualizations of race (see the essay by John Rex, 'Convergences in the Sociology of Race Relations and Minority Groups', in Tom Bottomore, Stefan Nowak and Magdalena Sokolowska, eds., *Sociology: the State of the Art* [London: Sage Publications, 1982]), and about the relation between feminism and Marxism (see Michèle Barrett, *Women's Oppression Today* [London: New Left Books, 1980]).

occurred in peasant societies which had then to undertake first of all capital accumulation and industrialization on a massive scale – which do not fit easily into a Marxist scheme of historical stages, and indeed may appear to contradict the whole theory of history to the extent that they resulted from the power of an ideology, channelled through a political party, rather than from the ripeness of economic and social conditions.

The question whether the existing socialist societies have the capacity to develop towards socialism in Marx's sense is equally intractable from the standpoint of classical Marxism, which provides no category into which such societies can be placed. Nevertheless, Marxists have attempted to deal with it. From the earliest years of Soviet society Marxist thinkers criticized its autocratic features,[111] doubted its socialist character,[112] and conveyed an uneasy awareness that a disturbing new factor had entered the historical process; but it was only after the Stalinist regime had become established that new terms were found to describe this form of society, as a 'deformed workers' state', 'totalitarian state economy', or more recently, 'state socialism'. These are, however, descriptions rather than concepts forming part of a theoretical scheme, and it seems doubtful whether any satisfactory conceptualization of the existing socialist societies could be incorporated into the original Marxist theory of the stages of social development without a very substantial revision of the whole theory. Many recent studies, in fact, implicitly or explicitly accept the need for such revision inasmuch as they argue that a new dominant class has emerged in the USSR and in other socialist societies,[113] and hence that the class system of capitalism has been followed historically, not by a classless

---

[111] See Rosa Luxemburg, *The Russian Revolution* (written 1918, first published 1922; English edn, Ann Arbor: University of Michigan Press, 1961).

[112] See Otto Bauer, *Bolschewismus oder Sozialdemokratie?* (Vienna, 1920), and the discussion of Bauer's views in Yvon Bourdet, ed., *Otto Bauer et la révolution* (Paris: Études et documentation internationales, 1968).

[113] See especially George Konrád and Ivan Szelényi, *op. cit.*: 'The social structure of early socialism is organized in keeping with the principle of rational redistribution . . . we regard this as a class structure, and indeed a dichotomous one. At one pole is an evolving class of intellectuals who occupy the position of redistributors, at the other a working class which produces the social surplus but has no right of disposition over it' (p. 145).

society, but by a new class system. On the other hand, some Marxist thinkers, while remaining extremely critical of the present state of affairs, regard the collective ownership of the major means of production as a fundamental advance which necessarily creates powerful forces working towards a more authentic socialism,[114] a phenomenon which has perhaps found expression in the successive waves of revolt in Eastern Europe. From this standpoint the transition to socialism may be conceived as a long-drawn-out process, marked by all kinds of false beginnings, setbacks and failures, in which future historians may nevertheless be able to discern some sort of pattern, as present historians do in the transition from feudalism to capitalism. But to assign this task to future historians is to recognize, quite correctly I think, the limitations of any sociological analysis of the present time, Marxist or other.

Finally, Marxist sociologists have come to devote increasing attention to a third field of inquiry, which concerns the relations between states in the world system. Here the main problems have been those of 'development' and 'underdevelopment', which became important subjects of study after the Second World War, when a process of decolonization began and newly independent states emerged in Asia and Africa. In the 1950s the mainstream of sociological theory treated these questions largely in terms of 'modernization'; it was broadly assumed that the new states were starting from a given condition of underdevelopment and that they would now follow a course of development similar to that in the Western capitalist countries at an earlier stage, by modernizing their economy and social structure, aided to some extent by Western capital and the transfer of technology.[115] Over the past two decades 'development studies' have multiplied and institutes for the study of development have proliferated, but during the same period the

---

[114] See the discussion in András Hegedüs, *op. cit.*

[115] This view was expressed in diverse ways in such works as W.W. Rostow, *The Stages of Economic Growth* (Cambridge: Cambridge University Press, 1960); B.F. Hoselitz, *Sociological Factors in Economic Development* (Chicago: Free Press, 1960); and S.N. Eisenstadt, *Modernization: Protest and Change* (Englewood Cliffs, N.J.: Prentice-Hall, 1966). A Marxist criticism of this kind of sociology of development, which locates its basis in the structural-functional theory of Talcott Parsons, is undertaken in John G. Taylor, *From Modernization to Modes of Production* (London: Macmillan, 1979).

earlier dominant model of modernization has been increasingly criticized, and to a considerable extent replaced by Marxist models.[116] Two principal currents of Marxist thought can be distinguished. One emphasizes the world capitalist system (especially the influence of multinational corporations and international financial institutions) and the process of 'dependent development', or even in some cases of 'active underdevelopment', particularly in the colonial period,[117] in which peripheral countries are dominated by the capitalist metropolitan centres.[118] However, this approach has been criticized more recently as paying insufficient attention to the economy and social structure of the developing countries themselves;[119] and the second current of thought has concentrated (partly under the influence of structuralist Marxism) on analysing the specific modes of production and social formations in these countries.[120] This has also allowed Marxist studies of development to be brought within the scope of a more general analysis of pre-capitalist modes of production, including the mode of production in tribal societies which had previously been little studied from a Marxist perspective.[121]

One question which has so far been neglected in the Marxist literature on development is that of the 'limits to growth'. This can be attributed, no doubt, to the strong historical connection between a Marxist view of society and a commitment to the

[116] A useful account of the changing theoretical orientations will be found in Neil Smelser, Arnaud Sales and Harry Makler, 'Recent Trends in Theory and Methodology in the Study of Economy and Society', in *Sociology: the State of the Art, op. cit.* The authors distinguish four main perspectives in current work: Marxist, Marxist-Weberian/ Marxist-functionalist, World system and dependency, Modernization; and they note the growing prominence of Marxism.
[117] See W. Rodney, *How Europe Underdeveloped Africa* (London: Bogle-l'Ouverture Publications, 1972).
[118] See Paul A. Baran, *The Political Economy of Growth* (New York: Monthly Review Press, 1957); A.G. Frank, *Capitalism and Underdevelopment in Latin America* (revised edn, New York: Monthly Review Press, 1969); and James D. Cockcroft, A.G. Frank and Dale L. Johnson, *Dependence and Underdevelopment* (New York: Doubleday Anchor Books, 1972).
[119] See, for example, Fernando H. Cardoso and Enzo Faletto, *Dependency and Development in Latin America* (Berkeley: University of California Press, 1979).
[120] See Taylor, *From Modernization to Modes of Production, op. cit.*
[121] See Maurice Godelier, *Perspectives in Marxist Anthropology, op. cit.*

maximum utilization of science and technology, industrialization, and economic growth, but the present balance between
world resources, population, and material levels of living
demands some rethinking of the issue; and this might well find
a point of departure in Marx himself, who thought of the
emancipation of human beings in terms of increased leisure and
a new structure of needs, much more than in terms of sheer
material progress.[122]

There is another obvious gap in Marxist studies of the world
system, and more generally, of politics; namely, the very
limited attention given to the nation state and nationalism.
Aside from the work of Otto Bauer, and to a lesser extent of
Karl Renner, mentioned earlier, Marxists have contributed
little in the way of analysis or research into these phenomena,
and have indeed tended to ignore or dismiss them as being of
minor significance.[123] But this is no longer, if it ever was, a
tenable view. Since the latter part of the nineteenth century in
Europe, and subsequently in other areas of the world, nationalism has competed with socialism as an ideology, and has
frequently proved stronger. More recently, nationalist movements within existing states (in Britain, Canada, Spain, for
example) have gained a mass following and had important
political consequences. Furthermore, it is evident that socialism does not automatically resolve all the issues involved in
nationalist aspirations or in the rivalry between nation states;
there have been serious conflicts between socialist nation
states, and within some socialist countries nationalist movements occupy a prominent place among the movements of
dissent.[124] Here, then, is a very broad field for future Marxist
research.

[122] See particularly the discussion in Agnes Heller, *The Theory of Need in Marx*
(London: Allison and Busby, 1976).
[123] See the comments in Tom Nairn, *The Break-up of Britain: Crisis and
Neo-nationalism* (London: New Left Books, 1977); and on the views of Marx
and Engels on nations and nationalist movements, Ian Cummins, *Marx, Engels
and National Movements* (London: Croom Helm, 1980).
[124] See the account of nations and nationalism in the USSR, in Hélène Carrère
d'Encausse, *L'Empire éclaté: la révolte des nations en U.R.S.S.* (Paris:
Flammarion, 1978).

A hundred years after Marx's death Marxism has become firmly established as one of the major paradigms in sociological theory; perhaps, in terms of its comprehensiveness and the explanatory power it has demonstrated (at least in certain areas), the pre-eminent paradigm. But like other sociological paradigms it is internally diverse, as I have shown in this essay, and there are important disagreements about the general principles of a Marxist sociology as well as about the proper analysis of particular issues. The disagreements and controversies, however, are not simply signs of disarray; they have helped to refine and develop important Marxist concepts, and perhaps to establish more clearly what are the fundamental concepts. At the same time, as I have suggested in the concluding part of this essay, there are many unresolved problems and unexplored areas of research, and it would be surprising indeed if Marxist sociology did not undergo further development and revision – on an even larger scale than in the past, because it is now so widely taught and debated – during the remainder of this century.

Politics

David McLellan

This necessarily brief survey of Marxist politics over the last century and more will be divided into three sections: first, the ideas of Marx himself; secondly, the classical Marxist conceptions from the death of Marx up to, and including, the Russian Revolution; and thirdly, the contemporary (in a wide sense) multifarious versions of Marxist politics that have emerged after the demise of the Stalinist monolith. In each section, I shall try to give an account of the three main elements that any Marxist political perspective must contain: an analysis of contemporary political power, and particularly the state, some conception of revolution and its agents, and an idea of the form a transitional socialist society will take.

1. *Marx: the theory of the bourgeois state*

In Marx's earliest writings, politics occupies a central place. As soon as the growing repression of the Prussian government made it clear that he could not pursue an academic career, Marx turned to journalism. As editor of the *Rheinische Zeitung* in 1842/3, Marx criticized the Prussian state in a series of articles which combined a radical Hegelianism with the mordant rationalism of Voltaire. Underlying his critique lay the possibility of forming a truly free association of citizens in a state conceived, on the Hegelian model, as the incarnation of reason.

However, the suppression of his paper following the publication of articles exposing the destitution of the Moselle wine growers led Marx to concentrate on what he called 'the objective character of the relationships'[1] that underlay state activity. He 'withdrew into his study'[2] in the summer of 1843 and wrestled with Hegel's main political work *The Philosophy of Right*, producing a lengthy commentary that remained unpublished in his lifetime. Hegel had rightly, thought Marx, perceived the menace of atomization and war of all against all as the growth of capitalism produced a 'civil society' in which the economic self-interest of the individual was destroying the social cohesion of previous ages. But his own experience as a newspaper editor and Feuerbach's critique of Hegel's idealism led Marx to reject Hegel's solution that the tensions of civil society could be harmonized by the state acting, through its organs of monarchy, bureaucracy and legislation, as some sort of superior ethical sphere. By contrast, Marx proposed 'true democracy' which he characterized as follows:

> In all states that are not democracies, the state, the law, the constitution is the dominant factor without really dominating, i.e. materially penetrating all the other spheres that are not political. In a democracy the constitution, the law and the state itself are only a self-determination of the people and a particular content of them in so far as it is a political constitution.[3]

Although in the same work Marx hinted at the socio-economic basis of all political activity and at the necessary disappearance of the state, his conception of 'true democracy' remained vague.

The direction of Marx's ideas became clearer in an essay entitled 'On the Jewish Question' published soon after his arrival in Paris whither he had emigrated to make contact with incipient socialist movements. This essay contains Marx's clearest indictment of classical liberal ideas. Marx claimed that the typically liberal solution to the Jewish question advocated by his colleague Bruno Bauer was insufficient. Bauer thought

[1] 'Defence of the Moselle Correspondent', in Karl Marx, *Selected Writings*, ed. D. McLellan (Oxford, 1977), p. 24.
[2] 'Preface to *A Critique of Political Economy*', *Selected Writings*, p. 389.
[3] 'Critique of Hegel's *Philosophy of Right*', *Selected Writings*, p. 29.

that the problem would be solved by the granting to Jews of equal political rights in a secularized state. But, according to Marx, this proposal, already exemplified in the French revolutionary constitutions and the constitutions of the United States, was no solution but simply a perpetuation of the problems that Hegel had diagnosed in civil society. Marx wrote:

> The right of man to freedom is not based on the union of man with man, but on the separation of man from man. It is the right to this separation, the right of the limited individual who is limited to himself ... The right of man to property is the right to enjoy his possessions and to dispose of the same arbitrarily, without regard for other men, independently from society, the right of selfishness. It is the former individual freedom together with its latter application that forms the basis of civil society. It leads man to see in other men not the realization but the limitations of his own freedom.[4]

The only true solution would be to ensure that those notions of freedom and equality had some reality in the social and economic world:

> Man must recognize his own forces as social forces, organize them and thus no longer separate social forces in the form of political forces. Only when this has been achieved will human emancipation be completed.[5]

In other words, it was no use having the right to access to the Grill Room of the Ritz if you couldn't afford the bill.

As soon as Marx had worked out his materialist conception of history in 1845/6, he could give a historical and materialist dimension to his idea of the divorce between the state and civil society under capitalism and the way in which the bourgeois state and its attendant ideas of political rights and common

---

[4] 'On the Jewish Question', *Selected Writings*, p. 53.
[5] Ibid., p. 57.

national interest functioned, like religion, as an opium, an illusory compensation and thus a support for the injustices of civil society. At the same time, there was an additional emphasis: whereas before Marx had concentrated on the gap between the state and civil society, he now emphasized the connection between the two:

> The social structure and the state continually evolve out of the life process of definite individuals, individuals ... as they work, produce materially, and act under definite material limitations, presuppositions, and conditions independent of their work.[6]

This statement comes from *The German Ideology*, Marx's most extended account of his theory of history. In this work (also unpublished during Marx's lifetime) he traced the origin of the state, together with other social institutions, to the division of labour: the state was in contradiction to the real interests of all members of society, constituting as it did an illusory community serving as a screen for the real struggles waged by classes against each other. In the course of history each method of production gave rise to a typical political organization further-ing the interests of the economically dominant class. The large-scale industry and universal competition of modern capitalism had created their own political organization – the modern state – which was dependent on the bourgeoisie for taxes and public credit. The state in turn moulded other social institutions:

> Since the state is the form in which the individuals of a ruling class assert their common interests and the entire civil society of an epoch is epitomized, the state acts as an intermediary in the formation of all communal institutions and gives them a political form. Hence, there is the illusion that law is based on will, that is, on will divorced from its real

---

[6] *The German Ideology, Selected Writings*, p. 164.

basis, a free will. In similar fashion, right in turn is reduced to statute law.[7]

This view found its classical summary in *The Communist Manifesto* with its statement that 'the executive of the modern state is but a committee for managing the common affairs of the whole bourgeoisie.'[8]

But the view of politics as subordinate to economics and, in particular, of the state as an instrument of class domination is subject to subtle qualification in Marx's specific analyses. He was, of course, aware that the state might be controlled by only part of a class or even by a class, such as the Whig aristocracy in England, who were acting in the interests of another class, or that, in countries such as India or China, such an analysis might be inapplicable since the absence of private property in land meant that 'the despot here appears as the father of all the numerous lesser communities, thus revealing the common unity of all.'[9]

The complexity of Marx's approach is particularly evident in the two lengthy articles he wrote on the French revolution of 1848 and its aftermath – *The Class Struggles in France* and *The Eighteenth Brumaire of Louis Bonaparte*. In Britain and the United States parliamentary democracy appeared to be the political form appropriate to the development of capitalism: France, however, was following a different path. Particularly in *The Eighteenth Brumaire* Marx tried to explain the rise to power of Louis Bonaparte and his apparent independence of class forces: 'France seems to have escaped the despotism of a class only to fall back beneath the despotism of an individual and, what is more, beneath the authority of an individual without authority. The struggle seems to be settled in such a way that all classes, equally impotent and equally mute, fall on their knees before the rifle butt.'[10] Stressing the enormous bureaucratic centralism of French government since the days

---

[7] *The German Ideology*, in Karl Marx, *Writings of the Young Marx*, ed. L. Easton and K. Guddat (New York, 1967), p. 470.
[8] *The Communist Manifesto*, *Selected Writings*, p. 223.
[9] *Pre-capitalist Economic Formations*, ed. E. Hobsbawm (London, 1964), p. 69.
[10] *The Eighteenth Brumaire of Louis Bonaparte*, *Selected Writings*, pp. 315f.

of the absolute monarchy, Marx noted that 'only under the second Bonaparte does the state seem to have made itself completely independent,' but continued immediately: 'and yet the state power is not suspended in mid-air. Bonaparte represents a class, and the most numerous class of French society at that, the small-holding peasants.'[11] Bonaparte could appear to represent the peasants as their mode of production forced upon them an isolation which meant that they could not act for themselves as a cohesive political force. Bonaparte was thus put in a position whereby he could play the role of mediator between different class forces. As Marx wrote later, Bonapartism 'was the only form of government possible at a time when the bourgeoisie had already lost, and the working class had not yet acquired, the faculty of ruling the nation.'[12]

It has sometimes been claimed[13] that Marx has here a different theory of the state – as a force sometimes independent of class control. And Engels to some extent supported this view by considering the absolutist monarchies of Europe as owing their existence to the equilibrium between declining feudalism and the rising bourgeoisie.[14] But Marx was quite clear that even Bonaparte's freedom of political manoeuvre was curtailed by class interests and that, economically, his regime gave a dramatic boost to the interests of French capital. And his complex account has served as a pioneering model for the analysis by Marxists of twentieth-century authoritarian regimes.[15]

During the last thirty years of his life, Marx devoted himself to the mammoth task of discovering the 'laws of motion of capitalist society' and his theoretical considerations on politics were incidental. In his projected work on economics, he intended to devote a whole book to the state. This work was

---

[11] Ibid., p. 31f.

[12] *The Civil War in France, Selected Writings*, p. 541.

[13] See, for example, J. Sanderson, *An Interpretation of the Political Ideas of Marx and Engels* (London, 1969), ch. 4.

[14] For a critique of this view, see P. Anderson, *Lineages of the Absolutist State* (London, 1974), pp. 15ff.

[15] Particularly the neo-structuralists, as in N. Poulantzas, *Political Power and Social Classes* (London, 1973).

never completed and Marx confined himself to general statements. In the *Grundrisse*, for example, he wrote that

> In all forms of society there is one specific kind of production which predominates over the rest, whose relations thus assign rank and influence to the others. It is a general illumination which bathes all the other colours and modifies their particularity. It is a particular ether which determines the specific gravity of every being which has materialized within it.[16]

The extent and form of the determination of politics by economics – and even whether one can separate the two – is, of course, the central problem in Marx's historical materialism. In *Capital* he insisted, in a determinist vein, that

> It is always the direct relationship of the owners of the conditions of production to the direct producers – a relation always naturally corresponding to a definite stage in the development of the methods of labour and thereby its social productivity – which reveals the innermost secret, the hidden basis of the entire social structure, and with it the political form of the relation of sovereignty and dependence, in short, the corresponding specific form of the state.[17]

Nevertheless, in this area, as in so many others, Marx's ideas were still tentative. As he admitted to his friend Kugelmann, 'the relationship of the different forms of the state to the various economic structures of society' was the one aspect of his work where he had not given sufficient directions for his followers to be able to complete his work.[18]

[16] *Grundrisse*, ed. M. Nicolaus (London, 1973), pp. 106f.
[17] K. Marx, *Capital* (London, 1972), vol. 3, p. 791.
[18] Marx to Kugelmann, in K. Marx and F. Engels, *Werke* (Berlin, 1957ff), vol. 30, p. 639.

2. *Marx: party and revolution*

Although Marx laid considerable stress on the way in which political options were severely limited and canalized by material circumstances, he did not neglect the more subjective side of the political process. Already in 1844 his study of the French revolution had convinced him that, just as the bourgeoisie had instigated the revolution of 1789 under the cover of the apparently universal slogans of freedom and equality, so now the proletariat was destined to overthrow capitalist society on principles that really would apply to the whole of humanity. The merely political revolution of 1789 had held that it was open to everyone to emancipate himself by becoming a bourgeois, but by definition not everyone could do so and the inevitable result was the exploitation of one group in society by another. Hegel's idea of the bureaucracy as a 'universal class' that could harmonize the interests of the whole of society was an illusion: the really universal class was the proletariat whose needs and aspirations coincided in the long run with those of humanity as a whole. In *The Communist Manifesto* Marx painted a striking picture of the increasing numbers and impoverishment of the proletariat producing radical social upheaval:

> All previous historical movements were movements of minorities, or in the interest of minorities. The proletarian movement is the self-conscious, independent movement of the immense majority, in the interests of the immense majority. The proletariat, the lowest stratum of our present society, cannot stir, cannot raise itself up, without the whole superincumbent strata of official society being exploded into the air.[19]

Although Marx was ready to concede that the proletariat might need allies – the peasantry, the petty bourgeoisie – in the revolutionary cause, he never wavered in his confidence in the proletariat as the agent of revolutionary change. Marx did not have to face the problem that has bedevilled so many of his later

[19] *The Communist Manifesto, Selected Writings*, p. 230.

followers in the West – the apparent lack of enthusiasm for revolution among the workers. He paid perhaps too little attention to a crucial difference between the position of the rising bourgeoisie in feudal society and that of the proletariat in capitalist society: the bourgeoisie could, in their towns, to some extent develop their own economic bases, their own culture and ideas in relative isolation from feudal society whereas no such option was open to the proletarians enmeshed as they were in a capitalist society of which it was especially true that 'the ideas of the ruling class are in every epoch the ruling ideas.'[20] Indeed, his own insightful analysis at the beginning of *Capital* of the fetishism inherent in capitalist society – whereby the relationships between things or commodities assume a mystifying reality obscuring the relationships between human beings – has consequences for the growth of proletarian revolution,[21] consequences that Marx failed to draw.[22]

Nor did Marx have to contend with the second (and obviously closely related) great crux of the Marxist movement – the relationship of leaders or party to the class that they allegedly represent. The growth of mass political parties only got under way towards the end of Marx's life, in line with the extension of the suffrage in Western Europe. The only 'party' that Marx ever belonged to was the Communist League of the late 1840s, a semi-clandestine propaganda organization with only a few hundred members and very few of them proletarians in the strict sense. The majority were artisans whose enthusiasm for 'communism now' was a corollary of their outright opposition to the capitalism that was destroying their traditional livelihood. And it is interesting to note how changeful were Marx's tactics in the only revolutionary situation in which he participated – Germany in 1848/9. On the one hand, his materialist conception of history, with its notion of stages, led him to think that Germany was not ripe for a socialist revolution and that, as he

[20] *The German Ideology, Selected Writings,* p. 176.
[21] For a recent attempt to apply Marx's concept of fetishism to the contemporary state, see D. Wells, *Marxism and the Modern State* (Hassocks, 1981).
[22] See further, C. Johnson, 'The Problem of Reformism and Marx's Theory of Fetishism', *New Left Review,* Jan./Feb. 1980.

said in his quarrel with the artisan leader Wilhelm Weitling, 'the bourgeoisie must first come to the helm.'[23] And this view was echoed in his support for the radical bourgeoisie as editor of the *Neue Rheinische Zeitung*. On the other hand, the imminence of the proletarian revolution proclaimed at the end of *The Communist Manifesto* and the tone of the 1850 *Address to the Communist League* were more in tune with the anti-capitalist sentiments of the artisan majority of the League.[24]

Nevertheless, Marx's response to the feelings of the German artisans does not justify regarding him as a Jacobin, if by that is meant one advocating revolution engineered by a minority accompanied, if necessary, by the use of terror. It is true that Marx considered force to be usually the midwife of revolution, but he never (except briefly in 1848 and under Tsarist conditions in Russia) approved of the use of revolutionary terror. Indeed, he strongly criticized the use of terror by the Jacobins in the French revolution; terror was for him a sign of the weakness and immaturity of a revolution which had to try to impose by sheer force what was not yet inherent in society. Occasionally Marx even envisaged the possibility of socialism being brought about by peaceful means. In 1872 he spoke of his belief in the possibility of a peaceful revolution in America, England and Holland. He took the same line in 1878 when he wrote: 'A historical development can only remain "peaceful" so long as it is not opposed by the violence of those who wield power in society at that time. If in England or the United States, for example, the working class were to gain a majority in Parliament or Congress, then it could by legal means set aside the laws and structures that stood in its way.'[25] This does not mean, of course, that Marx ever became a convert to parliamentary democracy, only that in certain political cultures he considered parliamentary democracy to be an appropriate transitional vehicle for the assertion of proletarian political power.

[23] M. Hess, *Briefwechsel* (The Hague, 1959), p. 151.
[24] This view is elaborated in R. Hunt, *The Political Ideas of Marx and Engels* (London, 1974), vol. 1. For a more Leninist reading of Marx at this time, see A. Gilbert, *Marx's Politics* (London, 1981).
[25] 'Konspect der Reichstagsdebatte über das Sozialistengesetz', *Werke*, vol. 34, pp. 498f.

As indicated above, Marx was vague about the timetable of revolution. In the early 1850s his young disciples would pull his leg about his repeated predictions of the imminence of industrial crisis.[26] But his more serious pronouncements were far less precise. The main thrust of his materialist conception of history led to the view that the advanced countries of the capitalist West were the ripest for revolution. Yet Marx realized that European revolutions were becoming more dependent on the general world situation. And later in his life he came to believe that Russia might prove the starting point of the revolution which 'begins this time in the East, hitherto the invulnerable bulwark and reinforcement of the counter-revolution'.[27] Of Russia he said a year before his death: 'If the Russian revolution becomes the signal for a proletarian revolution in the West, so that both complete each other, then the present Russian system of the community ownership of land could serve as a starting point for a communist development.'[28] When this central drama would be played out in the West was unclear. For there seems to be a tension between the long-term view of the *Grundrisse* and the prospects of a fairly imminent revolution implicit in some of Marx's later political writings. For in the *Grundrisse* the view seems to be that there is no prospect of a proletarian revolution until capitalism has exhausted all its capacities for the extraction of surplus value and that this would be a very long process. On the other hand, in such writings of the 1870s as the drafts for *The Civil War in France* or his remarks on Bakunin's *Statism and Anarchy* Marx's view seems to be that the proletariat can expect to lead a successful revolution, even where it is not a majority of the population, by the introduction of measures that would gain peasant and lower-middle-class support.

[26] Cf. *Karl Marx: Interviews and Recollections*, ed. D. McLellan (London, 1981), p. 44.
[27] Marx to Sorge, *Werke*, vol. 34, p. 296.
[28] 'Preface to the Russian edition of *The Communist Manifesto*', *Selected Writings*, p. 584.

3. *Marx: transitional society and communism*

There are two general points to be borne in mind when
considering Marx's sketchy remarks on post-revolutionary
society. First, Marx always refused to write 'recipes for the
cookshops of the future',[29] and this was reasonable enough in
his own terms: the materialist conception of history showed
how all ideas were conditioned by socio-economic reality and
speculation about the precise nature of communist society
could only be the result of the spinning of ideas that had no
empirical reference, no root in any observable reality –
something for which Marx had already severely criticized the
Utopian socialists. Secondly, Marx anticipated the major
revolutionary upheaval as happening in the advanced industrial
West. Thus post-revolutionary political arrangements would
take place in societies where capitalism had already generated
enormous wealth, the main trouble being that the conditions
under which this wealth was produced prevented its being
deployed for the benefit of society as a whole. Where there
were enough resources broadly to satisfy everyone's needs, it
was not merely wishful thinking to suppose some kind of
democratic political process to be possible. In the event,
however, Marxist political parties have, to date, come to power
in countries which did not enjoy the huge wealth generated by
capitalism, where there was not enough to go round and some
would have to go to the wall. Under such circumstances, the
very jostling for insufficient resources (let alone the necessity
for primitive capital accumulation) implied the necessity of
authoritarian government, irrespective of its political ideology.

In Marx's view the form of government that would be set up
following a successful revolution was a dictatorship of the
proletariat, and the most detailed information on its programme
is contained in the tentative ten points listed at the end of the
second section of *The Communist Manifesto*. The expression
'dictatorship of the proletariat' was seldom used by Marx and
never in documents for publication. In a letter to his friend

[29] K. Marx, *Capital* (Moscow, 1954), vol. 1, p. 17.

Weydemeyer, Marx claimed as one of his contributions to socialist theory to have that 'the class struggle necessarily leads to the dictatorship of the proletariat; that this dictatorship itself is only a transitional stage towards the abolition of all classes.'[30] And in the 'Critique of the Gotha Programme' Marx wrote that when capitalist society was being transformed into communist society, there would be 'a political transition period during which the state can be nothing but the revolutionary dictatorship of the proletariat'.[31] It should also be noted that the word 'dictatorship' did not have quite the same connotation for Marx that it does for us. He associated it principally with the Roman office of *dictatura* where all power was legally concentrated in the hands of a single man during a limited period in a time of crisis. Although Marx seldom discussed the measures that such a government would enact, the fullest account – the ten-point programme outlined in *The Communist Manifesto* – is in many respects a fairly moderate programme.

There is here a profound ambivalence in Marx's thought that was to return to haunt his successors. It is true that his statement in 1850 that 'the workers must not only strive for a single and indivisible German republic, but also within this republic for the most determined centralization of power within the hands of the state authority'[32] refers to such centralization as a precondition for a successful bourgeois democratic revolution and not a proletarian revolution. Nevertheless, the general tone of the remarks at the end of the second section of *The Communist Manifesto* and his statement in *The Eighteenth Brumaire* that 'the demolition of the state machine will not endanger centralization'[33] implies a perspective that Marx was later to modify. The remark in *The Eighteenth Brumaire* was omitted in the second edition. And in a hurriedly written Preface to a re-edition of *The Communist Manifesto* in 1872, there was one particular point on which he wished to emend his former views: 'One thing especially was proved by the Commune, viz., that the working class cannot simply lay hold

---

[30] Marx to Weydemeyer, *Selected Writings*, p. 341.
[31] 'Critique of the Gotha Programme', *Selected Writings*, p. 565.
[32] 'Address to the Communist League', *Selected Writings*, p. 284.
[33] K. Marx and F. Engels, *Selected Works* (Moscow, 1962), vol. 1, p. 340.

of the ready-made state machinery, and wield it for its own purposes.'[34] The state was not some kind of neutral instrument that could pass unmodified from class to class.

It was the Paris Commune that prompted Marx's most specific reflections on post-revolutionary politics. The Commune was 'the political form at last discovered under which to work out the economic emancipation of labour'.[35] Summarizing what he took to be this 'political form', Marx wrote:

> The majority of its members were naturally working men, or acknowledged representatives of the working class. The Commune was to be a working, not a parliamentary, body, executive and legislative at the same time. Instead of continuing to be the agent of the Central Government, the police was at once stripped of its political attributes, and turned into the responsible and at all times revocable agent of the Commune. So were the officials of all other branches of the Administration. From the members of the Commune downwards, the public service had to be done at workmen's wages. The vested interests and the representation allowances of the high dignitaries of state disappeared along with the high dignitaries themselves. Public functions ceased to be the private property of the tools of the Central Government. Not only municipal administration, but the whole initiative hitherto exercised by the state was laid into the hands of the Commune.[36]

Whether, in Marx's mind, the Commune was an example of the dictatorship of the proletariat is a question of some dispute. Engels was quite emphatic later in identifying them.[37] Ten years after the Commune Marx drew attention to the Commune's local character as against the necessarily national dimensions of the dictatorship of the proletariat: the Commune was 'merely the rising of a city under exceptional circumstances' and 'the

---

[34] 'Preface to the Second German Edition of *The Communist Manifesto*', *Selected Writings*, p. 559.

[35] *The Civil War in France*, *Selected Writings*, p. 544.

[36] Ibid., p. 542.

[37] 'Introduction to *The Civil War in France*', *Selected Works*, vol. 1, p. 485.

majority of the Commune was in no way socialist, nor could it be.'[38] But however limited the actual achievements of the Commune there can be no doubt that its existence provided Marx with practical evidence for the solution to the problem which had been with him since his 1843 essay 'On the Jewish Question': the separation of the state and civil society. In words strikingly echoing his previous work, Marx saw the Commune as 'the reabsorption of state power by society as its own living forces instead of as forces controlling and subduing it, by the popular masses themselves, forming their own force instead of the organized force of their suppression – the political form of their social emancipation.'[39] The principle that all officials – legislative, executive, judicial – should be elected, revocable and mandated was the implementation in the sphere of politics of the abolition of the division of labour. This deprofessional-ization of governmental functions would achieve Marx's aim of 'converting the state from an organ superimposed upon society into one completely subordinated to it'.[40]

It also becomes clearer from the above what Marx had in mind when he talked of the abolition of the state. (The biological metaphor of 'withering away' comes in fact from Engels who was always readier than Marx to draw parallels between the natural and social sciences.) It is of course important to remember that at the time of Marx's writing the state did much less than it did now: there were virtually no social services provided. Industry was all in private hands, and state organiz-ation of education was only just beginning, so that there was proportionately less to 'abolish'. With the gradual disappear-ance of classes, 'the public power will lose its political character', for 'political power, properly so called, is merely the organized power of one class for suppressing another.'[41] Of course there would still be public power in a future communist society, but 'when class rule will have disappeared, there will no longer be any state in the present political sense of the

[38] Marx to Domela-Nieuwenhuis, *Selected Writings*, p. 594.
[39] 'Drafts for *The Civil War in France*', *Selected Writings*, p. 555.
[40] 'Critique of the Gotha Programme', *Selected Writings*, p. 564.
[41] *The Communist Manifesto*, *Selected Writings*, pp. 237f.

word.'[42] Thus for Marx the abolition of the state involved the abolition of a professionalized state apparatus in which an essentially irresponsible legislative and judiciary ensured the invulnerability of the bureaucracy.

4. *The Second International*

During the four decades after Marx's death, the innovating forces in Marxist theory and practice were moving Eastwards, though this was not apparent at the time. The clear political heirs of Marx were the parties which made up the Second International founded in 1889, pre-eminent among them the German Social Democratic Party (SPD). In its Erfurt Programme of 1891 the party reiterated the traditional doctrines of the trend to monopoly capitalism, the decline of the middle class, the impoverishment of the proletariat and the inevitability of the socialization of the means of production in a classless society; the second half contained such immediate demands as universal suffrage, freedom of expression, free schooling and a progressive income tax. But the very success of the party in terms of numbers of members, organizational growth, and electoral support produced problems for its Marxism: the increasing membership tended to mean the diffusion of a simplified Marxism, the party's growing bureaucracy was less inclined to endanger itself by revolutionary enterprise, and involvement in electoral politics meant that reform rather than revolution became the dominant theme. The compromises of the SPD took place in the context of an aggressively expanding capitalism controlled by a military-bureaucratic elite and the party had inherited very little Marxist theory equipped to cope with such a situation.

Shortly before he died in 1895, Engels had written:

We can count even today on two and a quarter million votes.

[42] 'On Bakunin's *Statism and Anarchy*', *Selected Writings*, p. 563.

If it continues in this fashion, by the end of the century we shall conquer the greater part of the middle strata of society, petty bourgeois and small peasants, and grow into a decisive power in the land, before which all other powers will have to bow, whether they like it or not. To keep this growth going without interruption until it of itself gets beyond the control of the prevailing governmental system, not to fritter away this daily increasing shock force in vanguard skirmishes, but to keep it intact until the decisive day, that is our main task.[43]

Although Engels' text had been considerably toned down by the Berlin party leadership, it was exploited by some as a reformist charter. Edward Bernstein, who was the principal spokesman for what came to be known as Revisionism, considered many of Marx's prognostications to be wrong: 'peasants do not sink; middle class does not disappear; crises do not grow even larger; misery and serfdom do not increase.'[44] He drew the conclusion that Social Democracy was not only the chronological but also the intellectual successor to liberalism: 'there is actually no really liberal conception that does not also belong to the elements of the ideas of socialism.'[45] Although Kautsky, the dominant Marxist theorist of the time, showed many of Bernstein's sociological views to be short-sighted and insisted on the reality of class struggle, the political situation in Germany and the general intellectual climate did not allow the emergence of a viable alternative. The generally determinist attitude of the SPD and the belief in the inevitability of a proletarian victory became an argument for inaction as the conditions were never thought to be 'mature' enough for intervention.

The only SPD leader who managed to articulate something nearer Marx's own original political perspective was Rosa Luxemburg. According to her, Bernstein's confidence in

[43] 'Introduction to *The Class Struggles in France*', *Selected Works*, vol. 1, p. 135.
[44] Quoted in P. Gay, *The Dilemma of Democratic Socialism* (New York, 1962), p. 350.
[45] E. Bernstein, *Evolutionary Socialism* (New York, 1961), p. 151.

political democracy was misplaced for democratic institutions had 'largely played out their role as aids in bourgeois development'.[46] While not wishing to deny the importance of parliamentary struggle, Luxemburg pointed out that capitalist society was characterized by the fact that wage labour was not a juridical but only an economic relation: 'in our whole juridical system, there is not a single legal formula for the present class domination.'[47] This meant that the kind of political and legal reforms advocated by Bernstein could not possibly tackle the problem. Luxemburg conserved a faith in the potential of the masses, given creative leadership, for radical political action. Central to her conception of revolution was the idea of spontaneity, i.e., that the proletariat forged its consciousness of itself as a revolutionary class in the course of struggles which were themselves determined by the logic of capitalist development. The embodiment of spontaneity for Luxemburg was the mass strike which was the one proletarian revolutionary action which fused both economic and political elements. Her ideas, however, failed to make much impact on German Social Democracy – though they flared briefly into prominence in the abortive German revolution of 1919 whose failure was the chief factor in sealing the fate of the Russian Revolution.

5. *Lenin: party and revolution*

As regards his prognosis for revolution, Lenin's version of Marxism was not regarded by his colleagues in the Second International as being radically different from their own until the cataclysm of 1914. Although his ideas were tailored to the specific conditions prevailing in Russia, they all had some foundation in the Marxist tradition.

Lenin was without doubt pre-eminently a man of politics; but

[46] R. Luxemburg, 'Social Reform or Revolution', in *Selected Political Writings*, ed. D. Howard (New York, 1971), p. 110.
[47] Ibid., p. 116.

he always based his strategy on a careful analysis of socio-economic circumstances. In 1899 he published a lengthy and detailed study entitled *The Development of Capitalism in Russia* which documented the emergence of capitalism out of feudalism in Russia. Lenin argued that Russia, though undoubtedly underdeveloped, was already capitalist. The stage of usury capital and merchant capital outlined by Marx had already in some places been superseded by manufacturing capital – capital applied directly to the productive system – and the next stage of industrial capital was already on the horizon. From this Lenin concluded that the proletariat held a unique position in that they were the only class fully to appreciate and be able to articulate the exploitation of all Russian labourers – including the artisans and the rural proletariat. This idea of the proletariat leading the whole of the exploited population in a revolutionary struggle governed Lenin's political thinking up to 1914.

But what sort of a revolution could the proletariat justifiably aim at? Lenin was faced with a situation that was roughly parallel to that confronting Marx in Germany in 1848: autocratic monarchy, weak bourgeoisie, small and concentrated proletariat, and large peasant mass. Lenin's response, in *Two Tactics* written amid the upheavals of 1905, was to propose 'a revolutionary democratic dictatorship of the proletariat and peasantry'. He viewed the peasantry more optimistically than Marx and could claim to be the first Marxist to propose associating the peasantry in political power, thus placing them in the position of the liberals in the classical West European Marxist schema. On the other hand, the revolution would be 'democratic' because Lenin was clear about the fundamentally bourgeois nature of the next stage of revolution. He wrote:

The democratic forms in the political system, and the social and economic reforms that have become a necessity for Russia, do not in themselves imply the undermining of capitalism, the undermining of bourgeois rule; on the contrary they will, for the first time, really clear the ground for a wide and rapid, European not Asiatic, development of capitalism; they will, for the first time, make it possible for the bourgeoisie to rule as a class.[48]

The idea of a revolution spearheaded by the proletariat yet remaining bourgeois in its social and economic form seems disturbingly hybrid.

In the event, Lenin's proposals were never put to the test for in 1917 he adopted the more radical perspective that Trotsky had been advocating from as early as 1906. In his conception of 'permanent revolution' (an expression which, again, echoed the Marx of 1850) Trotsky argued that the particular social and economic configuration of Russia meant that any successful proletarian party could not stop at presiding over a capitalist revolution. As divisions among the peasantry emerged following the redistribution of land, the proletariat would be forced to adopt socialist attitudes. The proletarian government would find that increasingly radical measures would be forced upon them and that 'immediately power is transferred into the hands of a revolutionary government with a socialist majority, the division of our programme into maximum and minimum loses all significance both in principle and in immediate practice.'[49] At the same time, the internal opposition to such measures would ensure that 'without the direct state support of the European proletariat the working class of Russia cannot remain in power and convert its temporary domination into a lasting socialist dictatorship.'[50] In the event, of course, it was precisely this sort of support from the European proletariat that was not forthcoming once the Russian Bolsheviks had seized power in 1917.

Lenin's most enduring contribution to Marxist theory was to fill an evident gap in Marx by delineating the relationship of the proletarian party to the class it represents. Here the fundamental work is *What is to be Done?*, written in 1902. Basing himself on the conclusions of his *Development of Capitalism in Russia*, Lenin declared that the emergence of a national capitalism in

---

[48] V. Lenin, *Two Tactics*, in *Collected Works* (Moscow, 1972), vol. 9, p. 48.
[49] L. Trotsky, *The Permanent Revolution and Results and Prospects* (New York, 1969), p. 78.
[50] Ibid., p. 105.

Russia demanded a national centralized political organization. This political organization could gain an intensive knowledge of the socio-economic situation and prospects of every class, a knowledge which was inaccessible to the proletariat whose 'economic' struggle was too narrow for it to achieve this form of consciousness. Lenin quoted Kautsky at length and continued:

> Since there can be no talk of an independent ideology formulated by the working masses themselves in the process of their movement, the only choice is either bourgeois ideology or socialist ideology ... The spontaneous development of the working-class movement leads to its subordination to bourgeois ideology ... for the spontaneous working-class movement is trade-unionism, and trade-unionism means the ideological enslavement of the workers by the bourgeoisie.[51]

Thus the party, in order to fulfil its tasks, would have to be an all-Russian organization that would have the attributes of secrecy, centralization, specialization, exclusivity and, above all, a membership composed of professional revolutionaries who were fully trained and devoted themselves full time to party work. Lenin was not against mass organizations – quite the contrary – but he insisted that they must be quite separate from the party. Nor was Lenin against inner-party democracy. But the conditions prevailing in Russia made it impossible and meant that the leadership would have to be chosen through the oligarchical principle of co-option.

Lenin's views in *What is to be Done?* had the support of all his colleagues in the leadership of the Russian Social Democratic Labour Party. But at the Second Congress of the party in 1903 a split occurred between the Bolsheviks and Mensheviks. The latter opposed the exclusive professionalization of the Bolsheviks. The Mensheviks also distrusted the peasantry more than Lenin and were more favourable to alliances with the

[51] V. Lenin, *What is to be Done?*, *Selected Works* (Moscow, 1960), vol. 1, pp. 156f.

liberals and participation in elections. Both Luxemburg and Trotsky also published biting criticisms of Lenin's organizational proposals.[52] Nevertheless, Lenin himself was not unduly attached to the letter of *What is to be Done?* Particularly during the revolutionary upheavals of 1905 and 1917, his attitude was much more flexible. But this flexibility did not survive the rigours of the civil war of 1918–21. At the Tenth Party Congress meeting in March 1921 only weeks after the brutal suppression of the Kronstadt rising, Lenin himself proposed, first, 'the immediate dissolution of all groups without exception formed on the basis of one platform or another'; and secondly, in a spirit quite alien to the confidence in the masses expressed in 1917, that 'only the political party of the working class, i.e., the Communist Party, is capable of uniting, training and organizing a vanguard of the proletariat and of the whole mass of the working people that alone will be capable of withstanding the inevitable petty-bourgeois vacillations of this mass, and the inevitable traditions and relapses of narrow craft unionism or craft prejudices among the proletariat.'[53] On becoming the Party General Secretary shortly afterwards, Stalin canonized *What is to be Done?* The story, so brilliantly told by Deutscher,[54] of how Trotsky's expulsion was facilitated by the alterations in organization that he had himself helped to create is a tragedy in the original sense of the word.

The fact that Lenin was able to conceive of the possibility of a thoroughgoing socialist revolution in 1917, in face of the opposition of the rest of the Bolshevik leaders, owes much to his analysis of the reasons for the debacle of 1914 and in particular his studies of imperialism. Lenin's refusal to believe that the German SPD could have voted for war credits in August 1914 is simply the most striking example of how many an optimistic Marxist perspective has subsequently been overshadowed by the obstinate cloud of nationalism. Marx's own outlook had, of course, been firmly internationalist and

[52] Cf. R. Luxemburg, 'Organizational Questions of Russian Social Democracy', *Selected Political Writings*, pp. 290ff, and B. Knei-Paz, *The Social and Political Thought of Leon Trotsky* (Oxford, 1978), pp. 197f.
[53] V. Lenin, 'Preliminary Draft Resolution for the Tenth Congress', *Collected Works*, vol. 32, pp. 244, 246.
[54] I. Deutscher, *The Prophet Unarmed: Trotsky 1921–1929* (Oxford, 1959).

Luxemburg claimed that the advent of international monopoly capitalism rendered all national groupings obsolete. For Lenin, on the other hand, the question of national autonomy was purely one of tactics:

> We concern ourselves with the self-determination of the proletariat in each nationality rather than with the self-determination of peoples or nations ... As to support of the demand for national autonomy, it is by no means a permanent and binding part of the programme of the proletariat. This support may become necessary for it only in isolated and exceptional cases.[55]

This emphasis on class rather than nation was used to justify subsequent Soviet policies that often seemed to others to have a strong nationalistic element.

Lenin came to terms with the phenomenon of nationalism, explained the catastrophe of 1914 and provided a framework for his policies in 1917 through his renewed study of the world economy that culminated in the publication of his *Imperialism, the Highest Stage of Capitalism* in 1916. According to Lenin, the phenomenon of imperialism was tied to the growth of monopoly capitalism which had superseded competitive capitalism at the beginning of the twentieth century when the advanced economies came to be dominated by finance capital controlled by banks which were themselves concentrated in cartels or trusts. The former type of capitalism was typified by the export of goods: monopoly capitalism exported capital. The surplus capital could not be used at home (for this would mean a decline in profits for the capitalists) and so was employed 'for the purpose of increasing profits by exporting capital abroad to the backward countries. In these backward countries profits are usually high for capital is scarce, the price of land is relatively low, wages are low, raw materials are cheap.'[56] This in turn led to the *de facto* division of the world into the various spheres of

[55] V. Lenin, 'On the Manifesto of Armenian Social Democrats', *Collected Works*, vol. 6, p. 327.
[56] V. Lenin, *Imperialism, the Highest Stage of Capitalism, Collected Works*, vol. 22, p. 241.

influence of international cartels. Lenin made specific reference to the English liberal economist Hobson who had claimed that colonial expansion was due to a lack of home investment opportunities. But his chief source was Hilferding's *Finanzkapital* of 1912. In his lengthy analyses of changing capitalism Hilferding claimed that once finance capital had eliminated internal competition, there was pressure for tariff protection against external competition in order to enforce a monopolistic price policy. This required a strong state power thoroughly opposed to classical liberal principles. The increasingly powerful and aggressive nature of capitalist states, supported by the ideologies of nationalism, racialism and militarism, led to heightened international tension through growing competition to monopolize markets and sources of raw materials. This in turn led to economic warfare between nations and armed expansion into underdeveloped regions to enlarge the potential market in a process in which freedom, democracy and equality were the first casualties. Lenin's most immediate source was Bukharin's *Imperialism and the World Economy* which stressed, as against the view prevailing in German Social Democracy, that imperialism was a necessary feature of contemporary capitalism and that it necessarily led to war and revolution. In the crucial eighth chapter of his pamphlet, Lenin pointed to two internal effects of imperialism. Firstly, monopoly – the foundation of imperialism – created a tendency in the West for profits to retard and stagnate. Secondly, and more importantly, the super-profits of imperialism made it possible 'to bribe the upper strata of the proletariat, and therefore to foster, give shape to, and strengthen opportunism.'[57] Here lay the explanation for the treacherous politics of the Second International.

Lenin's analysis of imperialism also convinced him (in contrast to his pre-1914 views) of the possibility of socialist revolution in Russia. The imperialist war had brought world finance capitalism to its final stage and introduced the objective and subjective preconditions for worldwide socialist revolution. 'For socialism is merely the next step forward from

[57] Ibid., p. 281.

state-capitalist monopoly. Or, in other words, socialism is merely state-capitalist monopoly which is made to serve the interests of the whole people and has to that extent ceased to be capitalist monopoly.'[58] Unfortunately Lenin did not go into the questions of how many workers had been bought off by the fruits of imperialism, why the whole proletariat of the relevant countries should not be affected, and what effect this would have on *world* revolution. Convinced as he was that the era for proletarian revolution in Russia had dawned and that 'the revolution will *not* be limited to Russia,'[59] Lenin devoted himself to reflecting on what forms the proletarian state should adopt.

6. *Lenin: the transition to communism*

Lenin's major work on political theory entitled *The State and Revolution* had its origin in his argument with Bukharin in the summer of 1916 over the existence of the state after a proletarian revolution, an argument that was itself a rehearsal of the different perspectives contained respectively in Marx's *The Communist Manifesto* and *The Civil War in France*. Bukharin had emphasized the 'withering' aspect, whereas Lenin insisted on the necessity of the state machinery to expropriate the expropriators. In fact, it was Lenin who changed his mind, and many of the ideas of *State and Revolution*, composed in the summer of 1917 – and particularly the anti-statist theme – were those of Bukharin.[60]

Lenin's direct and simple definition of the state was that 'the state is a special organization of force: it is an organization of violence for the suppression of some class.'[61] Hence his

[58] V. Lenin, *Collected Works*, vol. 25, p. 362.
[59] V. Lenin, 'Farewell Letter to Swiss Workers', *Collected Works*, vol. 23, p. 373.
[60] Cf. S. Cohen, *Bukharin and the Bolshevik Revolution* (New York, 1973), pp. 39ff.
[61] V. Lenin, *The State and Revolution*, *Selected Works* (Moscow, 1960), vol. 2, p. 320.

denigration even of parliamentary democracy which was influenced by what he saw as the recent increase of bureaucratic and military influences:

> To decide once every few years which member of the ruling class is to repress and crush the people through parliament – this is the real essence of bourgeois parliamentarism, not only in parliamentary-constitutional monarchies, but also in the most democratic republics.[62]

Thus, following Marx's conclusions on the Paris Commune, which Lenin took as his model,[63] Lenin declared that the task of the revolution was to smash the state. Although for a period under communism 'there remains for a time not only bourgeois right but even the bourgeois state without the bourgeoisie',[64] Lenin believed that after a successful proletarian revolution the state had not only begun to wither, but was in an advanced condition of decomposition. But Lenin also called the state 'the armed and ruling proletariat'. Did this, too, wither? Yes, it did, insofar as it was in any way a power separate from, and opposed to, the masses. (The influence on Lenin of his recent experience of the Soviets is clear here.) He had little to say of the institutional form of this transition period. There was a strong emphasis on the dictatorship of the proletariat:

> A Marxist is solely someone who extends the recognition of the class struggle to the recognition of the dictatorship of the proletariat. This is what constitutes the most profound distinction between the Marxist and the ordinary petty (as well as big) bourgeois. This is the touchstone on which the real understanding and recognition of Marxism is to be tested.[65]

But there was little analysis of the shape this dictatorship might

[62] Ibid., p. 338.
[63] Cf. his very different view of the Commune as 'a government such as ours should not be' in *Two Tactics, Collected Works*, vol. 9, p. 81.
[64] V. Lenin, *The State and Revolution, Selected Works*, vol. 2, p. 381.
[65] Ibid., p. 328.

take, which is all the more tantalizing as Lenin's strong insistence on the withering of the state immediately after the revolution has libertarian or even anarchist overtones. His general view seemed to embody the classic socialist formula dating from Saint-Simon that the government of people could give way to the administration of things:

> We ourselves, the workers, will organize large-scale production on the basis of what capitalism has already created, relying on our own experience as workers, establishing strict, iron discipline backed up by the state power of the armed workers; we will reduce the role of the state officials to that of simply carrying out our instructions as responsible, revocable, modestly paid 'foremen and accountants' (of course, with the aid of technicians of all sorts, types and degrees). This is our proletarian task, this is what we can and must start with in accomplishing the proletarian revolution. Such a beginning on the basis of large-scale production will of itself lead to the gradual 'withering away' of all bureaucracy, to the gradual creation of an order without quotation marks, an order bearing no similarity to wage slavery, an order in which the functions of control and accounting – becoming more and more simple – will be formed by each in turn, will then become a habit, and will finally die out as the special functions of a special section of the population.[66]

In the political sphere, what is most striking is the absence of reference to the agent of revolution – the party itself. In his one serious reference to the party Lenin said:

> By educating the workers' party, Marxism educates the vanguard of the proletariat which is capable of assuming power and of leading the whole people to socialism, of directing and organizing the new order, of being the teacher, the guide, the leader of all the workers and exploited in the

[66] Ibid., p. 341.

> task of building up their social life without the bourgeoisie,
> and against the bourgeoisie.[67]

It is ambiguous (but crucial) here whether it is the vanguard or the proletariat which 'is capable of assuming power and leading...' Lenin's general cast of thought would tend to the former, but he nowhere enlarged on the apparent clash that this entailed with his more liberal statements.

Events, however, quickly resolved the ambiguity of Lenin's text. With the defeat of revolution in Germany in 1919 and in 1923, the international dimension of Marxism failed, for the second time, to live up to theory. The nascent Soviet republic was beset by civil war and foreign intervention, circumstances which required the highly authoritarian war communism rather than the Commune model of *State and Revolution*. The gradual shift from dictatorship of the proletariat to dictatorship of the party was aided and abetted by three main factors. First, the party found power thrust into its hands as the only cohesive force capable of governing in the chaotic situation following the revolution. Their success in 1917 took the Bolsheviks by surprise: they had had no time to lay plans as to the future form of government and virtually everything had to be improvised. As the popular basis of the new regime contracted so the party, which had been small and ineffective in late 1917, was obliged to assert its power and authority in the face of increasing social and political difficulties. The dissolution in January 1918 of the Constituent Assembly, for which the Bolsheviks had obtained only twenty-five per cent of the vote, was unavoidable given that the party claimed to be pursuing a proletarian socialist revolution. For the largest party in the Assembly represented peasant interests and its whole structure was much more appropriate to a bourgeois democracy and incompatible with the slogan of 'all power to the Soviets'. The civil war and militarization of public life soon led to the eclipse even of Soviet power. The parlous state of the republic produced a tendency to equate anti-Bolshevism with the counter-revolution and soon led to the suppression of all opposition political parties. The

[67] Ibid., p. 322.

Social Revolutionaries, representing as they did the better-off peasantry, were basically hostile to the Bolshevik programme; but this was not the case with the Mensheviks, whose popular support (despite Bolshevik harassment) tended to grow. In June 1918 they were excluded from the Pan-Russian Congress of Soviets and systematically suppressed at the end of 1920. Parallel with this external repression was the growing monolithism of the party itself, which prevented the expression of effective grass-roots working-class opinion. Workers' control had been introduced in principle in November 1917 but began to be abandoned after a few months. Strikes were seen as illogical in a state 'belonging' to the workers and the trade unions gradually became simply an arm of political authority.

What most distressed Lenin in his last years was the growth of bureaucracy which was encouraged by the increasing nationalization programme caused by confiscations and the war effort. There was also the influence of the traditional bureaucratic methods of Russian autocracy, and the desire to find work for the increasing number of unemployed by absorbing them into the state machine. By the end of 1920 this administrative machine had swollen to almost six million employees – a growth that was in inverse proportion to the productive capacity of the economy. Although Lenin was in favour of recruiting bourgeois technicians and specialists and indeed giving them special privileges, he was incessant in his conflict with bureaucracy. 'All of us', he wrote, 'are sunk in the rotten bureaucratic swamp of "departments".'[68] By early 1921 Lenin characterized the Soviet Union as 'a workers' state with bureaucratic distortion'.[69] And a year later, at the last Party Congress he attended, Lenin admitted:

If we take that huge bureaucratic machine, that gigantic heap, we must ask: who is directing whom? I doubt very much whether it can truthfully be said that the communists

---

[68] Lenin to Tsyurupa, *Collected Works*, vol. 36, p. 566.
[69] V. Lenin, 'The Party Crisis', *Collected Works*, vol. 32, p. 48.

are directing that heap. To tell the truth they are not directing, they are being directed.[70]

The final irony was when the famous Rabkrin, designed to be a popular watchdog over the swollen administration, became simply yet another addition to the bureaucracy with all the deficiencies it was supposed to combat.

Why did the Russian revolution fail? Trotsky himself was undoubtedly right, in *The Revolution Betrayed*, in pointing to backwardness as a major cause:

The basis of bureaucratic rule is the poverty of society in objects of consumption with the resulting struggle of each against all. When there are enough goods in the store the purchasers can come whenever they want to. When there are little goods, the purchasers are compelled to stand in line. When the lines are very long, it is necessary to appoint a policeman to keep order. Such is the starting point of the power of Soviet bureaucracy.[71]

But this very consideration prompts the query as to whether the title of Trotsky's book is itself misconceived and whether the whole enterprise of a genuinely democratic and socialist revolution in a backward country was itself mistaken from the start. A defender of the Bolsheviks would no doubt claim that the major reason for the rise of Stalinism and the attendant domination of politics over social and economic factors was the failure of their fellow revolutionaries in Germany to support them at the crucial moment: the German Marxists were too involved in one way or another with their own bourgeois society to be able to deliver in 1919 and 1923; and had the German working class been led by a party of the Leninist type, things would have turned out very differently. . . . But such essays into counterfactual history are notoriously difficult to get to grips with and many would find it difficult to see how such a party,

[70] V. Lenin, 'Report of the Central Committee to the Eleventh Congress', *Collected Works*, vol. 33, p. 288.
[71] L. Trotsky, *The Revolution Betrayed* (London, 1937), p. 110.

so specific to the conditions prevailing in Tsarist Russia, could have emerged in Wilhelmine Germany.

7. Marxist critiques of the Soviet Union

With the consolidation of Stalinism in the Soviet Union, Marxist political theory faced a new problem. No longer was it sufficient to analyse the workings of the capitalist state and consider the best means of affecting a transition to socialism. In the case of the Soviet Union a society had emerged which seemed to be neither capitalist nor socialist. For the Soviet leadership itself, of course, and for their orthodox followers worldwide, the Soviet was a genuinely socialist society that, despite possible Stalinist aberrations, was still preparing the advent of communism. Among more critical Marxists, however, there have emerged two main currents which lean to one side or the other of the capitalist/socialist divide.

In 1939 Bruno Rizzi, an Italian ex-Trotskyist, put forward the view that the Soviet bureaucracy had turned into a new ruling class based on a mode of production that involved a kind of exploitation akin to that found in slave societies. This society Rizzi called 'bureaucratic collectivism' which was summarized by Deutscher as follows:

> The working class has shown itself incapable of accomplishing the socialist revolution which Marxism had expected it to accomplish. Yet capitalism too had shown itself unable to function and survive. But as the working class had failed to cope with this task, the bureaucracy was performing it; and not socialist but bureaucratic collectivism was superseding the old order.[72]

This view, with its emphasis on the power of technological

[72] I. Deutscher, *The Prophet Outcast: Trotsky 1929–1940* (Oxford, 1963), p. 466.

factors to supersede both traditional capitalism and socialism, was reiterated by James Burnham in his *The Managerial Revolution*. But it received its classic exposition in Milovan Djilas' *The New Class*. Djilas defined ownership as 'nothing other than the right of profit and control' and concluded that 'the communist states have seen ... the origin of a new form of ownership or of a new ruling and exploiting class,'[73] the core of which consisted of the party.

From a more strictly Marxist point of view, Djilas' use of the notions of property and class was too loose. A more precise account of the Soviet Union as state capitalism has been offered by Tony Cliff. In his *State Capitalism in Russia*, he saw the Soviet Union as subject to the same dynamic as contemporary capitalism. In capitalism there was an increasing tension between the productive forces and the social relations of production, and the bourgeoisie was compelled to socialize more and more areas through nationalization. There was a difference of degree but not of the kind in Russia where, under state planning, 'the bureaucracy, transformed into a personification of capital, for whom the accumulation of capital is the be-all and end-all here, must rid itself of all remnants of workers' control, must substitute conviction in the labour process by coercion, must atomize the working class, must force all socio-political life into a totalitarian world.'[74] The political conclusion from this view was that the Soviet Union stood in need of just as thoroughgoing a proletarian revolution as any envisaged in the West.

The thesis that the Soviet Union is a state capitalist society has received support from the Chinese communists and their Maoist followers. The Chinese Communist Party has stated that the Twentieth Congress of the Soviet Communist Party in 1956 and the subsequent rise to power of Krushchev marked the restoration of capitalism in the Soviet Union. A subtle elaboration of this theme is to be found in the work of Bettelheim who claims that capitalist relations can be shown to exist in the Soviet Union in that the workers are separated from

[73] M. Djilas, *The New Class* (London, 1957), p. 35.
[74] T. Cliff, *State Capitalism in Russia* (London, 1974), p. 153.

the means of production which are effectively owned by the managers of separate state enterprises exchanging with each other. Thus, too, a bourgeoisie exists in the Soviet Union for if the state apparatus 'is dominated by a body of functionaries and administrators, and if it escapes the control and direction of the working masses, then this body of functionaries and administrators effectively becomes the proprietor (in the sense of a relation of production) of the means of production. This body then forms a social class (a state bourgeoisie) because of the relations existing between itself and the means of production, on the one hand, and the workers on the other.'[75]

The second approach to the Soviet Union takes its inspiration from Trotsky, who, in the crucial ninth chapter of *The Revolution Betrayed*, rejected the idea that Russia could be described as state capitalism. For the bureaucracy did *not* constitute a new class. They did not own the means of production or accumulate and pass on their wealth like capitalists. The bureaucracy was recruited and had no independent property roots in the economic structure. Their role was therefore not an example of class exploitation but of social parasitism. The Soviet bureaucracy was not a class but only a caste whose power, status and material rewards depended entirely on the socialized relations of production inaugurated by the 1917 revolution. The state membership of the means of production meant that the Soviet Union continued to be a 'workers' state' albeit a degenerate one. Therefore the overthrow of the bureaucracy and the restoration of genuine proletarian democracy would require a political but not a social revolution.[76]

The most interesting recent contribution to this debate has come from the East German dissident Rudolph Bahro. His book *The Alternative in Eastern Europe* has more affinities with the Trotskyist tradition than with state capitalism in that he dismisses the idea that actually existing socialism is in any way capitalist and advocates a political revolution against the ruling

---

[75] C. Bettelheim, *Economic Calculation and Forms of Property* (London, 1976), pp. 98f.
[76] For a recent defence of these views, see P. Bellis, *Marxism and the USSR* (London, 1979).

bureaucracy. In contrast to Trotsky, however, Bahro sees Stalinism as inevitable and even progressive:

> It was ... because of the positive task of driving the masses into an industrialization that they could not immediately desire that the Soviet Union had to have a single iron, 'Petrine' leadership... The yawning gulf between material progress and socio-political emancipation was unavoidable ... we should not fail to recognize, however, that this is a justification of the same kind that Marx accorded the revolutionary activity of the bourgeoisie. It pertains to an antagonistic reality, in which 'the higher development of individuality is ... only achieved by a historical process during which individuals are sacrificed'.[77]

Now, however, that the material preconditions for an advance to socialism have been created, the old Stalinist politbureaucracies have outlived their role and Bahro calls for a 'cultural revolution' led by a loosely organized league of communists. Such a movement would not base itself on the working class, a concept which 'no longer has any definable object in our social system',[78] but would be 'the organization of those emancipatory interests that are characteristic of all people in all strata of society'[79] and would inaugurate a federative, decentralized society reminiscent of Marx's proposals deriving from the experience of the Paris Commune.

8. *China and Latin America*

Chinese communism has produced a version of Marxist politics in many ways strikingly different from the Soviet Union. On

---

[77] R. Bahro, *The Alternative in Eastern Europe* (London, 1978), pp. 116f. The quotation from Marx is from *Theories of Surplus Value* (London, 1969), vol. 2, p. 118.
[78] Ibid., p. 183.
[79] Ibid., p. 375.

attaining power in 1949 the Chinese Communist Party had several advantages: it could rely on the general goodwill of the populace, who were experiencing the first united government that China had enjoyed for forty years; there existed a well-organized and cohesive system of party cadres with experience of administration through long years of civil war – unlike the Soviet Union whose civil war followed revolutionary victory rather than preceded it; and (also unlike the Soviet Union) China had a large and powerful ally of sorts and was not therefore as isolated on the world stage as was Bolshevik Russia.

Before the achievement of power, Mao had anticipated, like the Lenin of *Two Tactics*, bourgeois revolution under proletarian hegemony. Mao went beyond Lenin, however, in stating that the dictatorship would be one of several revolutionary classes. He wished to emphasize the revolutionary character of the Chinese people as a whole. The emphasis on the bourgeois character of the revolution was satisfying to the peasantry which had no enthusiasm for socialism. And when he mentioned the proletariat what he really meant was the Chinese Communist Party, which was standing in for an 'absent' working class. The rapid transition to socialism and the China-centred nature of the post–1949 development, as evidenced in the Great Leap Forward of 1958, were not yet part of Mao's thinking.

In his eventual rapid implementation of socialist measures, Mao tempered Lenin's 'democratic centralism' with his own idea of the 'mass line'. In a classic passage, he wrote:

All correct leadership is necessarily 'from the masses to the masses'. This means: take the ideas of the masses (scattered and unsystematic ideas) and concentrate them (through study turn them into concentrated and systematic ideas), then go to the masses and propagate and explain these ideas until the masses embrace them as their own, hold fast to them, and translate them into action, and test the directness of these ideas in such action. Then once again concentrate ideas from the masses and once again go to the masses so that the ideas are persevered in and carried through. And so on, over and over again in an endless spiral, with the ideas becoming more correct, more vital, and richer each time. Such is the Marxist-Leninist theory of knowledge.[80]

But the involvement of the masses so characteristic of Chinese society remains purely functional as it is designed to enable the party better to exercise its leading role. Moreover, the very backwardness of China (which meant that initiatives would have to come from the party) was held by Mao to be an advantage. He believed strongly in the malleability of human nature and considered the Chinese people to be more malleable than most:

> China's 600 million people have two remarkable peculiarities; they are, first of all, poor, and secondly, blank. That may seem like a bad thing, but it is really a good thing. Poor people want change, want to do things, want revolution. A clean sheet of paper has no blotches, and so the newest and most beautiful words can be written on it, the newest and most beautiful pictures can be painted on it.[81]

The author of the text to be written on this blank page remained unquestionably the party. Indeed the most striking fact about the relationship of the party to the masses is the huge power of decision-making that resides in the upper echelons of the party with very little control from below. There was, for example, only one Party Congress between 1945 and 1969. Any form of participatory democracy is rendered impossible by the immense cloak of secrecy surrounding all deliberations at the top of the party. Differences of opinion among the leadership are simply not revealed and much less is known about their varying views than about those of the top of the Soviet party. The mysterious fall and rise of the currently influential Teng Hsiao-p'ing is an example. For the party has never completely escaped from the influence of Stalinism in the 1930s that affected all communist parties. This Stalinist influence was

[80] Mao Tse-tung, 'Some Questions concerning Methods of Leadership', *Selected Works* (Peking, 1965), vol. 3, p. 119.
[81] *The Political Thought of Mao Tse-tung*, ed. S. Schram (New York, 1963), p. 253.

reinforced by the fact that the party, cut off from the proletariat that it was supposed to be representing, was forced into the position of commanding rather than representing. This bureaucratic authoritarianism was reinforced by the position of Mao Tse-tung in the party hierarchy. The Chinese Communist Party did not enjoy the tradition of inner-party democracy that had initially been so strong among the Bolsheviks. The initiatives of the masses have tended to be not well received if they were regarded as not being impregnated by the policies of the leadership – as exemplified in the outcome of the Hundred Flowers campaign and of the Cultural Revolution.

Unlike the Soviet Union, China has aimed to develop the agricultural sector in harmony with the industrial sector. The peasantry were thus not the victims of development policy but mobilized in order to achieve it. China has therefore been able to be a model for most Third World countries as the Chinese Communist Party was indisputably a peasant party and the peasantry formed the vast majority of the population of most Third World countries. In addition Mao's doctrines on guerrilla war, evolved in the 1930s and based on the active cooperation of the peasantry, have had widespread influence in Third World countries. Nevertheless this influence has been largely confined to Asia and Africa: Latin America produced a distinctive form of militarized Marxism.

Because of uneven industrial development, Marxism in Latin America tended historically to be seen as protecting the interests of a relatively small industrial proletariat whereas the masses were more open to populist and corporatist ideas such as Peronism. The official communist parties have often become defenders of a particular interest group within the system rather than revolutionary parties of the Marxist-Leninist type. The success of Fidel Castro, however, seemed to present an alternative Marxist politics. There is, of course, much evidence that the Cuban revolution was highly specific and therefore unrepeatable. The initial aim of the revolution was merely a democratic reformist government; most of the peasants had already been proletarianized by large mechanized capitalist farms; there was an absence of intervention by the United States; and, finally, even the bourgeoisie was disaffected with the Batista regime. Nevertheless, Che Guevara in practice and Regis Debray in theory tried to export the Cuban experience to the Latin American continent. According to Debray the capitalist state could only be overthrown 'by means of the more or less slow building up, through guerrilla warfare carried out in suitably chosen rural zones, of a mobile strategic force, nucleus of a people's army and of a future socialist state.'[82] This led to a conception very different from the successful strategy of Mao for whom it was most important that the guerrillas should control permanent bases to which they could periodically retire. In Mao's view, these should be in areas that were geographically difficult of access – mountainous, bordered by swamps or deserts etc. In these areas the troops themselves should work the land and be active in production. They should help raise the productivity of the local inhabitants and, if possible, organize elementary social services. This would both avoid their being a burden on the locals and counter the boredom of periodic inactivity that sapped the morale of all traditional armies. For Guevara and Debray, on the other hand, Latin American circumstances required a different approach.

> Under certain conditions, the political and the military are not separate, but form one organic whole consisting of the people's army, whose nucleus is the guerrilla army. The vanguard party can exist in the form of the guerrilla *foco* itself. The guerrilla force is the party in embryo. This is the staggering novelty introduced by the Cuban revolution.[83]

This subordination of the political to the military and the consequent lack of serious political analysis in theories such as Debray's yielded little more than a combination of a Hispanic revolutionary ethic with an American concentration on the technical details of guerrilla warfare which were only linked by a military romanticism. It is an outlook which has affinities with recent urban terrorist movements in Western Europe such as the Baader-Meinhof group in Germany or the Red Brigade in Italy.

[82] R. Debray, *Revolution in the Revolution?* (London, 1968), p. 25.
[83] Ibid., p. 105.

9. *The capitalist state revisited*

The Chinese and Latin American varieties of Marxism do indeed seem to be far removed from the writings of Marx himself. So it is fitting, in conclusion, to look at the way in which Marxists in the West have recently returned to one of the central problems with which Marx grappled – the relation of the bourgeois state to the capitalist economy. The weakness of Marxist political studies in the West can be traced to the defeat of revolutionary movements there immediately after the First World War – a trend reversed in the more turbulent decade following 1968.

On a practical level, the most striking development has been the loss by Moscow of domination over the world communist movement and the consequent political evolution of the West European communist parties – an evolution that came to be known as Eurocommunism. The Eurocommunist outlook can be seen as having its roots in certain remarks made by Marx himself on the possibility of peaceful transition to socialism and as an attempt to patch up the old quarrel between Kautsky and Lenin. But the main inspirer of Eurocommunism is undoubtedly Gramsci (though it is by no means clear that he would have approved all the uses to which his ideas have been put) and it is no coincidence that the Italian Communist Party should be the pioneer of the new trends.

Gramsci has been called the theoretician of the superstructure and he certainly opposed all forms of economic determinism by laying emphasis on the importance of political and ideological aspects of the class struggle. This emphasis, he thought, was particularly important in the West where the cultural and ideological weapons at the disposal of the bourgeoisie were, at least initially, more important than reliance on pure force. In a well-known passage, Gramsci drew a sharp distinction between Russia and the West on this count:

> In Russia the state was everything, civil society was primordial and gelatinous; in the West, there was a proper relationship between state and civil society, and when the state trembled a sturdy structure of civil society was at once

revealed. The state was only an outer ditch, behind which there stood a powerful system of fortresses and earth works.[84]

This implied different revolutionary strategies in East and West. In less developed societies the state should be the object of frontal attack; in more developed societies, it should be civil society. Borrowing terms from recent studies of military science, Gramsci termed the first sort of attack 'a war of movement or manoeuvre' in which artillery could open up sudden gaps in defences and troops be rapidly switched from one point to another to storm through and capture fortresses, and the second a 'war of position' in which enemies were well balanced and had to settle down to a long period of trench warfare. The French bourgeoisie, for example, preceded its success in its 1789 revolution by a war of position in the shape of a lengthy cultural assault on the ideological supports of aristocratic power. And Gramsci considered that the war of position became more important as capitalism developed. The war of movement was so costly to the working class that it should only be launched when absolutely necessary, and Gramsci warned against the simplistic assumption that a Leninist strategy could be applied unproblematically: any frontal assault on state power would have to be preceded by a long period in which the proletariat and their allies had largely dismantled the cultural hegemony of the bourgeoisie.

The broad perspectives of Gramsci were given practical form by the Italian communist leader Togliatti who had been his close friend and collaborator. Togliatti had always maintained a fairly independent line, but the Krushchev speech of 1956 gave him the opportunity of broadening his position by declaring, first, that the mere criticism of Stalin as a person was too superficial an approach to the phenomenon of Stalinism; secondly, that the construction of socialism was possible in a multi-party state; and thirdly that the whole communist movement had become a polycentral system in which Moscow no longer had the

[84] A. Gramsci, *Selections from the Prison Notebooks*, ed. Q. Hoare and G. Nowell-Smith (London, 1971), p. 238.

undisputed right to dictate policy. Togliatti's ideas, buttressed by an interpretation of Gramsci favourable to their policies, were given wide currency by the Communist Party of Italy in recent years, and have led to the famous 'historic compromise' in which the PCI, in the hope of extending its own power base, has been willing to give qualified support to parties whose basic orientation is not socialist.

The French and Spanish Communist Parties have, in the 1970s, followed the Italian lead and consolidated the concept of Eurocommunism. The French party decided, in 1976, to drop the aim of 'dictatorship of proletariat' from its programme, and its tactics in the 1978 elections gave rise to unprecedented criticism of the lack of open debate inside the party, led by prominent party intellectuals such as Althusser and Ellenstein. To date, the most outspoken has been the Spanish Communist Party. Its General Secretary, Santiago Carillo, in his controversial book *Eurocommunism and the State*, lays stress on the achievement and extension of democratic liberties and human rights and sees the gaining of an electoral mandate as an essential step in the struggle to transform capitalism. In a passage which obviously refers to the Soviet Union, Carillo goes as far as to say:

> In actual fact the lack of democratic 'credibility' of us communists among certain sections of the population in our countries is associated – rather than with our own activity and policy – with the fact that in countries where capital ownership has disappeared, the dictatorship of the proletariat has been implanted, with a one-party system, as a general rule, and has undergone serious bureaucratic distortions and even very grave processes of degeneration.[85]

At its 1978 Congress, the party even decided, in spite of strident opposition from Moscow, to abandon specific reference to Leninism in its self-definition.[86]

[85] S. Carillo, *Eurocommunism and the State* (London, 1977), p. 155.
[86] Further on Eurocommunism, see E. Mandel, *From Stalinism to Eurocommunism* (London, 1978), and C. Boggs and D. Plotke, *The Politics of Eurocommunism* (Boston, 1980).

At a more abstract level, three main trends can be discerned among contemporary Marxist theories of the state. First there is the approach influenced by neo-structuralism. The notion that 'relatively autonomous' spheres – economic, political, ideological – in society can be viewed as a system structured only 'in the last instance' by the economic has been popular among communist party intellectuals as it provides some sort of theoretical underpinning for party policies. It is also an approach which owes a lot to structural-functionalism and to Weber's analysis of bureaucracy, and, at a less elevated level, has affinities with the work of Burnham referred to earlier. The studies of Poulantzas, the leading exponent of this view, attempt rigorously to systematize the concepts of class, economy, power and state by defining the 'precise status and functioning of the current economic role of the state, without at the same time abandoning the separation of the political and the economic.'[87] In so doing Poulantzas is trying to combat the orthodox communist position known as 'state monopoly capitalism' which sees a fusion between the political (state) and the economic (monopoly capitalism). For him, the role of the state is 'a factor of cohesion between the levels of a social formation . . . and the regulating factor of its global equilibrium as a system'.[88] Thus the contemporary capitalist state is a class state in that the social formation which it functions to maintain is one dominated, at various levels, by the capitalist class – irrespective of what positions of political power etc. may be held by representatives of that class. The main difficulties connected with such an approach are first that it is so theoretical that it tends to escape from any empirical control, and secondly the emphasis on impersonal structures tends to be unable to cope with accounts of change, let alone revolution.

A sharp contrast to the neo-structuralists is offered by the 'state derivation' school which attempts to break down the dichotomy between economics and politics by working out an analysis of the bourgeois state which derives directly from the 'anatomy of civil society' that Marx provided in *Capital*. Marx's

[87] N. Poulantzas, 'The Capitalist State: a Reply to Miliband and Laclau', *New Left Review*, Jan./Feb. 1976, p. 81.
[88] N. Poulantzas, *Political Power and Social Classes* (London, 1973), pp. 44f.

critique of political economy describes capitalist social relations and thereby uncovers those political categories which are their forms. The state derivationists wish thus to undercut the traditional opposition of economic base to political superstructure by seeing the very separation between the two as rooted in the nature of capitalist social relations. Broadly speaking, individual competing capitals need a state to ensure the general interest of total social capital and reproduce the necessary social relations of production that would disintegrate in a capitalist free-for-all. As Altvater, one of the leading exponents of this view, has written:

> Capital cannot itself produce through the actions of the many individual capitals the inherent social nature of its existence; it requires at its base a special institution which is not subject to its limitations as capital, one whose transactions are not determined by the necessity of producing surplus value, one which is *in this sense* a special institution 'alongside and outside bourgeois society', and one which at the same time provides, on the undisputed basis of capital itself, the immanent necessities that capital itself neglects . . . The state cannot be grasped therefore merely as a political instrument, nor as an instrument set up by capital, but only as a special form of establishment of the social existence of capital alongside and outside competition, as an essential movement in the *social reproduction process* of capital.[89]

Thus, like the neo-structuralists (although through a very different approach), the state derivation theorists are concerned to reject the idea of state monopoly capitalism by emphasizing both the capitalist nature of the state and the distinction between capital and state. Despite the obvious difficulties of attributing to the state excessive insights into the general requirements of capital and not leaving much space for class struggle, the state derivation school does at least try to link contemporary politics to some of Marx's basic concepts.

[89] E. Altvater, 'Some Problems of State Interventionism', *State and Capital: a Marxist Debate*, ed. J. Holloway and S. Picciotto (London, 1978), p. 42.

More fruitful than either of the above approaches is that pioneered by authors such as Habermas, Offe or O'Connor which starts from the contradictory part played by the modern state in trying both to ensure capitalist accumulation and preserve its legitimacy.[90] The most impressive work in this area, Habermas' *Legitimation Crisis*, starts from this basic contradiction and outlines a typology of the crises inherent in contemporary capitalist society: an economic crisis, a crisis of rationality, of legitimacy, and of motivation. In Habermas' view a crisis in contemporary capitalism is not inevitable. But the steps taken by the state to avert it entail a crisis of rationality. For the conflict of interests inherent in late capitalism and the contradictory demands on state intervention tend to mean that state aid is dysfunctionally distributed. This in turn creates a crisis of legitimacy, for state intervention means opening up the question of control and choice. The only solutions are buying off the most powerful parties or the creation of a new legitimizing ideology. In addition, growing public intervention involves lessening the scope of the private sphere which has motivated bourgeois society and thereby produces a crisis in motivation. Summarizing his conclusions, Habermas declares:

> Economic crises are shifted into the political system through the reactive-avoidance activity of the government in such a way that supplies of legitimation can compensate for deficits in rationality and extensions of organizational rationality can compensate for those legitimation deficits that do appear. There arises a bundle of crisis tendencies that, from a genetic point of view, represents a hierarchy of crisis phenomena shifted upwards from below. But from the point of view of governmental crisis management, these crisis phenomena are distinguished by being mutually substitutable within certain limits. These limits are determined by, on the one

[90] See, for example, J. Habermas, *Legitimation Crisis* (London, 1976); C. Offe, *Essays in Stress and Contradiction* in L. Lindberg *et al.*, eds., *Modern Capitalism* (Lexington, 1975); J. O'Connor, *The Fiscal Crisis of the State* (New York, 1973). A good account of recent work by Americans on this theme is to be found in the essay by M. Kesselman in B. Ollman and E. Vernoff, eds., *The Left Academy* (New York, 1982), pp. 82ff.

hand, the fiscally available quantity of value – the shortage of which cannot be validly predicted within crisis theory – and on the other by supplies of motivation from the socio-cultural system. The substitutive relation between the scarce resources, value and meaning, is therefore decisive for the prediction of crisis.[91]

Although Habermas rejects much of Marx's own analysis he shares with the Marxist tradition a radical disjuncture between analysis of the present and proposals for the future. It is characteristic of Marxist politics, for Marx onwards, that comments on the past and present are almost invariably hard-headed and illuminating whereas the outlines of the necessarily misty future are usually tinged with rose. If it is true that 'man must prove the truth, i.e. the reality and power, this worldliness of his thinking in practice',[92] then performance has, so far, not lived up to promise.

[91] J. Habermas, *Legitimation Crisis*, p. 93.
[92] K. Marx, 'Theses on Feuerbach', *Selected Writings*, p. 156.

Economics

Ernest Mandel

1. *The key contributions*

Marx's economic theory starts from the historically limited and therefore relative character of economic phenomena and problems. It rejects out of hand the assumption of any eternal economic law and limits itself to the discovery of specific economic laws, applicable to specific social systems. Most of Marx's analysis concerns the economic laws of the capitalist mode of production. But Marx views capitalism as generalized commodity production. Therefore, his research contains many elements for determining laws governing partial commodity production, i.e., pre-capitalist societies in which simple commodity production already has attained a certain maturity, and post-capitalist societies in which commodity production has not yet withered away.

Underlying Marxist economic theory is an anthropological paradigm: man is a social animal; the human species can only survive through social labour. In each specific society, there is a specific way of organizing social labour (specific relations of production) and a specific way of appropriating surplus labour (labour over and above that part of the available labour potential which is used to maintain [to reproduce] the labour potential of the producers and their instruments of labour).

All human societies have to balance output and needs (taking into account fluctuations of available stocks). The *law of value* is the objective mechanism through which in a market economy (under commodity production), socially recognized needs (i.e., those supported by available purchasing power) and socially necessary labour balance each other out, in spite of the fact that social labour is performed in the form of private labour, and that the private producer does not exactly know what precise needs (quantitatively and qualitatively) his output is supposed to satisfy.

The law of value governs the exchange of commodities. While commodities can only be sold at a price, i.e., against money, once commodity production is solidly established, the fluctuations of prices are governed in the last instance by fluctuations of the values of the commodities. For Marx, labour is not just a *numéraire* making different commodities commensurate with each other. It *is* value. The value of a commodity is determined by the fraction of the total available labour power in a given society, devoted to the production of that given commodity. The fluctuations of the values of commodities are governed by the fluctuations of productivity of labour in each sphere of production. But they are also linked to the fluctuations of aggregate social demands. If current output is larger than socially recognized needs, productive resources will be withdrawn from that sector of production. If current output is insufficient for satisfying demand for a given commodity, additional productive resources will be transferred to that sector.

The law of value thus governs not only the exchange of commodities but also the distribution of labour power and material resources between different sectors of economic activity, under conditions of commodity production and private ownership of the means of production. But private ownership, even when generalized, does not tend to reproduce itself indefinitely for all. Through a series of social and economic upheavals – the most important of which were the commercial revolution, the agrarian revolution and the industrial revolution – owners of means of production and people owning neither means of production nor means of livelihood (having no access to land where they could produce their own food) appear alongside each other. The second group (the proletariat, the working class) is forced to sell its labour power to the first group (the capitalist class, the bourgeoisie). This is the basic social relation of the capitalist mode of production.

Why is the capitalist class interested in buying labour power from the proletariat under conditions of 'equal exchange', i.e., at the real value of that labour power (without taking into consideration cheating, theft etc.)? Here appears Marx's main economic discovery, his *theory of surplus value.* Under capitalism, the worker's labour power has become a commodity. Like all commodities, this labour power is sold at a price – the worker's wage – which is not arbitrary but is in the last analysis governed by its value. Now the value of that special commodity – labour power – is determined, like the value of all commodities, by the amount of labour socially necessary to produce it, i.e., by its reproduction costs at a given level of productivity of labour in the consumer-goods-producing branches.[1] Like all commodities, labour power has at the same time value (exchange value) and use value, a given set of physical qualities which the buyers of that commodity want to enjoy. But the specific use value of the commodity labour power is precisely *its capacity to produce new value.* Living labour, working with raw materials and tools (machinery), incorporates into the value of these raw materials (and the fraction of the value of machinery which is maintained through current production) new value, additional value. If this 'value added' is just equal to the workers' wages, there will be no surplus value, no profit for the capitalists. But if the 'value added' to the value of the material by the workers engaged in the process of production is larger than the workers' wages, there appears additional value which the capitalist can appropriate simply through being owner of the finished products of the workers. This additional value is called surplus value by Marx. Its existence is the precondition for the capitalist hiring the worker. And its source is simply the difference between the total new value produced by the worker and the reproduction costs of his own labour power.

The precondition for the appearance of that difference is, obviously, a level of productivity of labour in the consumer-goods-producing sectors (in the first place agriculture) which enables the workers to produce the goods necessary for keeping

[1] Marx explicitly rejected the idea that these reproduction costs had only to cover physiological needs. They have to provide the workers with a set of consumer goods and services which have become historically incorporated into the socially recognized average wage. Marx called that part of wages its 'moral-historical' element.

them alive in only a fraction of the normal workday. If they needed the whole workday just to produce the goods without which they could not continue to work, no surplus value could appear.

Surplus value is appropriated by the capitalists. It is divided into two basically different categories. Part of it is *unproductively consumed*. This is used for the upkeep of the capitalist class and its hangers-on (including the upkeep of the bourgeois state). Another part is *productively invested* i.e., used to buy additional raw materials, additional machinery and additional labour force for *expanding production*. But under capitalism, production can only grow if capital expands. For under capitalism, additional raw material and machinery, and additional manpower take the form of *additional capital* (additional constant capital in the first place, additional variable capital in the second place). So capitalism lives under constant pressure of the *law of capital accumulation*. In order to survive, it must grow. Capital can only exist if more capital is being accumulated.

This is true above all because of competition. Capital appears in the form of many capitals in competition with each other, as it is based upon private property. Capitalist production is production for an anonymous market. To triumph in this competition, each capitalist, or more correctly, each capitalist firm, must reduce production costs. In order to reduce production costs, it is necessary to produce on a larger scale, to use more up-to-date machinery, to rationalize the labour and production process. All this demands more capital. Hence the constant drive to increase capital accumulation. And as surplus value is the only source of capital, the constant drive to increase capital accumulation implies a constant drive to increase the mass of surplus value.

Starting from all these premises, Marx discovered what he thought to be the basic economic contradiction of the system: the *tendency of the rate of profit to decline*. Profit originates from surplus value. Surplus value is produced by living labour, and by living labour only, i.e., by that part of capital which is used to buy labour power, and which Marx calls variable capital. But accumulation of capital, through technical progress, is not neutral with regard to the division of total capital between variable capital and constant capital. It tends to increase the latter more than the former (it tends towards the growth of the organic composition of capital, i.e., of the relation between constant and variable capital). Now as profit is only produced by variable capital, if variable capital becomes a smaller and smaller part of total capital, the relation between profit and total capital (which Marx calls the rate of profit) will tend to decline, all other things remaining equal.

Of course all other things do not normally remain equal; otherwise capitalism would have disappeared a long time ago together with the decline of profit. The same force – technical progress, increase in the productivity of labour – which leads to the increase in the organic composition of capital also leads to a constant cheapening of wage goods. This in turn makes it possible to produce the equivalent (counter-value) of these wage goods in a smaller and smaller fraction of the normal workday. This means that the rate of surplus value (the ratio between that part of the workday in which the worker produces surplus value, and that other part in which he reproduces the equivalent of his wage) tends to increase. The increase in the rate of surplus value can neutralize the effect of the increase in the organic composition of capital upon the rate of profit.

Nevertheless, Marx assumed that, in the long run, this compensation would not operate in a complete way. There are limits to the increase in the rate of surplus value, whereas the organic composition of capital can grow without limits. When living labour disappears under automation, the organic composition of capital becomes endless; but the rate of surplus value becomes zero, because only living labour produces surplus value. When overaccumulation (overheating) occurs, both the amount of capital accumulated and the relative scarcity of manpower leading towards an increase in real wages make the rate of profit decline. Under capitalism, a decline in the rate of profit induces a decline in productive investment, a decline in economic growth, an economic crisis, bankruptcies and massive unemployment. At the same time, through massive devalorization (destruction) of capital and wage cuts, the crisis creates conditions for relaunching the process of capital accumulation, once the rate of profit picks up again.

The tendency of the rate of profit to decline therefore does not operate in a linear way, but through successive phases of ups and downs, i.e., in a *cyclical way*. It governs the stages of the trade cycle (the business cycle) which is the specifically capitalist form of economic growth: a succession of stages of economic recovery, prosperity, boom, overheating, crashes, depressions, recovery etc. And from the specific way in which that tendency operates, both through the business cycle and in the long run, a whole series of *laws of motion* of the capitalist mode of production can be deduced and tested in the light of empirical evidence, i.e., in the light of the actual socio-economic history of the last two hundred years.[2]

Marx's contributions to economic analysis lie essentially in the field of the theory of value and of surplus value on the one hand, and in the discovery of these laws of motion on the other hand. But the controversies his ideas have caused centre much more around the laws of motion than around the basic theoretical stepping stones leading up to them. This is understandable, and was rather cruelly predicted by himself in his Preface to volume 1 of *Capital*:

> In the domain of political economy, free scientific inquiry meets not merely the same enemies as in all other domains. The peculiar nature of the material it deals with, summons as foes into the field of battle the most violent, mean and malignant passions of the human breast, the Furies of private interest.[3]

It is true that the most serious opponents of Marx's economic theories – like the most serious opponents of socialism – tried to show that what they called the 'fallacies of Marx's predictions' had their roots in false basic analytical concepts or

[2] In E. Mandel, *Late Capitalism* (London, 1975), ch. 4, and in *Long Waves of Capitalist Development* (Cambridge University Press, 1980) I have tried to prove that at least three times, around 1848, 1893 and 1948 (1940 in the USA), there has been a sudden and durable upward swing of the average rate of profit in the international capitalist economy.

[3] K. Marx, *Capital* (London, 1954), vol. 1, p. 10.

methods. They went on from a critique of the laws of motion of the capitalist mode of production to a critique of the labour theory of value and of the theory of surplus value, to a critique of the law of the tendency of the rate of profit to fall, and to a critique of historical materialism in general. Nevertheless, the critique concentrated on the laws of motion for a wider public. The basic theoretical assaults were more limited and often hermetic in their scope and contents.

This is even more true for the controversies which reigned in the Marxist camp itself, where these laws of motion came first under attack because of their obvious political implications, while the stepping stones which led to them were, for a long time, considered taboo and treated with filial awe.

So it seems appropriate to deal with the first hundred years of Marxist economic theory by treating the critique of the laws of motion of capitalism before dealing with the critique of Marx's basic economic concepts – while logic would, of course, invite the reverse operation. This is not a sacrifice of the logical to the chronological sequence. It is a recognition of the fact that the formidable impact of Marx on contemporary history flows from the dynamics of class struggle and revolution,[4] which are directly linked to the laws of motion of bourgeois society, and only indirectly, and in the last instance, flow from the most abstract of Marx's analytical tools.

---

[4] 'Poland is also challenging the idea that lies right down at the roots of Marxism: the idea of the irreversibility of history . . . That could be the start of rescuing a large part of humanity from the cul-de-sac of history that Marx invented' (the *Economist*'s editorial, 11 July 1981). Needless to say, Marx never believed in any 'irreversibility' of history, no more than he believed in any linear development of human societies. The concept which lies 'at the roots' of Marxism is the concept of social change, of the temporary nature of all social institutions, including private property and market economy, and of the dependence of human progress upon changes in social structure, in the last analysis changes in the relations of production, brought about by social struggles. Such a view of human history certainly encompasses the possibility of social regression, if 'progressive' social classes are crushed in a given context where no others can rapidly arise. Be this as may be, it is striking that the arch-bourgeois and leading anti-Marxist weekly in Britain attributes to Marx's (presumably wrong) ideas the tremendous power of having led 'a large part of humanity' into a cul-de-sac. And when that same weekly acknowledges the possibility that the Polish revolution, clearly conducted and led by the working class, could reverse the course of history, it silently approves (should we add, tongue in cheek, 'unconsciously'?) Marx's vision about the key historical role of the industrial proletariat after the rise of modern industry.

2. *The laws of motion of the capitalist mode of production*

I. *Concentration and centralization of capital*

Does competition automatically lead to concentration and centralization of capital? Does free enterprise breed monopoly? Does 'free market capitalism' produce monopoly capitalism? The question was answered positively by Marx, and taken up forcibly by Engels in his *Anti-Dühring* and in his edition of volume 3 of *Capital*. This thesis hits right at the heart of the liberal-bourgeois credo, to wit that private property and the free market constantly extend the realm of human freedom. No, answer Marxists. Private property polarizes society between haves and have nots. It breeds progressive expropriation of small proprietors by big ones, of free entrepreneurs by gigantic economic trusts. It breeds concentration of economic power, hence corruption and oppression including in the political scene. It does so under the double pressure of technological progress – the constantly rising 'costs of entry' into large industry, banking, transportation, wholesale trade etc. – and of competition in which smaller and less efficient firms are eliminated (or absorbed) by larger and more efficient ones. And precisely because this law of concentration and centralization of capital hits at the heart of the bourgeois credo and the basic self-justification of bourgeois society, it was among the first to be violently challenged by critics.

These criticisms fall generally into three categories. The first one concentrates on empirical evidence which supposedly proves that there is no centralization of capital. The small industrial and banking firms are supposed to have a resilience which Marx strongly underestimated. The argument was taken up by the marginalist critics of Marx like Böhm-Bawerk, Pareto etc. It was relayed by the Russian 'legal Marxists' and their offspring Masaryk (the future President of the Czechoslovak republic), by some Catholic writers and especially by Bernstein and his supporters in the international social-democracy.[5] But it never had much ground to stand on. In the best of cases, it was an unfounded extrapolation of temporary developments in new branches of industry or in periods of great prosperity, traditionally prone to the growth of new firms.

It is sufficient to recall the historical fact of the trust movement, the creation of large industrial and banking combines in the USA as early as the mid-1880s, its spread to Germany, France, Japan, Britain, Italy, the emergence in all imperialist countries of finance groups controlling a large part of big industry through holding companies, and the reduction of the number of market-dominating firms in key sectors of industry (coal, steel, oil, copper, aluminium, automobiles, electrical machine building, paper, aerospace construction, petrochemicals, computer building, nuclear equipment building etc.), to acknowledge that this law of motion of capitalism is a real one, confirmed by history.[6] The emergence, especially after the Second World War, of the multinational corporation, is nothing but the verification of that same law now operating on an international scale: the *international* concentration and centralization of capital.

It has been objected that the so-called Gini curve remained fairly stable during the last decades. Abstraction made of the fact that the evidence is by no means clear for the key industrial sectors enumerated above, this objection would only prove that concentration and centralization of capital do not normally go beyond the point of *a few firms* dominating branches of

[5] See among others Eugen von Böhm-Bawerk, *Karl Marx und der Ausgang seines Systems* (1896; English edn, *Karl Marx and the Close of his System* New York: Augustus Kelley, 1949); Eduard Bernstein, *Die Voraussetzungen des Sozialismus und die Aufgaben der Sozialdemokratie* (1899; English edn, *Evolutionary Socialism* New York: Schochen, 1963); T.G. Masaryk, *Die philosophischen und Soziologischen Grundlagen des Marxismus* (Vienna, 1899); Michael Tugan-Baranovsky, *Theoretische Grundlagen des Marxismus* (Leipzig: Duncker and Humblot, 1905).
[6] To give but one example: in the West German conservative business publication *Wirtschaftswoche* we read (issue of 7 August 1981), 'Today, there is hardly any Japanese firm of importance which does not live under the protection of the six super-conglomerates and their ten satellites.' The six super-conglomerates, heirs to the prewar *Zaibatsu* are the finance groups Mitsubishi, Mitsui, Sumitomo, Fuyo, Sanwa, Dai-Ichi Kangyo Bank. They control more than 600 big firms. Recently, the Mitsui group took Toyota, Toshiba and Oji-Paper under its umbrella as satellites.

production, i.e. that monopolistic competition prevents the concentration of capital advancing up to the domination of branches of production by a single firm. But whether to call the result of the operation of that law of motion of capitalism 'oligopoly' or 'monopoly' is only a semantic problem. The substantial problem remains that 'free competition' as it operated in the first century after the industrial revolution gives place to market domination, with economic behaviour quite different from the first. And that was after all what Marx was really trying to prove: that as a result of competition, competition would decline, would turn into its opposite.

A second challenge concerned the so-called exceptional cases. It was argued successively that agriculture, the retail trade and the service industries were, for structural reasons, escaping the law of concentration and centralization of capital. Marx himself pointed out the specific reasons which retarded a full-scale normal development of the capitalist mode of production in these sectors. But he also stressed that, in the long run, the laws of motion of the capitalist mode of production would impose themselves in these sectors too. The premature generalizations of the critics were slowly but surely bypassed by events. In the epoch of agro-business, of giant retail chains and of the growing mechanization and semi-automation of one service branch after another, there is little doubt that he was right.

Finally a third objection notes that, while firms indeed grow gigantic, and the number of these market-dominating giants perforce declines as compared to the number of producing firms under 'free market' capitalism, this movement at the level of corporations is negated at the level of property of capital. Property becomes more and more diffused, especially after the emergence of joint stock corporations. Ownership and control get divorced from each other. It is not the concentration and centralization of capital property, but the concentration of expertise in management, which is said to wield real (be it concentrated) power in the final stage of capitalism.[7]

There is again a semantic confusion at the bottom of this objection. When Marx deals with centralization of capital, what he is talking about is the centralization of the decision-making power which capital property entails under the capitalist mode of production, not the centralization of formal capital property. On the contrary, Marx himself understood that the joint stock corporation was but a new form of expropriation of real capital owners, by their transformation into purely formal capital owners.[8] The joint stock corporation enables the top layers of the capitalist class to control capital far in excess of their own formal ownership. But those who do control these huge assets, of which they only own a narrow fraction, are themselves private owners of capital, sometimes (in the case of so-called top managers) great masses of capital, most often huge masses of capital.[9] No large corporation is controlled by people who do not own private wealth, who are not integrated into the rich sections of the capitalist class.

II. *Social polarization*

The law of progressive concentration and centralization of capital is so important in the Marxist analysis because it leads directly to a social and political conclusion. As the weight of small and medium-sized capitalists is progressively declining in bourgeois society, a declining fraction of the active population is composed of 'self-employed', a growing fraction of that society is composed of people selling their labour power to the capitalists and their state. Hence the tendency towards growing

[7] The classical work making that assumption is A.A. Berle and Gardiner C. Means, *The Modern Corporation and Private Property* (New York, 1933). See also James Burnham, *The Managerial Revolution* (New York, 1941), and J.K. Galbraith, *The New Industrial State* (Harmondsworth, 1968).

[8] See *Capital* vol. 3, ch. 23, which actually uses the very words 'the managing functions become more and more separated from the ownership of capital' in the joint stock companies.

[9] See, among different sources, Ferdinand Lundberg, *The Rich and the Super-Rich* (New York, 1968); S. William Domhoff, *Who Rules America* (Englewood Cliffs, 1967); C. Wright Mills, *The Power Elite* (New York, 1957); Anthony Giddens, *The Class Structure of the Advanced Societies* (London, 1979); Jay Gould, *The Technical Elite* (New York, 1966), etc.

polarization of society between a declining number of buyers of labour power and a constantly growing number of sellers of labour power.[10]

Empirical evidence fully bears out the correctness of that

Proletarization of the labour force in the United States (in %)[11]

Year	Wage-earners including functionaries	of which: leading managers and high functionaries	self-employed
1780[a]	20		80
1880	63.1	1.1	36.9
1890	66.2	1.2	33.8
1900	69.2	1.3	30.8
1910	73.7	1.8	26.3
1920	76.5	2.6	23.5
1930	79.7	2.9	20.3
1939	81.2	3	18.8
1950	82.2	4.4	17.9
1960	85.9	5.3	14.1
1969	90.8	7.2	9.2
1977[b]	91.3		8.7

a. The 1780 figures are extremely rough estimates, excluding slaves who represented, at that time, one fifth of the population.
b. These percentages are calculated upon the civilian labour force, not the total labour force, and based on the official figures of the *Statistical Abstract of the USA, 1978.*

---

[10] The definition of the proletariat as the sum total of those under economic compulsion to sell their labour power – given by Plekhanov and Lenin in the first programme of the Russian Social-Democratic Workers Party – situates outside the proletariat all those salary-earners (top managers, top functionaries of the bourgeois state, professional people like doctors and lawyers working under contract as hired labour etc.) whose income is high enough to enable savings, making possible accumulation of capital, and who actually own enough capital to live from the proceeds (interests, rents, dividends) thereof. If they sell their labour power, it is not because they don't have other means of livelihood, but for other reasons, i.e., out of a 'free choice'. This is precisely not the case for normal workers and employees, who have no choice in the matter.
[11] James F. Becker, *Economie politique marxiste* (Paris: Economica, 1980). English edn, *Marxian Political Economy: an Outline* (Cambridge University Press, 1979), p. 287, gives this table with sources. We have some reservations on the way the category 'managers and high functionaries' has been calculated.

prediction of Marx. In the key industrialized capitalist countries, the fraction of the active population composed of sellers of labour power has jumped from less than 50 or around 50 per cent to around 75 per cent within one generation. In another generation, it has jumped to 85–90 per cent, topping 90 per cent already in the USA, Britain and Sweden. There is no indication that this trend is being reversed, although of course its speed is slowed down, once a certain threshold has been passed.

Therefore, the attempts to question this law of motion of bourgeois society, discovered by Marx, have always been rather perfunctory. It has been alleged that Marx underestimated the resilience of the petty bourgeoisie (independent peasants, handicraftsmen, tradespeople) or the substitution of 'new' middle classes to old ones. For Marx, however, the argument turned essentially around the problem of the economic obligation to sell one's labour power. That a constantly rising part of the active population – never mind the rhythm at which this rise takes place – falls into that category can hardly be questioned on the basis of statistical evidence. And this law was derived by Marx from the very nature of value, surplus value, capital and capital accumulation, i.e., from the very structure of capitalism. It is because the capital needed to remain self-employed constantly increases in size, because even rising wages do not enable workers or salary-earners to accumulate capital, that only those who own more and more capital can continue to accumulate capital, i.e., remain capitalists.[12] All other economically active people progressively become part of the proletariat, i.e., have to sell their labour power.

Indeed, the main objection raised against that law of motion of bourgeois society is not that it is wrong, in and by itself, but that Marx read too much into it, i.e., made it the basis of sweeping political extrapolations. Granted that the number of

[12] Could the historical trend of centralization of capital, which implies that more and more capital is necessary for going into business or staying in business as self-employed, be reversed by the micro-chips? This remains to be seen. But even if this were to occur, it would still be a marginal economic phenomenon. The advantages of large-scale production in a society based upon private ownership and competition would remain overwhelming in the large majority of branches of output.

wage- and salary-earners grows more and more, critics state. But the more that mass grows, the more it becomes heterogeneous and unable of united organization and action. State employees and private-sector workers, productive and unproductive workers, employed and unemployed ones, male and female wage-earners, young and adult ones (not to speak of wage-earners in imperialist countries and those in semi-colonial and dependent ones) have increasingly divergent and not convergent interests. Therefore, the law of concentration and centralization of capital, and the law of increasing social polarization, do not tell us anything about an increasing capacity of the proletariat, even when defined as the sum total of all those compelled to sell the commodity labour power, to overthrow capitalism and to realize a socialist revolution. And some of the critics will even add: on the contrary, the larger the part of the total active population composed of wage- and salary-earners, and the greater the heterogeneity of the proletariat, the greater its integration in bourgeois society, and the lower its revolutionary potential.[13]

We believe the objection to be unfounded. The *main* trend, crisscrossed, of course, by several contradictory ones, is that of a *growing homogeneity* and not a growing heterogeneity of the proletariat as defined above. Today, the differences in income, in lifestyle and consumer habits, in social outlook and perspectives, between manual and intellectual workers, between unskilled workers and clerks or secretaries, between workers in the private sector and state employees, between male and female workers, are less and not greater than fifty or a hundred years ago. The clearest proof of that trend lies in the growth and growing homogeneity of *union organization*. While trade unions, the elementary class organizations of the proletariat, were in the beginning essentially restricted to skilled male manual workers, they successively drew in women workers, unskilled labourers, state employees, white-collar

[13] See, among others, P. Baran and P. Sweezy, *Monopoly Capital* (New York, 1966), André Gorz, *Adieu au Prolétariat* (Paris, 1980), etc.

workers, technicians.[14] In many capitalist countries, all these categories are today bound together in a single trade union federation. Indeed, in several we find representatives of white-collar unions, state employees or even technicians' unions at the head of the most militant trade unions, if not at the head of the trade union federation itself.

And this is by no means a purely formal trend. When we speak of growing unionization, we also speak of growing militancy and growing participation in strike action. The most sensational reversal of trends occurred among the technicians. They played a clear role as strike-breakers (the so-called *Technische Nothilfe*) in the German revolution and the Weimar Republic, as well as during the Spanish revolution of the 1930s and the French general strike of 1936. But they were largely integrated into the French general strike of May 1968 and the Italian, Spanish and British strike waves of the 1970s.[15]

The main problem, however, lies elsewhere. What Marx pointed out, when he linked the growing concentration and centralization of capital with the increasing trend towards social polarization, was another law of motion of the capitalist mode of production: the growing *objective socialization of labour*, its increasing conflict with private appropriation and the fact that all those involved in large-scale enterprise (whether in production, telecommunications, transportation, banking and finance, trade or state administration, including hospitals, schools and post offices) would be increasingly indifferent if not hostile towards private business, and increasingly subject to all those results of the socialization of labour which are preconditions for socialism: understanding of the key importance of cooperation, solidarity and capacity for collective action and self-administration.

[14] The successful efforts at initial unionization of unskilled women workers in England owe much to the role of Marx's daughter Eleanor. See Yvonne Kapp *Eleanor Marx* (New York, 1976), vol. 2. On progressive unionization of the white-collar workers, see C. Wright Mills, *White Collar* (Oxford, 1951). State employees had to fight for a long period for the right to organize and to strike, and as the recent case of the air controllers' strike in the USA shows, conquests in these fields are by no means irreversible.

[15] There was a correct premonition of this trend by Kautsky, *Das Erfurter Programme* (Stuttgart, 1892). See also Max Adler, *Der Sozialismus und die Intellecktuellen* (Vienna, 1919).

III. *Pauperization*

The increasing socialization of labour, growing out of the increasingly decisive role of large-scale enterprise in all key sectors of economic activity, only creates the *objective preconditions* for the working class in the broadest sense of the word reshaping society according to its own needs and interests, i.e., for a replacement of capitalism by socialism. But a mediating link is obviously needed between this objective preparation of the working-class for self-management and socialism, as the result of its very role in the capitalist mode of production, and its actual capacity to overthrow capitalism. In this mediation, the shaping of working class consciousness in an anti-capitalist sense, through organization, education and the experience of mass struggle, plays an essential role. And this evolution of working-class consciousness must in its turn be embedded on the rock of the proletarian condition, on the socio-economic conditions of life and labour of the working class. At this precise point of the analysis, a formidable controversy arose, which is still going on among commentators of Marx, supporters and critics alike. Is the growing misery of the working class a necessary precondition for shaping it into a revolutionary force? Can such an alleged growing misery by and large be reduced to a decline in wages, be it in value terms or even in terms of absolute standard of living?

The myth that Marx somehow defended an 'iron law of wages' theory – which in fact originated with Malthus and Ricardo, and was taken up in the socialist movement especially by Lassalle and consistently opposed by Marx – has been defended by many authors.[16] It has been refuted innumerable times.[17] Marx's theory of wages was an 'accumulation of capital' theory, in which the effects of lower and higher rhythms of accumulation *both on the supply and the demand of*

[16] E.g. Fritz Sternberg, *Der Imperialismus* (Berlin, 1926); Jürgen Kuczynski, *Die Theorie der Lage der Arbeiter* (2nd edn, Berlin, 1952 – after a 'self-criticism' imposed by the SED party leadership for incorrect formulations in the first edition!); Karl Popper, *The Open Society and its Enemies* (London, 1945), vol. 2; Akademie der Wissenschaften der UdSSR, *Politische Oekonomie, Lehrbuch* (Berlin, 1955); Wolf Wagner, *Verelendungstheorie – die hilfslose Kapital-ismuskritik* (Frankfurt, 1976), etc.

[17] The best refutation is that by Roman Rosdolsky, *Zur Entstehungsgeschichte des Marxschen 'Kapital'* (Frankfurt, 1968).

the commodity labour power are taken into consideration, within the framework of the combined operation of all the other laws of motion of the capitalist mode of production. Further-more, Marx explicitly stressed the partially autonomous nature of the fluctuations of wages, determined by the struggle (and the relations of forces) between Capital and Labour, as antagonistic fighting social classes, i.e., large groups of human beings.[18] The result of the interaction of all these factors is by no means a historical trend towards lower and lower wages, neither in every country nor on a world scale.

But neither is there any trend of a gradual and constant rise of wages in function, e.g., of the increase of the average productivity of labour under capitalism. What emerges is a fluctuation of real wages determined both by the secular and the short-term trend of the reserve army of labour (unemploy-ment), and by the relationship of forces between the classes. Cyclical crises of overproduction tend to depress wages. In periods of long booms, wages tend to increase. In countries with long-term structural massive unemployment (Western Europe in the first half of the nineteenth century; Central and Southern Europe in the second half of the nineteenth and the beginning of the twentieth century; the so-called 'Third World countries' until this very day), wages tend to remain low. In countries with secular scarcity of manpower (the USA until the end of the nineteenth century), wages tend to be from the beginning much higher than in others.

For these reasons, massive international movements of labour migration play an important role in the Marxist theory of wages.[19]

If, therefore, there is no such thing as a Marxist theory of 'absolute impoverishment of the working class', Marx certainly did deny that there would be, under capitalism, a linear

[18] I have tried to bring all these trends together towards sketching a Marxist theory of wages in my *Late Capitalism* ch. 5.
[19] The first author to make a systematic study of this key-factor in the fluctuation of wages – including international migrations – was Fritz Sternberg, *op. cit.* A subtle analysis of the different components of the reserve army of labour is to be found in Rosa Luxemburg, *Einführung in die Nationalökonomie* (Berlin, 1925). A similar study about the contemporary United States can be found in Michael Harrington, *The Other America* (New York, 1963).

improvement in the workers' lot. His thesis of a *cyclical* fluctuation of workers' wages, the strength of the labour movement and the welfare state notwithstanding,[20] has been impressively confirmed by the evolution of real wages since the second half of the 1970s, under the impact of the increase of massive structural unemployment in the imperialist countries during the 'long depressive wave' in the international capitalist economy, which set in in the late 1960s or the early 1970s.[21] This has been true for many imperialist countries. It applies also to many semi-industrialized dependent countries, the most striking example being Brazil.[22]

In what sense can one say that the workers' lot becomes worse under capitalism, even if real wages do not decline generally, except in periods of long depression and in countries with massive structural unemployment? Marx did formulate a theory of *relative impoverishment* of the working class, given the capitalist mode of production. This theory has two sides to it.

In the first place, there *is* a definite trend under capitalism for the productive workers – the only ones who produce value – to receive a gradually declining share of the value they produce. In other terms, there is a definite trend under capitalism for an increase in the rate of surplus value (the ratio of surplus value and the value of the workers' wages), brought about especially through steep increases in productivity of labour in the wage-goods-producing industries. Incidentally, it is this steep increase in productivity of labour which makes it possible for

[20] John Strachey, *Contemporary Capitalism* (London, 1956), and many other authors posited at the beginning of the long-term post-Second World War boom that rising real wages and social security allowances had become institutionally irreversible.

[21] See Ernest Mandel, *Late Capitalism* ch. 4, and *Long Waves of Capitalist Development*.

[22] The 1980–1 recession hit Brazilian big industry in a strong way, starting with January 1981. The rate of unemployment among previously employed wage-earners, i.e., without taking into account the huge mass of marginalized permanent unemployed, rose up to 20 per cent. As there is no state compensation for unemployed, and as capitalist firms only pay small compensation to fired workers (on average, one month's wage per year employed), a huge mass of persons appeared without any income whatsoever. Daily papers started to print advertisements of people willing to sell blood, kidneys and even one of their eyes as a means of getting money.

capitalism to achieve under certain conditions *both* a considerable increase in real wages (workers consumption) and in surplus value (capital accumulation). Increase in real wages is quite compatible with a decrease in the value of wages, if the rate of decline of the total value of wage goods is less than the rate of growth of productivity of labour in the consumer goods industries.

This thesis of the gradual increase in the rate of surplus value has been questioned by several critics who assert that there is, under capitalism, a definite trend towards *constant shares* of wages and RIP (rents, interests and profits) in the national income.[23] In order to oppose these so-called 'constant shares' to the law of a rising rate of surplus value, these critics are however forced to use aggregates which do not conform to Marx's categories. Especially the category 'aggregate wages' is meaningless to indicate anything regarding the rate of surplus value. For Marx, variable capital only encompasses wages of productive workers, who are likewise the only ones who produce surplus value. Wages of non-productive state employees, or wage-earners employed in the commercial and financial sector, do not come out of variable capital. They have to be deducted from aggregate wages in order to calculate the rate of surplus value.[24]

In the second place, even if real wages rise, they rise less quickly than do the *needs* which accumulation of capital – e.g., the development of new commodities by new branches of industry, and also the development of needs originated by transformation of the workers' lives as a result of industrialization, urbanization, the decomposition of the nuclear family, the speed-up, the nerve-racking home-job-home transportation etc. – itself provokes among workers.[25] There is therefore relative impoverishment of the workers in relation to their

[23] See among others Joan Robinson, *An Essay on Marxian Economics* (London, 1966).
[24] This is also what Joseph Gillman, *The Law of the Falling Rate of Profit* (London, 1957), fails to do.
[25] Insistence on *increasing needs* arising out of the intensification of labour is characteristic of Jürgen Kuczynski, *op. cit.* Rosa Luxemburg had already gone in the same direction (*Einführung in die Nationalökonomie*).

needs as consumers using up their labour power more intensively than before, not to speak about their needs as human beings who become conscious of the infinite possibilities of self-development.

IV. *Crises of overproduction*

If workers do not become constantly poorer and more miserable under capitalism, why should they question the survival of the system, even if their rate of exploitation goes up? One important link in the chain of Marx's reasoning in that direction is the inevitability of crises of overproduction, which periodically hit the system, do lead to declines in the workers' living and working conditions, and especially make it visible for an increasing number of wage- and salary-earners that the system is sick, cannot deliver the goods, should be replaced by a better one. For Marx, crises of overproduction were the *memento mori* of capitalism, again one of its fundamental laws of motion.

In spite of overwhelming historical evidence – twenty-one international crises of overproduction succeeding each other regularly since 155 years on the world market – this law of motion has been challenged at several levels. At the end of the nineteenth century (during the 'long expansive wave', 1893–1913), Bernstein and his supporters argued that while there was a *tendency* towards overproduction under capitalism, capitalist organization (monopolies, trusts etc.) would lead to a gradual decline of the gravity of these crises. In the light of the worst slump in capitalist history, that of 1929–32, this objection didn't remain popular for a long period. But it was revived in the 1950s and the 1960s, during the 'long expansive wave' of 1948–68, by a whole series of economists, who thought that state intervention using Keynesian techniques had definitely licked the system's propensity to produce periodic underemployment of men and machines. The present slump took care of answering that assertion better than any theoretician could have done.

On a more abstract general level, several theoreticians – above all the Russian 'legal Marxist' Tugan-Baranovsky, but also in a certain sense the Austro-Marxist Rudolf Hilferding and the Bolshevik N. Bukharin – argued that crises of overproduction did not grow out of the basic nature of the capitalist mode of production as *generalized commodity production* but only out of one of its specific features, to wit the tendency of competition to spur on disproportion between different branches of output, essentially between department I (producing producers' goods) and department II (producing consumers' goods). If and when capitalist organization – what Hilferding called a 'generalized cartel' – could overcome this *anarchy of production* characteristic for capitalism as it had functioned up to now, crises of overproduction would no longer occur.

This line of reasoning conflicts with Marx's view that crises of overproduction are being caused by *all* the basic aspects of capitalist mode of production taken together, and not only by anarchy of production (competition growing out of private property). The disproportion between consumption and production (the tendency of the development of productive capacity to grow without limit, as if the very nature of capitalist growth did not impose strict limits upon the growth of mass consumption as a result of the necessary rise in the rate of surplus value and the rate of accumulation, without which capitalist growth is impossible) is itself a basic aspect of sector disproportion under capitalism. But as long as that disproportion is not overcome by a 'generalized cartel' (and it *cannot* be overcome) crises of overproduction remain inevitable even under such a cartel. Indeed, Tugan-Baranovsky pushed his lack of understanding of this aspect of the problem to its ultimate and absurd consequence. He calmly envisaged a capitalist production with no consumption by final consumers whatsoever, i.e., with no living labour, not seeing that in such a situation there would also be no surplus-value production, no value production, no capital and no capitalism (not to say no human survivors).

Out of the scattered passages in Marx's writings about the causes and explanations of capitalist crises of overproduction, two basically divergent schools emerged. The first one, in the footsteps of Tugan-Baranovsky and Hilferding, saw in the anarchy of production (disproportionality) the basic cause of capitalist crises. The second one, following Kautsky and Rosa Luxemburg, Nathalia Moszkowska and Paul M. Sweezy, situates the cause of the crisis in the lack of development of mass consumption proportionate to the development of society's productive capacity (underconsumption). In the late 1920s, Henryk Grossmann developed his own analysis of capitalist crises, in which he tried to combine disproportionality and underconsumption as causes of crises around the central theme of overaccumulation (insufficient mass of surplus value, decline of the rate of profit) as the main cause of capitalist crises.[26]

It is generally recognized that the Marxist theory of crises has had an important influence upon academic business cycle theories. These fall into categories similar to Marxist theories of crises: theories of crisis of profit and overaccumulation, as represented by authors like Schumpeter, the neo-classical Austrian school especially von Mises and Haberler, A.C. Pigou, the father of welfare economics etc., all of whom contend that crises arise because too little profit (savings) is available for investment; and theories of underconsumption, whose ancestors were Malthus, Sismonde de Sismondi and the Russian populists, and whose most famous modern representatives are of course Keynes and the neo-Keynesians. More sophisticated developments of business cycle theory originating from the Keynesian school, under the influence of macro-economics (econometry), e.g., the theory of the multiplier and the theory of the accelerator, were wholly or partially integrated with Marxist economic concepts by the Polish school of political economy, especially Michal Kalecki and Oscar

[26] M. Tugan-Baranovsky, *Studien zur Geschichte und Theorie der Handelskrisen in England* (Yena, 1901); Rudolf Hilferding, *Das Finanzkapital* (Vienna, 1910); Otto Bauer, 'Marx' Theorie der Wirtschaftskrisen', *Die Neue Zeit* XXXIII, 1; Otto Bauer, *Zwischen zwei Weltkriegen?* (Bratislava, 1936); N. Bukharin, *Der Imperialismus und die Akkumulation des Kapitals* (Vienna, 1926); Rosa Luxemburg, *Die Akkumulation des Kapitals* together with *Antikritik* (Berlin, 1923); Nathalia Moszkowska, *Zur Kritik moderner Krisentheorien* (Prague, 1935); Nathalia Moszkowska, *Zur Dynamik des Spätkapitalismus* (Zürich, 1943); Fritz Sternberg, *Der Imperialismus, op. cit.*; Fritz Sternberg, *Der Imperialismus und seine Kritiker* (Berlin, 1929); Paul M. Sweezy, *The Theory of Capitalist Development* (New York, 1942); Henryk Grossmann, *Das Akkumulations- und Zusammenbruchsgesetz des kapitalistischen Systems* (Frankfurt, 1929); Karl Kautsky, 'Krisentheorie', *Die Neue Zeit* XX, 2; Michal Kalecki, *Selected Essays on the Dynamics of the Capitalist Economy* (New York, 1971).

Lange. It is striking to note that, contrary to the 1920s and the 1930s, the present 'long depression' has not given birth up till now to any significant new development of theoretical analysis, either in Marxist or in non-Marxist circles.[27] Whether this is because the theory of crisis (of business cycles) has already reached a high level of perfection, or whether it is due to an excessive preoccupation with immediate (and pragmatic) analysis, remains to be seen.

v. *Monopoly capitalism, imperialism*

While Marx and Engels clearly saw that competition would lead to monopoly, an additional phenomenon appeared before the end of the nineteenth century within the framework of the capitalist mode of production. Its *modus operandi* significantly changed under the impact of growing centralization of capital. Price competition receded more and more into the background. Market control came more and more into the forefront. What is generally called among Marxists – but not only amongst them – the period of monopoly capitalism or of imperialism, was ushered in. The division of the world between metropolitan imperialist countries on the one hand, and colonies and semi-colonies (underdeveloped countries) on the other, became consolidated from that time on.

Three broad explanations of these momentous changes have been offered among Marxist theoreticians, generally linked to similar explanations among academic economists and historians.

The first starts from decisive *changes in the realm of production*: the appearance of capitalist trusts and combines, and of finance capital, dominating national markets, dividing up among themselves international markets, and ultimately determining high levels of integration of concentrated economic and political power as well. The main representatives of this line of thought, among Marxists, are Rudolf Hilferding, V.I. Lenin

[27] Nevertheless, interesting conjunctural and broader theoretical analysis are contained among else in Elmar Altvater, T. Hoffmann and W. Semmer, *Von Wirtschaftswunder zur Wirtschaftskrise* (Berlin, 1979); Ernest Mandel, *The Second Slump* (London, 1979); André Gunder Frank, *Reflections on the World Economic Crisis* (London, 1980); Michel Aglietta, *Régulation et Crises du Capitalisme* (Paris, 1976).

and N. Bukharin.[28] International expansion and aggression, the subordination of foreign countries and whole continents, the drive to militarization and war, are seen as the outcome of a new qualitatively higher level of centralization of economic power inside the imperialist countries, as well as results of the specific needs arising out of the *export of capital* which becomes, more than the export of commodities (to which it remains however linked), the main driving force of capitalist expansion.

This close interlinkage between monopolization of production, capital export, foreign aggression and militarization has been challenged above all by Schumpeter, who saw imperialist militarization more as a result of the survival of semi-feudal elements in capitalism than as a product of capitalist development properly speaking.[29] The emergence of American imperialism as the main imperialist country, in which no trace of 'semi-feudal remnants in the sphere of the state' can be discovered, has been history's answer to Schumpeter's objection.

The second explanation starts from what is assumed to be a peculiar exchange between capitalist and non-capitalist spheres in the world. It is best represented by Rosa Luxemburg, although she had many followers, the most important of whom was Fritz Sternberg.[30] It alleges, in short, that 'pure' capitalism could not survive, that it will produce an unsaleable surplus of consumer goods, that capitalist expansion hinges upon the exchange of that surplus with non-capitalist revenues (revenues originating outside of the realm of the capitalist mode of production properly speaking). This comes down essentially to peasant revenues inside the capitalist countries, and the revenues of pre-capitalist classes of backward countries. Imperialism is therefore essentially *a phenomenon in the field of circulation of commodities and capital*, a drive of capitalism

[28] Rudolf Hilferding, *Das Finanzkapital, op. cit.*; N. Bukharin, *Imperialismus und Weltwirtschaft* (1914; here cited according to the German edition, Vienna, 1929); V.I. Lenin, *Imperialism, the Last Stage of Capitalism* (1917). These works were influenced by the book of Hobson, *Imperialism* (London, 1902).
[29] Joseph A. Schumpeter, *Zur Soziologie der Imperialismen* (Tübingen, 1919; English edn, *Imperialism and Social Classes* New York, 1951).
[30] Rosa Luxemburg, *Die Akkumulation des Kapitals op. cit.*; Fritz Sternberg, *Der Imperialismus op. cit.*; Paul M. Sweezy, *The Theory of Capitalist Development op. cit.*

to incorporate into its realm successive additional zones and layers of pre-capitalist classes.

The third explanation, of a more recent origin, sees the development of imperialism as determined by a specific relationship between the metropolitan centre and the under-developed periphery. This is essentially an exploiting relationship, through uneven exchange, a drain of resources from the periphery towards the centre, expressing itself above all in a 'freezing' of qualitatively different levels of wages in the centre and the periphery. The main representatives of this explanation of imperialism are André Gunder Frank, Samir Amin and A. Emmanuel.[31]

All of these explanations of imperialism are not mutually exclusive. But some of them are. There is an obvious contradiction in the explanation of underdevelopment by low wages (the same way as its academic counterpart, the theory of the so-called vicious circle of poverty, is contradictory), especially if, as is the case with Emmanuel, this is combined with the (strictly unproven) assertion that productivity of labour is not lower in underdeveloped countries than in developed ones. If both these assertions are taken for granted, then one sees no reason why capital would not flow more and more to underdeveloped countries, where the rate of profit and the scale of exploitation would be substantially and per-manently higher than in the metropolis, and why this flow would not end in situating most industries in the Third World. Instead of explaining underdevelopment, such a theory would explain it away, i.e., explain why it couldn't exist for a long time.

VI. *Capitalist collapse?*

In the period leading up to the First World War, theories of crises and theories of imperialism were often linked together in the so-called 'collapse' controversy. This was graphically expressed by Kautsky in his formula of the 'three Ks' (Krise,

[31] André Gunder Frank, *Capitalism and Underdevelopment in Latin America* (New York, 1967); Samir Amin, *L'Accumulation à l'echelle mondiale* (Paris, 1970); Gunder Frank and Samir Amin, *L'Accumulation dépendante* (Paris, 1978); Arghiri Emmanuel, *Unequal Exchange* (New York, 1972).

Krieg, Katastrophe – crisis, war and catastrophe) which would lead to a collapse of the system. In Marx's own writings, no such precise amalgamation of 'catastrophic' predictions exists. And when he endeavours, as in the famous passage at the end of chapter 24 (section 7) of volume 1 of *Capital* to make general predictions, he always carefully introduces *subjective factors* (the subjective reaction of the workers towards the general trends of the system) as a necessary mediating link for the downfall of capitalism. In the Kautskyan tradition, there was undoubtedly an excessive reliance upon pure economic determinism, the idea that certain objective laws would in and by themselves bring the system down and that all that socialists had to do was to organize the workers and educate them, waiting till the 'objective development' sounded the death-knell of the system (one must add, however, that Kautsky himself shied away from any automatic 'collapse' prediction).

This being said, the 'collapse controversy' was meaningful, and it retains its topical character more than ever in these days. Do the inner contradictions of capitalism tend to grow larger and larger, or do they tend to be progressively reduced? Does the system periodically lead to large-scale catastrophes, or do these become more and more unlikely? Can the system reproduce itself – adapt itself to new environments, overcome new contradictions – more or less *ad infinitum* or is there a definite historical end to capitalism as a socio-economic system? This question has, of course, to be separated from the quite different one, whether socialism is inevitable. Quite soon, in the framework of the collapse controversy, Rosa Luxemburg formulated the question in a more precise way: capitalism is certainly doomed to disappear; but whether it will lead to socialism or to a new barbarism remains to be seen. That will depend upon the outcome of the struggle between living social and political forces.

There is a certain historical rhythm – a 'cyclical movement' – of 'optimists' and 'pessimists' as to the historical perspectives of capitalism. This cycle is closely interconnected with the long waves of capitalist economic development themselves. During long waves of economic expansion (1893–1913, 1949–69) 'optimism' prevails. Prophets of doom are ridiculed. Bernstein and Strachey-Crosland proclaim that crises and wars – not to speak of catastrophes and collapse – are more and more unlikely.[32] Kautsky, who, after opposing these ideas, started to embrace them himself after 1910, had the misfortune to see an article, in which he asserted that international cartels made wars unlikely if not impossible (the so-called theory of ultra-imperialism), appear after the actual outbreak of the First World War. Rudolf Hilferding, another opponent of Bernsteinian optimism in the early twentieth century, asserted during the brief 'boom' of 1923–9 that international indebtedness (capital flows) would make a new European war impossible.[33] We know what happened afterwards.

During periods of long-term depression, on the contrary, the idea of unavoidable wars and catastrophic crises of capitalism prevails. The old Engels sketched some of these ideas under the influence of the long 1873–93 depression.[34] Under the impact of the First World War and the long depression of 1913–39, various Marxist economists like the Hungarian Eugen Varga, the German Fritz Sternberg and the Pole Henryk Grossmann rehabilitated the collapse hypothesis with a vengeance.[35] Grossmann even tried to give it a rigorous economic proof – 'absolute' lack of surplus value after a certain threshold of growth of the organic composition of capital, not only for assuring the accumulation of capital but even for feeding the bourgeois class and its hangers-on. This attempt was a failure. But after the deep crisis of 1929–32, the long depression of the 1970s and the 1980s reminds us of the growing difficulties of capitalism to reproduce expansion under 'normal' conditions. Cataclysms like runaway inflation, mass unemployment, wars,

[32] Eduard Bernstein, *Die Voraussetzungen des Sozialismus und die Aufgaben der Sozialdemokratie, op. cit.*; John Strachey, *Contemporary Capitalism, op. cit.*; Anthony Crosland, *The Future of Socialism* (New York, 1963).
[33] Karl Kautsky, *Der Imperialismus* in *Die Neue Zeit* 11 September 1914; Rudolf Hilferding, *Realistisches Optimismus* in *Die Gesellschaft* November 1924.
[34] The first article actually using the formula 'collapse theory' is by Heinrich Cunow, *Die Zusammenbruchstheorie* in *Die Neue Zeit* XVI (1898), 2.
[35] Eugen Varga, *Die Niedergangsperiode des Kapitalismus* (Hamburg, 1922); Henryk Grossmann, *Das Akkumulations- und Zusammenbruchsgesetz des Kapitalistischen Systems, op. cit.*; Sternberg's answer to Grossmann was published under the title *Eine Umwälzung der Wissenschaft?* (Berlin, 1930).

fascism and other forms of dictatorship occur with frightening regularity. They offer proof of the fact that the dilemma 'socialism or barbarism' has received quite some confirmation in actual history.

Among Marxist and non-Marxist participants in this controversy alike, the question has been posed whether, independently from its contents, 'organization' of the economy was not the way out of the dilemma. The main theoretician who came back again and again to this question was the Austro-Marxist Rudolf Hilferding. In his *magnum opus, Das Finanzkapital* written before the First World War, he visualizes 'organized capitalism' as capable of avoiding economic crises, but at the same time leading to social catastrophes. In the 1920s, he thought 'organized capitalism' as intrinsically leading to peace and prosperity, in the gradualist tradition of Bernstein. At the end of his life, under the impact of the traumatic shock of fascism, he thought 'organized capitalism' to be no more capitalism but a totalitarian society in which the law of value had ceased to reign.[36] Leon Trotsky, continuing the Bukharin-Lenin-Varga tradition of the 1914–20 period, visualized decadent capitalism as leading to war and fascism, but essentially remaining capitalism, the decline of capitalism covering a long historical period of revolutions and counter-revolution, but with increasingly sinister trends towards barbarism.[37]

While writers like von Hayek saw even in democratic socialism and any form of reformist state-intervention a 'road to serfdom', thereby reversing Rosa Luxemburg's dilemma (which, under their pen, became 'capitalism or barbarism'), Schumpeter took a more subtle approach. The decline of capitalism seemed to him more or less unavoidable. But whether this would lead to a totalitarian society or to a

[36] Hilferding had had an early intuition about the dialectical relationship between the growth of capitalist 'organization', organized capitalism and strong state power in *Organisationsmacht und Staatsgewalt, Die Neue Zeit,* XXXII, 2. He reversed that position in the 1920s, then came back to it in the 1930s.
[37] Leon Trotsky, *In Defence of Marxism* (New York, 1942), *Manifesto of the Emergency Conference of the Fourth International* (New York, 1940).

combination of socialism and some forms of democracy remained an open question.[38]

VII. *Is a socialist economy possible? How will it be built?*

As we have seen, the 'collapse controversy' more or less unavoidably leads to the question of whether socialism can succeed and (or) will succeed capitalism. This again leads to the question of what a socialist economy looks like. Even before the impact of the Russian revolution and of the Soviet experiment raised this question from the realm of theory to that of practice, and to judgments about the results of that practice, the more general question was posed: is a socialist economy in the strict Marxist sense of the concept possible?

The debate around this question was raised by opponents of Marx and of socialism more than by Marxists themselves, who shied away – as Marx did himself – from elaborating any form of blueprint of what a socialist economy would be like.[39] So the debate was above all represented by the controversy between Pareto, Barone and the Vienna School, about the impossibility of economic calculation under socialism – in the absence of a market. The school which declared socialism impossible obviously exaggerated the actual function of the market in real economic life – even under capitalism. Barone's answer was subtle, concentrating on the possibility for 'planning authorities' to *simulate* market mechanisms as the basis of economic calculation.[40]

Thirty years later, Lange and Taylor came back to the problem, expanding Barone's contribution.[41] Von Mises' objec-

[38] von Hayek, *The Road to Serfdom* (London, 1944); Joseph Schumpeter, *Capitalism, Socialism and Democracy* (New York, 1942).
[39] The main classical Marxist comments on socialist society are contained in Marx's 'Critique of the Gotha Programme' and Engels' *Anti-Dühring.* See also Karl Kautsky, *Die soziale Revolution* (Stuttgart, 1903).
[40] E. Barone, *The Ministry of Production in the Collectivist State* (1908), and L. von Mises, *Economic Calculations in the Socialist Commonwealth* (1920), both reprinted in F.A. von Hayek, ed., *Collectivist Economic Planning* (London, 1935).
[41] O. Lange and F. Taylor, *On the Economic Theory of Socialism* (University of Minnesota Press, 1938).

tion that you couldn't solve millions of equations, which such a simulation would involve, has in the meantime been taken care of by the computer. But somehow, all participants in that debate seemed to miss Marx's main point, to wit that resource distribution between different branches of output, and relations between resources and wants, need not be mediated through market mechanisms at all, neither 'real' nor 'simulated' ones. They can be decided by *conscious* preferences of consumers, which would give results quite different from choices determined by unevenly distributed purchasing power, publicity pressure, predetermined consumption patterns etc.

More important than the debate on the theoretical possibility of a socialist economy was the debate on the practical steps towards building such an economy, which came into its own only after the First World War, especially under the influence of the Russian and the German revolutions. Very rapidly, this debate fell into two parts: the debate in the capitalist countries on the main problems of the transition from capitalism to socialism: the debate inside the Soviet Union on the logic (the laws of motion) of building a socialist economy, once capitalist private property is by and large abolished.

The first debate centred around the specific problems of socialization of the economy. If we make abstraction of many interesting but conjunctural debates, essentially determined by problems of political tactics in given national situations, the main controversies arose around the following problem: what was the key field of socialization? The Austrian Karl Renner defended the view that it was easier to socialize the economy from the realm of circulation than from the realm of production as Marx and Marxists had traditionally argued. This idea had found many supporters among gradualists in the thirties and later on during the fifties and the sixties. What was the relative importance of property relations (nationalisation) and of production relations at factory level in the elimination of capitalism? The German left communist Karl Korsch appeared here as the forerunner of the Yugoslav school of self-managing socialism after 1950, while Gramsci's contribution on the role of workers' councils was very important. What was the importance of planning for overcoming capitalism? Here the contribution of the Belgian Hendrik De Man went in the direction of 'organized capitalism', with all the contradictions which we mentioned above.[42]

The debate in the Soviet Union, which was essentially centred around the laws of motion of a post-capitalist society in which commodity production has not completely disappeared – i.e., around the dialectics of plan and market – was conducted in a theoretically serious manner in two phases: in the 1920s and the 1960s, interrupted by the long night of Stalinism, during which no serious theoretical discussion of any kind was possible, the machine-gun being the key argument used against theoretical opponents by the faction in power. During the 1920s, the main participants in the debate were Eugene Preobrazhensky and N. Bukharin. Not by accident, the main subject of the debate was *primitive socialist accumulation* i.e., the objective laws of building up large-scale socialized industry in an essentially peasant milieu, with or without transfer of value (of quantities of labour) from agriculture to industry, with or without gradual collectivization of agriculture, with or without raising consumption for the mass of producers (workers, poor peasants, part of middle peasants).[43] During the 1960s, the controversy opposed essentially the Liberman faction of economists to the 'dogmatists' of the Strumilin school (one variant of which represented by the mathematician Nemchinov defending the 'objective automatism' of optimi-

[42] Karl Renner, *Die Wirtschaft als Gesamtprozess und die Sozialisierung* (Berlin, 1924); Karl Korsch, *Schriften Zur Sozialisierung* (originally published between 1919 and 1937; Frankfurt, 1969); Antonio Gramsci, *Philosophie der Praxis* (1919–21; Frankfurt, 1967); Edvard Kardelj, *Les contradictions de la propriété sociale dans le système socialiste* (Paris, 1976). See also Branko Horvat, *An Essay on Yugoslav Society* (New York, 1969); Hendrik De Man, *Au-delà du Marxisme* (Paris, 1929), *Réflexions sur l'économie dirigée* (Paris, 1932), *L'Idée Socialiste* followed by *Le Plan du Travail* (Paris, 1935).
[43] E. Preobrazhensky, *The New Economics* (1926; Oxford, 1965); N. Bukharin, *Le Socialisme dans un seul pays* (Paris, 1974).

zations realized by mathematical methods, i.e., by generalized use of the computer).[44]

This debate became more and more intertwined with debates on *planning techniques* in which the October revolution and the Gosplan had initiated a real breakthrough, with W. Leontief's input-output tables and Feldman's equilibrium-growth calculations.[45] But this combination obscured to a large extent the fact that at the basis of different rhythms and forms of 'socialist accumulation' (i.e., of economic growth in a post-capitalist society) there lay political-social choices and not purely technical ones.[46]

3. *Debates about the basic theoretical concepts*

I. *Critiques of the labour theory of value*
The appearance of *Das Kapital* coincided with a fundamental turn of academic political economy, away from the classics (Petty, Adam Smith, Ricardo) basing themselves on the labour theory of value to which Marx and Engels also adhered, although with substantial modifications, towards the so-called

---

[44] E.G. Liberman, 'The Plan, Profits and Bonuses', in *Pravda* 9 September 1962; Oscar Lange, *Problemas de la Economia Politica del Socialismo* (La Habana, 1966); Ota Sik, *Planning and the Market under Socialism* (New York, 1967); Wlodomierz Bruz, *Problèmes généraux du fonctionnement de l'économie socialiste* (Paris, 1968). The opposite thesis was defended by Strumilin, Kronrod, Gatovsky and others. Among the main contributors to the problems of mathematical calculations (including the use of computers), planning and market, see: V.V. Novoshilov, *The Problems of Planned Pricing and the Reform of Industrial Management* (Moscow, 1966); V. Nemchinov, 'Basic Elements of a Model of Planned Price Formation', in *Voprossi Ekonomiki* 1963, no. 12; L. Kantorovitch, *Mathematical Methods for Organizing and Planning Industry* (Leningrad, 1939); L. Kantorovitch, *The Best Use of Economic Resources* (London, 1955).

[45] See G.A. Feldman, *Zur Wachstumstheorie des Nationaleinkommens* (originally published in 1928; published in German, Berlin, 1969).

[46] A good example is the Stalinist so-called 'law of the priority development of heavy industry'. I have refuted that in *Marxist Economic Theory*, ch. 16. For a different position see Maurice Dobb, *On Economic Theory and Socialism* (London, 1955).

neo-classical, i.e., marginalist school. For a rather long period, this break of academic political economy with the labour theory of value had very little impact on the evolution of Marxist economic theory, except in the field of straightforward polemics.[47] It should be said also that the main marginalist theoreticians generally ignored Marx and Marxism.

The one exception was Eugen von Böhm-Bawerk, one of the founders of the neo-classical school, who, after the appearance of volume 3 of *Das Kapital* wrote a famous critique of the main concepts of Marxist economic theory, to which in turn Rudolf Hilferding wrote a no less famous reply. While this polemic hardly met an echo at the time of its appearance, it influenced the Cambridge school of neo-Keynesians, favourably disposed to Marxist politics and sociology but quite critical of Marxist economic theory, half a century later. In Joan Robinson's *Essay on Marxian Economics* we find basically the same argument of Böhm-Bawerk's, about the supposed contradiction, between volume 1 and volume 3 of *Capital*. In volume 1, a commodity's value is directly determined by labour inputs (quantities of socially necessary labour); in volume 3 it isn't. In volume 1, stable (stagnant, low) real wages are posited; in volume 3, real wages are fluctuating cyclically. Etc. etc.[48]

As Roman Rosdolsky convincingly demonstrated, these criticisms of Marx's economic theory are based on a misunderstanding about his method, which can be compared with that of the method of successive approaches, used in most sciences, natural and social ones alike.[49] In order to analyse a complex

---

[47] E.g., Bukharin's polemics with marginalism, *Economic Theory of the Leisure Class* (1914; New York, 1972).

[48] Eugen von Böhm-Bawerk, *Karl Marx and the End of his System, op. cit.* answered by Rudolf Hilferding, *Böhm-Bawerk's Criticism of Marx*; Tugan-Baranovsky, *Theoretische Grundlagen des Marxismus* (Leipzig, 1905); Joan Robinson, *An Essay on Marxian Economics, op. cit.*; Paul Samuelson, *Marxian Economics as Economics* (New York, 1967); Michio Morishima, *Marx's Economics* (Cambridge, 1973); Leszek Kolakowski, *Main Currents of Marxism* (Oxford, 1978), vol. I.

[49] Roman Rosdolsky, *Zur Entstehungsgeschichte des Marxschen 'Kapital', op. cit.* The publication of Marx's *Grundrisse* in 1939 passed nearly unobserved, because few copies reached the public outside of the USSR. The second edition in 1953 also got slow comments, but these received momentum in the 1960s and 1970s, especially after the appearance of Rosdolsky's book and the translation of the *Grundrisse* into French, Italian and English.

phenomenon, it is perfectly admissable first to assume that some constituent parts of that phenomenon are stable, in order to isolate a small number of variables which are essential for understanding the inner logic of the system (its structure). Once these have been discovered, it is possible to abandon progressively simplifying assumptions, to pass to a new level of abstraction lower than the previous one, to multiply the number of variables etc. This is what Marx has done in moving from volume 1 to volume 2 and 3 of *Capital*. And while volume 3 is less 'abstract' than volume 1, nearer to the 'appearances on the surface of economic life', it by no means covers all of these. Other unwritten volumes of *Capital* dealing with competition, the world market and the state, would have completed the job, which remains unfinished.

Those inside the Marxist camp who challenged some of the basic laws of motion of capitalism laid bare by Marx slowly started to question the validity of Marx's theory of value and of surplus value – or at the very least their relevance for 'concrete' economic analysis, not to say for the elaboration of socialist strategy and tactics. This was true, strangely enough, not only for the social-democrat Bernstein but also for the communist Graziadei.[50] One has to admit that this debate has had little or no effect on the mainstream of Marxist economic thought.

There remains, however, one field of the theory of value properly speaking in which Marxists have been faced with a challenge to which they have offered very little response up to now. This is the so-called reduction problem. According to Marx's theory of value, while all living labour engaged in production produces value, it is not completely homogeneous, i.e., one hour of labour is equivalent to another hour of labour only at the same level of simple skill. Higher skilled labour produces more value than unskilled labour. An hour of skilled labour can be reduced to a multiple of an hour of unskilled labour.

While the argument seems reasonable, the question arises:

[50] Tugan-Baranovsky, *Theoretische Grundlagen des Marxismus, op. cit.*; Bernstein, *op. cit.*; Graziadei, *Prezzo e Sovraprezzo nella Economia Capitalistica* (Torino, 1924).

how can this multiple be measured in a precise way? By what concrete multiple do you reduce skilled labour to universal quantities of unskilled (or low-skilled) simple labour? The answers to that question have been complicated by the fact that several authors have gone into obvious circular reasoning, by deducing (in the Adam Smithian tradition) the *higher quantities of simple labour produced* by skilled labour from the *higher wages payed* to skilled labour (which include, over and above the normal reproduction costs of labour power, the production costs of the skill itself). This is, of course, impossible from a logical point of view and contrary to Marx's analytical tradition.

The least one can say is that the answers to this problem remain by and large controversial, and that no solution has yet appeared which is generally accepted and integrated into the mainstream of Marxist theory.[51]

II. *The 'transformation problem'*

Much more important and much more ponderous than the debates about the labour theory of value properly speaking have been the controversies unleashed by a critique – among non-Marxists and Marxists alike – of the way in which Marx, in volume 3 of *Capital* 'transformed' values into prices of production. This 'transformation problem' is not a simple 'technical' aspect of Marx's economic theory, i.e., it is not simply a question of using mathematics in a correct way. It is related to key aspects of the theory itself.

While under simple commodity production exchange is essentially an exchange of commodities, produced with stable production techniques, and therefore the socially necessary quantities of labour contained in each commodity are proportional to the actual labour time spent in their production, this is no longer the case under capitalism. In the capitalist mode of production, commodities are commodities produced by 'many capitals', in constant competition with each other

[51] See I.I. Rubin, *Essays on Marx's Theory of Value* (1929; Detroit, 1972); the contributions of Böhm-Bawerk, Hilferding and Bob Rowthorn in Nutzinger and Wolfstetter, eds., *Die Marx'sche Theorie und ihre Kritik* (Frankfurt, 1974), vol II, part 5 (*Das Reduktionsproblem*).

and under conditions of *constantly changing production techniques*. Indeed, one could make a good case for the statement. that, under 'pure capitalism', it is not commodities which are circulating but segments of capital (commodity capital is but one of the many metamorphoses of capital as such).

But capitalist commodity production is production for profit. While each capital strives to receive the maximum amount of profit, the end-result of that strife is the tendency towards an equalization of the rate of profit for all capitals. This equalization in turn implies a redistribution of surplus value between different capitals (branches, firms), each of them not receiving the amount of surplus value produced by 'their' workers, but a part of total surplus value roughly proportional to that part of total capital which each of these capitals represents (this analysis does not of course take the problems of monopoly into consideration). Therefore, while total profit calculated in value terms[52] is necessarily equal to total surplus value (no surplus value can be created outside of the realm of production), the profit accruing to each specific commodity-producing sector of production is not necessarily identical to the surplus value produced in that sector. Therefore, the 'price of production' (costs of production plus average profit calculated upon total capital spent) of the given commodity is not necessarily identical to its value.

Again, while the reasoning is convincing – it has, however, been questioned several times – the concrete calculations involved in the transformation of values into prices of production by Marx in volume 3 of *Capital* were quite rapidly

---

[52] The problem of values calculated in value terms being equal or unequal to prices of production calculated in money terms is a false one, as it implies comparing incommensurable quantities. In order to give meaning to that problem, the fluctuations of the value of gold, i.e., of the marginal productivity of labour in the gold-mining industry, have to be introduced into the calculation.

challenged.[53] The first main challenge – on which most of the subsequent ones are still based – came from the Prussian statistician von Bortkiewicz, who influenced Marxist authors such as Paul M. Sweezy. Especially since the 1940s, a large controversy has developed, in which many alternative solutions to the 'transformation problem', different from that of Marx, have been offered by authors such as Winternitz, Seton, Garignani etc. This controversy became increasingly interwoven with more substantial debates about the theory of value, initiated by Piero Sraffa's critique of the neo-classical capital and value theory, but implying a return to a neo-Ricardian and not a Marxist labour theory of value. Disconnected from the theory of value, the theory of exploitation loses its firm foundations, although it must be admitted that some neo-Ricardians, as well as authors trying to establish some form of synthesis between neo-Ricardianism and Marxism, have tried to salvage that theory without using the concept of surplus value.[54]

Marxists were at first slow to answer the challenge, limiting themselves to making some obvious general theoretical points. In later years, this has progressively changed. Various Marxist authors have now come up not only with an intrinsic criticism of the von Bortkiewicz-Sraffa-Steedman solution of the transformation problem, but also with a more convincing analysis of the real economic problems lying behind that problem. The

[53] The bibliography of all the contributors to that debate is too long to quote. Here are those which I consider the most important: L. von Bortkiewicz, 'Zur Berichtigung der grundlegenden theoretischen Konstruktion von Marx im Dritten Band des "Kapital"', in *Jahrbücher für Nationalökonomie und Statistik* (July 1907); J. Winternitz, 'Values and Prices: a Solution of the So-called "Transformation Problem"', in *Economic Journal* (June 1948); F. Seton, 'The Transformation Problem', in *Review of Economic Studies* (1957), vol. 24; C. Garignani, *On the Theory of Distribution and Value in Marx and the Classical Economists* (1977); C.C. von Weiszäcker, 'Notizen zur Marx'schen Wertlehre', in Nutzinger and Wolfstetter, eds., *Die Marx'sche Theorie und ihre Kritik* (Frankfurt, 1974); Gilles Dostaler, *Valeur et Prix, Histoire d'un débat* (Paris, 1978); G. Abraham-Frois and E. Berrebi, *Théorie de la valeur, des prix et de l'accumulation* (Paris, 1976); J. Steedman, *Marx after Sraffa* (London, 1977); Pierre Salama, *Sur la Valeur* (Paris, 1975). Piero Sraffa's basic work is *Production of Commodities by Means of Commodities* (Cambridge, 1960).
[54] See Willi Semmler, *Zur Theorie der Reproduktion und Akkumulation* (Berlin, 1977); James F. Becker, *Marxian Political Economy, op. cit.*, and others.

contribution to single out is that of Anwar Shaikh, who, by applying the itinerative method, shows convincingly not only why prices of production have to deviate from values, but also that these deviations are themselves in the last analysis *governed* by the law of value.[55] By assuming from the outset a uniform rate of profit, the neo-Ricardians make the real difficulty which is to be solved disappear before even beginning the analysis. For on theoretical grounds as well as on the basis of empirical facts, the starting point for the real movement which has to be explained is that of *uneven rates of profit* between different branches of production, as well as a tendency towards overcoming that unevenness, through capital competition and capital mobility.

III. *Is there a real tendency for the organic composition of capital to grow?*

The basic economic contradiction of the capitalist mode of production is the tendency of the rate of profit to decline. As we have seen, this tendency is challenged above all on empirical grounds. But a deeper theoretical challenge has been raised, again, among Marxists as well as among non-Marxists. The declining rate of profit derives directly from the tendency of the organic composition of capital to increase. But is the assumption of such a tendency proven?

Those critics who deny the existence of that tendency argue above all that it confuses two different trends: the trend to more and more advanced (mechanized) techniques of production; and the trend to increasing value (or costs) of machinery and raw material as against wages. The first trend is an obvious feature of capitalist development. Each specific technique, as Marx pointed out when he analysed the concept of the organic composition of capital, implies a *physical relation* between a set of machines, a quantity of raw material and a number of workers. The efficient use of a Bessemer steel oven, or of an oxygen-fed LD oven, needs a certain *amount* of iron and a given *number* of workers. It also implies a given *value* of both

[55] See Anwar Shaikh's contribution in a forthcoming book, *The Transformation Problem: Essays in the Memory of Robert Langston*: 'The Transformation from Marx to Sraffa'.

constant and variable capital, inasmuch as for each given production cycle, or in each given year, the value of a steel oven, of x tons of iron, and of a given number of workers' wages, can be considered data, and not a set of variables.

But from all this, the critics continue, it does not follow at all that technical progress, which implies an increasing number (or complexity) of machines, and an increasing amount of raw material fed to them, also automatically implies that the costs (the value) of these machines and raw materials will increase more quickly than the value of the labour power necessary to put them into motion. In other words: the tendency of the organic composition of capital to increase presupposes a *labour-saving bias of technical progress in value terms* and this supposedly is not proven. Indeed, some of the same critics argue, a capital-saving-biased technical progress is perfectly possible, and is indeed supposed to have occurred at several epochs in the twentieth century. A 'neutral' technical progress was another possibility. Closely related to such an assumption is the one of a slowly declining capital/output ratio, which would tend equally to disprove any tendency for the organic composition of capital to grow.

The empirical data are inconclusive, to say the least.[56] Among most of the participants in this debate, the use of macroeconomic aggregates like the 'total wage bill' obscures the distinction between productive and unproductive labour, as it does in the debate, referred to above, about the alleged 'stable shares' in the national income. It is easy to correct such mistaken impressions, by examining branches of production one by one, instead of operating with aggregates. One cannot find a single

[56] Roy Harrod (*Economic Essays* [London, 1953]) seems to be the main author to have substantiated the idea of a 'neutral' technical progress. For empirical evidence in the opposite sense see R.J. Gordon, *A Rare Event* in *Survey of Current Business* (July 1971) and the same author's articles in *Review of Economics and Statistics* (November 1968) and in *American Economic Review* (June 1969); see also Anne P. Carter, *Structural Change in the American Economy* (Harvard University Press, 1970). For another confirmation see A.E. Ott, 'Technischer Fortschritt', in *Handwörterbuch der Sozialwissenschaften* (Göttingen, 1959), vol. 10: 'If one finally asks, which of the seven cases of technical progress occurs most often in real life, it is evident that labour-saving technical progress with additional expenditure of capital ... represents that form of technical progress typical for the development of capitalism.'

branch in which there is a secular tendency for wages to become an increasing part of total production costs. If this were not the case, how could one interpret the meaning of semi-automatization, not to speak of full automatization, which is, after all, the basic trend of contemporary production technique?

N. Okishio, a representative of the Japanese school of Marxism, has raised a logical objection to the tendency for the organic composition of capital to increase and the tendency of the rate of profit to decline.[57] Every single capitalist only introduces new production techniques in order to cut production costs and increase profits. How could it happen that what is true for each individual capitalist would suddenly turn into its opposite for all capitalists taken together?

This objection implies a misunderstanding about the very nature of the average rate of profit. Under a generalized market economy, i.e., capitalist commodity production, the law of value *imposes* the value (price of production) of the commodities, after a certain time-lag, *behind the backs of the* '*economic agents*', capitalists and workers alike, independently of their will. This time-lag is, roughly, that of the business cycle, i.e., between the moment when, in an investment wave (which covers the period of economic recovery and prosperity), new production techniques are introduced, and the moment of crash and depression, when under the pressure of overaccumulation, overproduction and capital devalorization, the value of the commodities is reduced to the level implied by these new production techniques. When the new technique is being introduced, it gives the innovators surplus profits (profits above average profit). This is of course why they introduce it; in this Okishio is right. But when, under the influence of overaccumulation, the value of the commodities is reduced, surplus profits disappear. Those who utilize the new production techniques

[57] N. Okishio, 'Technical Changes and the Rate of Profit', in *Kobe University Economic Review* (1961), vol. 7; N. Okishio, 'A Mathematical Note on Marxian Theorems', in *Weltwirtschaftliches Archiv* (1963), vol. 91; Makatoh Itoh, 'Marxian Crises Theories', in *Bulletin of the Conference of Socialist Economists* (February 1975), vol. IV, no 1. Older representatives of the Japanese Marxist school include Tsuru and Kozo Uno. A more recent one is Koshimura.

only receive the average rate of profit, and, moreover, an average rate lower than in the beginning of the cycle. In not understanding that side of the process, Okishio does not see how an objective law (the law of value) imposes itself in spite of the intentions of individual capitalists.[58]

IV. *The source of monopoly profits*

In the framework of capitalist industry, surplus profits are normally originated only as a result of *temporary* advantages enjoyed by innovating firms (superior techniques, more 'rational' organization of labour etc.). As long as the *weighted* average of productivity of labour determining the value of the commodity in a given branch of production is not modified, those firms producing at a higher productivity of labour receive a surplus profit.[59] This is generally wiped out at the end of the business cycle, during the phase of crash and depression.

Can *durable* surplus profits arise under capitalism, not in spite but in function of the operation of the law of value? Marx answers 'yes' in volume 3 of *Capital* when he deals with ground rent. Structural, institutional obstacles to the mobility of capital – which is the objective force imposing the equalization of the rates of profit between different branches – can lead to situations where branches of production with a lower organic composition of capital than the social average will enjoy a rate of profit higher than the average rate, i.e., will receive surplus profits during a long period (absolute ground rent). Likewise, conditions of structural, institutional scarcity, which cannot be simply overcome by the successive influx of capital into those sectors, will lead to situations where the productive unit operating with the lowest productivity of labour determines the value of the commodity, and receives the average rate of profit. Those units of production enjoying productivity of labour

[58] For sophisticated mathematical inquiries into the interrelationship between the evolution of the organic composition of capital, the evolution of the rate of surplus value, the evolution of productivity of labour in both departments etc., see G. Stamatis, *Die spezifisch kapitalistischen Produktionsmethoden und der tendenzielle Fall der allgemeinen Profitrate bei Karl Marx* (Berlin, 1977), and Willi Semmler, *Zur Theorie der Reproduktion und Akkumulation* (Berlin, 1977).
[59] Karl Marx, *Capital* vol. 3, ch. 10.

higher than the marginal one can also sell their products at the level of that price of production, thereby receiving a surplus profit over and above the average rate of profit (differential ground rent).

The question can now be posed: is this argument of volume 3 of *Capital* only applicable to agriculture and mining – it has today obvious applications in the fields of oil and gold production! – or could it be applied to industrial output also? Isn't it merely a particular example of a more general case, that of monopolized branches of production? Cannot monopoly capitalism be defined as characterized by growing obstacles to the 'perfect' mobility of capital, arising out of capital concentration and centralization (difficulties of entry resulting from size, patents etc.), capacity to limit competition and output (market control), growing unevenness of technology etc.? Wouldn't in that case monopolistic rents, cartel rents, technological rents arise identical in origin and nature to the ground rent or mining rents analysed by Marx?

This line of reasoning implies that monopolistic surplus profits arise both from the redistribution of surplus value between monopolized and non-monopolized branches of production, and from situations in which the marginal and not the average firms determine the value (price of production) of a certain number of commodities (in which, therefore, the total amount of value and surplus value produced is higher than it would be under conditions of free competition). The tradition within Marxism which defends that point of view starts with Hilferding's *Finanzkapital* which developed the concept of *cartel rent* and is represented among others by E. Varga, Paul M. Sweezy and E. Mandel. It leads logically to the idea of two average rates of profits under monopoly capitalism, one in the non-monopolized and one in the monopolized sectors of the economy. These two rates would 'equalize' only during time-spans much longer than the normal business cycle, possibly during a 'long wave'.

That line of reasoning has been challenged by other Marxists, especially the Soviet author Wygodsky, some of his East German colleagues, E. Altvater and partially A. Emmanuel. According to those authors, monopolistic surplus profits, inasmuch as they are real and not simply apparent, would be the result not of a redistribution of surplus value but of more surplus value produced within the monopolized sectors themselves. The function of monopolies would consist essentially in preventing these exceptional situations from becoming erased rapidly (e.g., institutional obstacles to a worldwide mobility of labour as compared to a much higher national mobility of capital). But the law of value would do away with any branch rate of profit over and above the average rate. In other words: surplus profits would appear more like advantages of firms *within* given branches of production, than advantages of monopolized branches as compared to non-monopolized ones.[60]

Needless to say, this debate, which parallels similar debates in academic circles, is only in its infancy, and has not reached the point where it can be said to have been solved in a satisfactory way for the bulk of those accepting the conceptual framework of Marxist economic theory.

v. *Uneven exchange*

Whether a Marxist accepts the idea of transfer of values between monopolized or non-monopolized sectors of the economy will greatly influence his view of what lies at the bottom of uneven (unequal) exchange on the world market. That such an uneven exchange has occurred, is occurring, and has greatly influenced the present polarization of the international capitalist economy between 'developed' and 'under-developed' countries can hardly be denied. That the analysis of volume 3 of *Capital does* imply transfers of values between branches – the whole procedure followed by Marx in his calculation of the equalization of the rate of profit is based upon such transfers – is equally obvious. Indeed, academic economics, following Marxist analysis, have gradually generalized the concept of 'terms of trade' (implying the notion of long periods

[60] Rudolf Hilferding, *Das Finanzkapital, op. cit.*; E. Varga and L. Mendelson, eds., *New Data for Lenin's Imperialism* (New York, 1940); E. Mandel, *Late Capitalism, op. cit.*; Wilhelm Brenner, *Zur politischen Oekonomie des Monopols* (Köln, 1975); S.L. Wygodsky, *Der gegenwärtige Kapitalismus* (Köln, 1972); Paul Boccara, ed., *Le Capitalisme Monopoliste d'Etat* (Paris, 1971) etc.

of adverse evolution of these terms for certain participants in exchange) from a concept applicable only to relations between nations, to a concept applicable to inter-regional relations within a single country, to relations between agriculture and industry, or even to relations between skilled and unskilled labour.[61]

Marx himself clearly stated that on the world market, labour from more advanced countries (i.e., countries with a higher level of productivity of labour) is valued as more intense, i.e., as producing more value than labour from underdeveloped countries. This means that on the world market, when two quantities of goods are exchanged (e.g., at one million dollars each), the one exported by the backward country can represent 30,000 hours of (less intensive) labour, while the other one only represents 20,000 hours of labour spent in the industrialized country.

Does this analysis imply that there is an actual 'drain' of value (of quantities of labour, and, in the long run, of economic resources, of 'potential for economic growth') from the underdeveloped to the developed country?[62] At first sight, one could believe that this is simply a question of defining the sphere in which value-recognition occurs. If this sphere is the *world* market, then, it follows, that part of the less intensive labour spent in the underdeveloped countries has not been recognized as 'socially necessary labour' on the world market. If this sphere is the *national* market, however, it follows that all labour which is spent at the average productivity of a given country is value-producing (is socially necessary labour). In that case, through uneven international exchange, part of that value will not be realized within that country but to the advantage of the importers and (re-)users of commodities produced by that labour, i.e., will be transferred to the more advanced countries through uneven exchange.

From there on, one could construct a *Marxist theory of foreign trade* (which is still in its infancy), following Marx's developments in volume 3 of *Capital*. Commodities would fall

[61] James F. Becker, *Marxian Political Economy, op. cit.*
[62] See especially Paul A. Baran, *The Political Economy of Growth* (New York, 1957). But there is an ample literature on the subject.

roughly into three categories. There would be those commodities essentially produced for 'national' markets, and which would therefore have different 'national values' (prices of production), inasmuch as the average productivity of labour and the average rate of profit is quite different in different countries. Only relatively small surpluses of these commodities would be exported. 'World market prices' of them would be different from 'national prices' and would be oscillating widely (e.g., the world market price of wheat as compared to the price of wheat in India on the one hand and in Canada on the other hand), determined by the least productive production unit which succeeds in having its labour recognized as socially necessary labour *on the world market*. Secondly, there would be those commodities essentially produced in a single country (or in a small number of countries). In that case, it would be the 'national value' (or the weighted 'national values') of that commodity which would simultaneously determine its national price and its world market price. And, finally, there would be those commodities produced by many countries, but essentially *for* the world market, for export. In that case, world market prices would be the determining factor for 'internal market prices', i.e., only those quantities of labour recognized on the world market as socially necessary would be value-producing.[63]

Further consideration will, however, lead to the conclusion that even if the hypothesis of different spheres of determination of the value (price of production) of commodities is abandoned, and with it the hypothesis of transfers of value, the question of the 'drain' through international trade, i.e., of the relative impoverishment of underdeveloped compared with developed countries as a result of 'unequal exchange', is by no means eliminated. One can give and should give great weight to given social structures (relations of production, class relations, property relations etc.) as relative motors or relative brakes upon the process of mobilization of material and human

[63] I developed this in *Late Capitalism* ch. 11. For alternative interpretations see Christian Palloix, *L'économie mondiale capitaliste* (Paris, 1971), 2 vols.; Heinz-Dieter Meier, *Der Konkurrenzkampf auf dem Weltmarkt* (Frankfurt, 1977).

resources for the purposes of economic growth (of increasing the average social productivity of labour). One can argue at length whether the survival of pre-capitalist and semi-capitalist social structures has been encouraged by imperialism, and to what extent this uneven and combined development has reduced actual modernization and economic growth in so-called 'Third World' countries. One can even reduce the whole logic of that combined and uneven development to the pressure of the world market, i.e., the stranglehold of imperialism upon the Third World's society and economy. But whatever be the main stress one puts on this or that 'cause' of underdevelopment, it remains true that, from a Marxist point of view, underdevelopment is in the last analysis underemployment, in a quantitative as well as in a qualitative sense. Underemployment in that broad meaning implies simultaneously lower wages (under the pressure of an immense surplus of labour) and lower prices of food and raw materials (although higher than could be obtained with more capital investment, all other things remaining equal). Whether the more industrialized capitalist countries' ruling classes profit from these uneven levels of world prices and world wages directly (through favourable terms of trade) or indirectly through easier access to these raw materials, and surplus profits resulting from capital investment in these countries) is not decisive. What is decisive is that part of the profits realized by the imperialist ruling class *does* originate in the Third World. And that is hard to deny.

VI. *The nature of the post-capitalist economy*
Marx and the Marxist tradition are unambiguous on the subject: socialism, as 'the first phase of communism', is characterized by the absence of commodity production. Nobody denies, on the other hand, that commodity production still exists in the Soviet Union and in all other countries calling themselves socialist. What conclusion should one draw from this apparent discrepancy between theory and reality? Was Marx's theory wrong? Is the definition of these countries as 'socialist countries' wrong? What is the social nature of their economy? A debate amongst Marxists has been raging around that basic

issue practically since the day of the October revolution of 1917.

We shall leave aside here the epistemological (philosophical) aspect of the debate, and concentrate on the issue of economic theory involved. For Marx and Marxists, there are only two basically different ways in which needs and resources can be balanced in any given society: either *a priori* in a conscious way (regardless of whether this is done democratically or despotically, based upon prejudice, magic rites, religion, habit, tradition, or based upon the application of science, whether it is 'irrational' or 'rational'); or *a posteriori* through the operation of the law of value, i.e., objective laws operating behind the backs of the 'economic agents'. Schematically, and in the last analysis, *a priori* adaptation of social resources to social needs implies social property of the means of production and labour which is directly recognized as social labour. *A posteriori* adaptation of social resources to social needs implies private property, implies labour which is spent in the form of private labour and which is not immediately and directly recognized as social labour. Only to the extent that the commodity it produces is sold at its value (under capitalism to the extent its owner receives, through its sale, the average rate of profit) is private labour recognized as social labour.

One can therefore only argue that commodity production still prevails under socialism if one argues that under socialism, there is still private labour. And this then immediately implies that planning, i.e., conscious *a priori* determination of social needs and husbanding of social resources to fulfil these needs, is impossible. For you can't have commodity production without the rule of the law of value, and you can't have the rule of the law of value with real planning.

Up to now the debate has been dominated by the tendency of most of its participants to approach the problem in a formal-mechanistic way of 'either or': either socialism or capitalism; either social property or private property; either social labour or private labour etc. This formalistic approach has obvious political, ideological and therefore social-interest functions, on which we do not need to dwell. We only want to stress the unsolvable theoretical contradictions to which it leads in the field of Marxist economic theory. For what we are dealing with is, obviously, a phenomenon of *transition* of a new form of society *arising out of* an old one, having not yet achieved its own intrinsic logic of development, but developing in constant struggle with an adverse environment. Capitalism, after all, still rules in the major part of the world.[64] Any attempt to draw conclusions as to the nature of mature forms from immature, hybrid, transitional phenomena can only lead into a blind alley.

This was true for all those, starting with the Russian Mensheviks, who declared that, because socialism was impossible under the socio-economic and political conditions of backward Russia, capitalism and only capitalism could emerge from the October revolution.[65] This was difficult to argue under the conditions of war communism, but with the emergence of the NEP and the restoration of commodity production, the Mensheviks thought they could triumph: capitalism had, after all, come back to Russia. Left communist critics of the NEP (and later of Stalinism) adopted similar positions, the most consistent being Amadeo Bordiga. That Soviet society is some form of state capitalism has been an opinion widely held ever since among many circles considering themselves Marxist (including the Chinese communists in the 1960s and 1970s).[66]

On the other extreme of the spectrum, all those supporters or apologists for the existing regimes in the USSR, Eastern

[64] This is the historical background against which the 'socialism-in-one-country' controversy of the 1920s in the Soviet Union has to be seen. Those who contend that commodity production (and the state) in the Soviet Union cannot disappear as long as imperialism survives thereby admit that what they call 'socialism' is not the society described by Marx and Engels, in which there was no commodity production, no state and no classes. They thereby implicitly admit that socialism, as described by Marx and Engels, is impossible in one country.

[65] Throughout the 1920s and 1930s, there was an interesting debate in the Second International between Otto Bauer and Karl Kautsky on that subject, a debate in which Bauer ended up by considering the Soviet economy socialist or semi-socialist.

[66] The list of contributions to that subject is too long to be quoted in full. Let me limit myself to four authors: Amadeo Bordiga, *Structure Economique et Sociale de la Russie d'aujourd'hui* (Paris, 1975); Tony Cliff, *Russia, a Marxist Analysis* (London, 1962); Charles Bettelheim, *On the Transition to Socialism* (New York, 1971), and *Class Struggles in the USSR* (New York, 1976, 1978), 2 vols. The official Chinese position: *How the Soviet Revisionists Carry Out All-round Restoration of Capitalism in the USSR* (Peking, 1968).

Europe and China have strenuously defended the idea that these are socialist countries, in spite of the survival of commodity production, money, different social classes and the state, if necessary by stating frankly that Marx and Engels were wrong on what socialism would be like, or could not predict it exactly. Their definition of socialism is reduced to a single argument: the prevalence of social property of the means of production. This reduction of socialism to a single aspect of social organization has been repeatedly submitted to severe criticism which is by and large correct. We would add to that traditional criticism that the survival of commodity production implies many limitations to the nature of social (collective) property too, which makes it incongruent with the substance of social property characteristic for a socialist society.

The solution of the difficulty lies, in our opinion, in understanding the nature of the post-capitalist societies as societies in transition between capitalism and socialism, in which commodity production still survives but is no more generalized, in which the law of value still operates but no more rules, in which planning is already possible but perforce still imperfect. The emergence of a privileged bureaucracy which manages the state, the society and the economy of these countries has frozen their progress towards socialism and compounded the contradictions inherent in the transition period.

The repeated debates in the USSR on the nature of 'socialist' commodity production – the latest phase of which is the Kronrod controversy, in which the old Soviet economist actually argues that the law of value is not a capitalist survival or the product of a dual property system, state property and cooperative property in agriculture, but an organic product of socialism itself[67] – only testifies to the objective nature of the contradiction and the impossibility to 'think it away', whatever the political and material needs to try and do so.

These needs – i.e., the severe limitations on free critical scientific analysis and debate imposed by the rule of the

[67] See Marie Lavigne, 'La société socialiste avancée', in Marie Lavigne, ed., *Economie politique de la planification en système socialiste* (Paris: Economica, 1978).

bureaucracy – have until recently inhibited any creative development of Marxist thought inside the post-capitalist societies themselves. Since the late 1960s and the early 1970s this has changed, however, and in Yugoslavia, the GDR, the Czechoslovak Socialist Republic, Poland, Hungary and China, independent Marxist thinkers have appeared who try, with the tools of Marxist analysis, to understand the reality and the laws of motion of the economy of their own countries. The most impressive of them, up to now, has been Rudolf Bahro, although a special mention should also be made of the sociologists around the Yugoslav *Praxis* group, the Czech Petr Uhl, and several of the more radical socialist economists and sociologists emerging in and around *Solidarnosc* in Poland.[68]

It is fitting to conclude that, after one hundred years of development determined both by its own inner logic and by the impact of world history on it, Marxist economic analysis still basically evolves around key questions of human destiny. Is the subordination of humanity to severe and alienating 'objective social laws' the definite and unavoidable price it has to pay for its increasing emancipation from dependence upon blind natural forces? Can mankind become master of its own social fate, consciously determine its own future, mould its own nature? Can exploitation of man by man, oppressive class society, social inequality, social division of labour, the state, massive violence, wars, be overcome? Marx's answer was: yes, through a regime of associated producers, on a high level of development of the productive forces, with the withering away of commodity production and money, i.e., through world socialism. Nothing in the historical evidence of the last hundred years disproves the scientifically realistic nature of that assumption. But final proof will only come from practical corroboration.

[68] Rudolf Bahro, *Die Alternative* (Berlin, 1978); Petr Uhl, *Le Socialisme emprisonné* (Paris, 1980).

Philosophy

Roy Edgley

Some questions

Marx died a hundred years ago but is still very much alive and kicking. Though he did some of his greatest work in the British Museum, Marx's work is no museum-piece. It lives on in Marxism. It is for that reason, as the founder, with Engels, of Marxism, that Marx is commemorated. But Marxism did not spring complete from Marx's head. It developed, through his own life, in relation to the European culture that was the historical antecedent and contemporary context of his work; and since his death it has continued to develop in the real movement in which Marx's work has survived and grown in the work of others. Marxism is a contemporary reality. In Marx's own day communism haunted Europe. Today Marxism haunts the whole globe.

What then is the relation between the work of Marx and of Marxism on the one hand, and philosophy on the other? How did his work respond to the European philosophical tradition as it had developed up to and into his own lifetime, and how has Marxism responded since? In particular, how does Marxism relate to philosophy today, in our own time and place? It goes without saying that in relation to the richness and diversity of the material my account will necessarily be highly selective and schematic. My main purpose is to identify significant continuities and discontinuities between Marxism and philosophy in ways that will enable me to bring them to focus in a Marxist critique both of some dominant themes in contemporary English philosophy and of some recent Marxist philosophy.

Marxist philosophy? The chief question to be raised is: is there any such thing? The reality of Marxism is most obviously and centrally political. It is a form of socialism, the political movement of working-class struggle for emancipation from capitalism. But what distinguishes Marxism as a type of socialism is its commitment to both scientific theory and a comprehensive radicality in practice and theory: the radical practice of revolutionary politics united with the radical theory of a science of society. The nature of that relation, that unity of theory and practice, is itself a key problem for Marxist practice and theory. Marx himself both exemplified this unity in his own life's work and theorized its necessity in the massive corpus of theory transmitted to us in his writing. It is for that theoretical work that Marx is distinguished. But that theory is centrally science, social science. Though science is a feature of bourgeois and pre-bourgeois culture, in its modern dominant form arising with the birth and growth of capitalism itself, Marx and Engels are firmly committed to the scientific mode of investigating and understanding reality, and indeed regard their type of socialism as superior to other types chiefly on the ground of its scientificity: Engels identifies it as 'scientific socialism'.[1] As such, Marxist theory raises the question raised by the establishment of science in general in European culture: the question whether science supersedes philosophy as a form of thought, as it seems to supersede religion; and if not, what the place and role of philosophy is in Marxism, in particular its relation to Marxist science; and thus the relation of both to political practice, especially the Marxist practice of revolutionary politics. The question is not simply that of the relation of Marxist science to a possible Marxist philosophy, but also the question of the relation of Marxist theory, including its philosophy if any, to philosophy in general, including non-Marxist and specifically bourgeois philosophy. Marx and Marxism, as Marx himself frequently acknowledges, are heavily indebted to the European philosophical tradition, especially to Aristotle, to the materialism of the Scientific Revolution and the Enlightenment, and to Hegel. Nevertheless, Marxism radically transforms this inheritance and in crucial ways opposes it. Just as Marxist political practice opposes

---

[1] K. Marx, F. Engels and V. Lenin, *The Essential Left* (London: George Allen and Unwin, 1960), p. 105.

bourgeois political practice, so Marxist theory in general opposes bourgeois theory. If Marxist social science opposes bourgeois forms of thought and theory in economics, politics, sociology and historiography, is there a Marxist philosophy that opposes bourgeois philosophy?

- There seem to be three general possibilities. Either there is a distinctive Marxist philosophy that opposes bourgeois philosophy, perhaps as Marxist social science opposes the bourgeois social sciences. Or there is a philosophy in Marxism that is not distinctively Marxist, a philosophy Marxism shares with bourgeois thought, the opposition between Marxist and bourgeois theory being at the scientific level. Or there is no such thing as philosophy of any kind in Marxism because Marxism opposes bourgeois philosophy by opposing philosophy as such. Only the first possibility would allow us to claim clearly and unequivocally that Marx and Marxism make a contribution to philosophy. The second would deny that. The third might allow the claim, but only in a Pickwickian sense: it would imply that Marx's contribution to philosophy was a contribution to its supersession.

The existence of a Marxist philosophy, it must be admitted, is more doubtful than the existence of a Marxist social science. Nevertheless, Marxist social science does not exist as a Marxist form of the special social sciences, of economics, political science, sociology and history; and it does not oppose these bourgeois social sciences in a straightforward way. Thus there is no Marxist economics in the sense in which there is bourgeois economics, and that for a general reason that divides into two, namely the specialization of intellectual labour in our class-divided society. This specialization is, on the one hand, a division not only between intellectual and manual labour but also between theory and practice, particularly political practice; and on the other hand a multiple division within the field of intellectual labour or theory, the division in which the various 'subjects' or 'disciplines' are constituted. Thus bourgeois economics is an academic subject, an intellectual discipline on its own understanding sharply separated both from other subjects, such as political science and history, and also from political practice. The opposition of Marxism to the bourgeois forms of thought in these specialist subjects is partly opposition to their very form as specialist subjects. Marxism thus does not oppose these disciplines on their very own ground, establishing an alternative set of such specialisms. That ground, this specialist form, is itself, according to Marxism, mystificatory. At the theoretical level Marxism develops a unified theory in which the real relations between the economic, the political and the historical are made explicit and understood. It is for this reason that the subjects most hospitable to Marxism under capitalism have been sociology and history. Sociology aims to be a social science that is general and comprehensive. History studies the specific and concrete, and when it resists its consequent anti-theoretical tendencies finds an application for ideas from any of the special sciences. But even these subjects standardly remain academically theoretical, remote from acknowledged and explicit involvement in practical politics.

Oddly enough, there is here, arising from that original doubt about the existence of a Marxist philosophy, the beginning of an argument for a significant and positive relation between Marxism and philosophy, and one that has in it some truth about the actual relation between them as it occurs both historically and within Marx's own development. To see what this relation might be, I must first outline a preliminary answer to the question that can't be any longer kept at bay: what is philosophy? That itself is a heavily contested problem of a historico-philosophical kind, set by the changing shapes that philosophy has taken both in its explicit conception and implicitly in the practices of the philosophers. Moreover, these changes have been changes not simply in philosophy itself but also in the rest of the intellectual and cultural formation and even the rest of the social order. A history of philosophy must also be, at least in part, a history of science, of religion, of morality, of politics, of art, in a word of those 'subjects' that have been considered sometimes part of philosophy, sometimes different from it, and sometimes themselves as objects of philosophical inquiry. If we take philosophy in its explicit intellectual and linguistic form, as a type of argumentative thought and theory, the most general historical change that has occurred has been the effect of the growing division of intellectual labour, the development of specialisms. Having begun as an all-embracing intellectual practice, philosophy, partly as a result of its own activity in the establishment of distinctive specialisms, especially science, is now one subject among others, its scope drastically reduced. Nevertheless, through all its historical variations it has tended to display certain constant characteristics that can indicate if not define it relatively to other non-philosophical types of inquiry and argument.

Etymologically the word 'philosophy' is Greek and means 'love of wisdom'. Wisdom was the exercise of reason in deep and persistent questioning. What philosophy questioned, and thus both presupposed and defined itself by opposition to, were ordinary everyday untheoretical ideas commonly taken for granted. Being the exercise of wisdom and reason, philosophy claimed intellectual authority or supremacy, but was not restricted to any special field of inquiry. This initial generality reflected a conception of philosophy as a (potentially) unified synoptic system of ideas about a unified total reality, the cosmos. However, the unity of both thought and cosmos was differentiated, and different philosophers explored and emphasized different areas. For the three greatest philosophers of ancient Greece, Socrates, Plato and Aristotle, the notion of wisdom, and thus philosophy, was centrally that of practical wisdom, and thus moral and political philosophy. This type of wisdom was understood as self-knowledge, knowledge of the self in society by contrast with knowledge about the rest of the cosmos. But theories about the rest of the cosmos, the cosmologies (as we now call them) of such thinkers as Thales and Anaximander, were still identified as part of that single unity, philosophy.

This distinction within philosophy was later formalized as a distinction between 'ethics' and 'natural philosophy'. At the same time a third branch of philosophy was recognized, metaphysics. 'Metaphysics' was originally a name given to a work of Aristotle's that came after his *Physics*, but it came to designate a subject that studies a reality beyond physics, an eternal and unchanging world accessible not to the senses but only to pure thought or reason, *a priori*. This idea of metaphysics, though that of one branch of philosophy among others, was in some way implicit in the whole project of philosophy in general. Even when concerned with practical questions, as in ethics, the enterprise of philosophy was always an expression of discontent with ordinary commonsense ideas, and involved an attempt to think things out more rationally and adequately, and thus at a more fundamental or radical level, often explicitly at the linguistic level of key concepts or categories such as 'justice' or 'knowledge'. The effect was a move towards theory, towards generality and abstractness, towards the definition or redefinition of basic categories and principles; and a tendency to regard this process as disclosing, as its source of authority, a genuine supersensible reality beyond the superficial appearances of perception which satisfied everyday ideas. Such a reality was often thought of as in nature akin to ideas themselves. With or without this metaphysical ontology, philosophy came to be primarily or wholly a study of *ideas*. This tendency was confirmed in the modern period, as natural philosophy developed into natural science. Through the Cartesian 'way of ideas' philosophy became centrally and dominantly epistemology, either rationalist as in Descartes or empiricist and psychological as in Hume.

The dichotomies involved in these processes of philosophy, between sense-perception and reason, concrete and abstract, particular and universal, contingency and necessity, change and permanence, material and ideal, reality and thought, practice and theory, superficial and fundamental, and appearance and reality, are richly present in classical philosophy, and not simply as distinctions but as hierarchical distinctions, of inferiority and superiority, subordination and authority. They have formed the staple themes of philosophy ever since. As Marxists were later to point out, their material condition, a condition of the emergence of philosophy itself in ancient Greece, was a hierarchically divided class society, with a top layer of aristocratic citizens and a bottom layer of slaves or workers, the slaves performing 'menial' manual labour to provide material necessities and thus freeing their masters to engage in intellectual labour. Among the consequences of this class division of labour was a tendency for practical questions to appear in the thinking of the classical philosophers, indeed of philosophers ever since, not as questions of material production but focally as questions of moral and political practice, even of the philosophical 'practice' of contemplation, types of activity suitable for gentlemen. What is also evident, however, is that the dualities I have listed as emerging into focus in classical philosophy are also pervasively present in Marx's thought, though transformed from a philosophical into a social scientific key.

To return, then, to that question of Marxism's mode of opposition to the bourgeois social sciences: there are two relevant constant characteristics that philosophy has tended to display throughout its variations. First is its intellectual depth, its aim and claim to be basic or fundamental in the whole order of thought, and thus in authority over the rest of thought. Second, connected closely with that, is its generality and thus interconnectedness or unity. Philosophy asks questions whose answers are otherwise presupposed or taken for granted, typically over a wide field of discourse; and consequently it tries to unearth, in our basic categories of thought, buried assumptions of a general kind, to question them, and perhaps to consider possible alternatives. In the process it seeks for itself the unity of a 'synoptic view', studying the relations of matters otherwise considered separately. In opposing the divided specialisms of bourgeois social science Marxism has a 'philosophical' character in these respects. It seeks unity, both within theory and between theory and practice, and in doing so it opposes the bourgeois social sciences at a fundamental or radical intellectual level. Specifically Marxist theory opposes bourgeois economics, for example, not, or not only or centrally, at the level of observed fact, but at the deeper conceptual level, the level of the concepts or language in terms of which those observations are interpreted and theoretically appropriated. Thus, for instance, whereas bourgeois thought separates the economic from the political, Marxism reveals their internal interconnection, and in the process develops a conceptual framework very different from that of bourgeois economics and political science. This conceptual differentiation may extend down to those theoretically basic categories that philosophy has taken as *a priori* and thus as its own object of inquiry, such as knowledge and reason. Would it follow that Marxism, in opposing the bourgeois social sciences at the scientific level, opposes the philosophy embedded in those bourgeois sciences by incorporating its own distinctive philosophy? Or could it be the case that just as Marxism opposes the bourgeois social sciences not on their own ground but on some other, so it opposes bourgeois philosophy, both within and outside social science, not on its own ground, as philosophy, but on some other?

Within the Marxist movement itself the latter option, with its implication that there is no Marxist philosophy, Marxism opposing philosophy as such, has maintained a fairly constant if sometimes shadowy presence. It has been explicitly and enthusiastically seized by various types of 'vulgar Marxism', more or less anti-intellectual, which have tended to portray all abstract ideas, or perhaps all non-scientific ideas, as pejoratively ideological. But it also occurs in more respected versions of Marxism in uneasy partnership with the former option, with its claim that there is a distinctive Marxist philosophy. Indeed, in Marxism since Marx's death it is this view that has been dominant, and it moreover provides us with a widely accepted way of classifying historically the main phases of the Marxist movement. At a very general level, there have been two influential forms that this Marxist philosophy has taken, the earlier more closely connected with the later work of Engels, the later with the earlier work of Marx.

Dialectical materialism

The earliest view to develop and become influential in the Marxist movement was that Marxist philosophy is dialectical materialism ('diamat') and that this philosophy is related to Marxist science, namely historical materialism, in one or more ways, as the philosophy of that science: as a 'world-view' generalized from and supported by that science, or as an ontology on which that science is based, or as an epistemological foundation or methodology of that science. The first generation of Marxism after Marx's death, up to the Russian Revolution, was dominated by the two most famous and influential books of the founders, Marx's *Capital* and Engels' *Anti-Dühring*, and these two books were widely thought of in accordance with that division of labour, the former the basic science of Marxist economics, the latter the related philosophy of Marxism.

Dialectical materialism is the union of the two main streams of philosophy that Marx inherits and transforms: the materialism of the Scientific Revolution, especially in its English and French Enlightenment forms, and the dialectics of Hegel. The combination of these in dialectical materialism involves Marx's rejection both of traditional scientific and Enlightenment materialism as non-dialectical, i.e., as 'metaphysical' or 'mechanical', and of Hegel's dialectics as idealist. The element of scientific materialism claims that reality is wholly or basically material, not basically, or constituted by, thought or ideas, as Hegel holds, and is governed by natural laws that science seeks to discover. The element of dialectics claims that this reality is neither a static substance, nor a mass of atoms or subsystems that are related to one another purely externally, nor a process of cyclical or repetitive change, nor a process of merely gradual evolutionary change; on the contrary, it is a causally interconnected totality, both internally unified and contradictory, driven by its contradictions in a process of inevitable developmental change, revolutionary as well as evolutionary, and in its revolutionary changes bringing forth genuine qualitative novelty. The laws governing nature, society and human thought are dialectical in that sense, and science is the attempt to discover them. As a scientific study of capitalism, *Capital*, for instance, discloses that bourgeois society has a material base, its economy, which is subject to irreconcilable contradictions, and that the gradual intensification of these contradictions will inevitably produce a revolutionary transformation of the whole society from capitalism to socialism. *Capital* is an attempt to formulate the laws of such development.

This account raises many problems. The most relevant one

here is whether, and if so how, it sustains the claim that there is a distinctive Marxist philosophy. It's clear that the formulation of diamat as a unique combination of materialism and dialectic was first put forward and argued for in Marxism, and that it has remained more or less peculiar to the Marxist tradition. However, there is a way in which the very content of diamat itself both resists the claim that it is distinctively philosophical and suggests that its confinement to Marxism is a historical contingency. For the laws of dialectical materialism are said to characterize the whole of reality and thus to be validated by science in general, including the natural sciences, at least as they advance from their earlier 'mechanical' and ahistorical phase into their mature modern forms. Dialectical materialism is consequently not a philosophy in any sense in which philosophy is distinct from science, nor is it distinctive even of Marxist science.

Engels in fact provides a view about philosophy and its relation to science that throws light on this aspect of the matter. In some passages in the *Anti-Dühring* he argues that philosophy has been superseded by science and in particular is no longer necessary to Marxism.[2] It's strange, on the face of it, that a book with such a theme should be regarded as formulating a Marxist philosophy. However, under the surface of the text, and more or less explicit in the so-called 'Old Preface', written originally for the first edition of *Anti-Dühring* but rejected in favour of another and later assigned to Engels' materials for his *Dialectics of Nature*, is the germ of an idea that might give some support to the claim that there is a philosophy in Marxism, and one capable of being given a Marxist twist. Apparently conceiving of science as having typically employed 'the methods of empiricism', i.e., observation and experiment, and, possibly in consequence, being typically divided into specialisms, independent fields of scientific investigation, Engels distinguishes science from 'theory' and 'theoretical thinking', which is 'the sphere of what hitherto was called philosophy'. This 'theory' seeks

  to bring the individual spheres of knowledge into the correct

[2] F. Engels, *Anti-Dühring* (London: Lawrence and Wishart, 1955), pp. 40, 56.

connection with one another. In doing so, however, natural science enters the field of theory and here the methods of empiricism will not work, here only theoretical thinking can be of assistance ... This natural capacity [for theoretical thinking] must be developed, improved, and for its improvement there is as yet no other means than the study of previous philosophy.[3]

The implication of the whole passage is that philosophy can supply two connected necessities for the fuller development of science: a mode of thought that is non-empirical and which, being so, can bring the separate scientific specialisms into coherent unity. Speculating, we can say that this philosophical and theoretical mode of thought would be conceptual rather than observational and experimental: it would examine the currently established results in the various special sciences and try to discern structural analogies between the different areas or aspects of reality as described by them, identifying these analogies in terms of very general concepts or categories. It is this mode of thought that is exemplified by Engels' own argument. His defensive references to 'natural philosophy' might be regarded as allowing this title to be adapted to refer to this theoretical thinking. He seems to regard classical formal logic and the 'metaphysical' materialism of the Scientific Revolution's 'mechanical philosophy' as jointly constituting the 'natural philosophy' of an earlier stage of science, now superseded by the latest stage, in which the sciences have begun to develop into dialectical form. Dialectical materialism would be 'natural philosophy' in this sense.

The anti-empiricist view that science has theoretical levels and concepts that are not reducible to empirical elements is one that Engels shares with Marx, as we shall see. It is an idea that has become familiar in recent English-speaking philosophy of science through the works of Kuhn and Feyerabend.[4] Engels'

---

[3] The passage from which these quotations are taken is in Engels, *op. cit.*, pp. 457-8.

[4] T. Kuhn, *The Structure of Scientific Revolutions* (Chicago and London: The University of Chicago Press, 1962), and P. Feyerabend, *Against Method* (London: New Left Books, 1975).

account differs from theirs in two important respects, Marx agreeing with him on the latter but not on the former. First, he is enough of an empiricist to regard 'the methods of empiricism' as adequate for the special sciences and to suppose that it is only at the level of their unification that they are not appropriate. Second, as a materialist he rejects tendencies towards idealism:

> ... in theoretical natural science ... the interconnections are not to be built into the facts but to be discovered in them, and when discovered to be verified as far as possible by experiment.[5]

Engels means, I take it, that theoretical natural science, though it constructs the concepts of those interconnections, does not constitute the interconnections themselves but asserts that they exist, independently of such theory, in material reality. Combined with the claim that these interconnections are not (wholly) empirical, and that they must be verified by experiment '*as far as possible*', this view reveals itself as a version of the 'scientific realism' that has lately been emerging in English-speaking philosophy of science in reaction to Kuhn and Feyerabend.[6] In that case, 'theoretical natural science' would be a more accurate name for what Engels has in mind than 'natural philosophy'. For though philosophy might supply the perspective of conceptual unification, the resulting concepts and theories could not be regarded as authorizing, or providing a foundation for, the empirical content of the special sciences. On the contrary, the argument would run in the opposite direction. It would not be the case that the theory was a generalization of which the results of the special sciences were instances, but it would nevertheless be those results that

[5] F. Engels, *op. cit.*, p. 464.
[6] R. Harré, *Principles of Scientific Thinking* (London: Macmillan, 1970) and *The Philosophies of Science* (Oxford University Press, 1972); R. Bhaskar, *A Realist Theory of Science* (Leeds: Leeds Books, 1975) and *The Possibility of Naturalism* (Brighton: Harvester Press, 1979); R. Keat and J. Urry, *Social Theory as Science* (London: Routledge and Kegan Paul, 1975); T. Benton, *Philosophical Foundations of the Three Sociologies* (London: Routledge and Kegan Paul, 1977).

supported the theory, not vice versa. That would be compatible with Engels' heuristic conception of the role of philosophy and with the theme of the supersession of philosophy by science.

Would there, in any case, be anything distinctively Marxist about this dialectical materialism? As far as the content of the theory is concerned, there would not, as I have said. That content, according to Engels, is not peculiar to Marxism but evolves in the natural sciences independently of Marxism. It is Engels' *argument* that is Marxist. It is an argument for dialectical materialism that is at the same time an argument for Marxism. Its success depends precisely on the claim that the content of dialectical materialism is not distinctively Marxist. What then is the overall structure of that argument? As a science of society, Marxism opposes other existing forms of social science, branding them as bourgeois ideology. But as a science of society it does not oppose the existing forms of natural science. On the contrary, though these also have been developed within bourgeois society by bourgeois intellectuals, and even in positive interrelationship with the technology of the capitalist mode of production, Marxism ascribes to them a cognitive success and authority that it needs for its own purposes. The social sciences in general, beginning their development in the late eighteenth and early nineteenth centuries, some two centuries after the birth of modern natural science, inevitably tended to take the natural sciences as their model and thus sought to share that cognitive authority. Marxism itself relies on that authority in claiming to be genuinely scientific and in this respect superior to both other forms of socialism and other social theories. Engels' argument is one way of trying to justify that claim: of seeking to recruit the cognitive authority of the natural sciences to the support of Marxism, and at the same time depriving of such support other cultural and political tendencies currently claiming it, such as Dühring's work, or 'social Darwinism'.[7] In sharing dialectical materialism with the advanced natural sciences, Marxism shares their claim to scientificity. In particular, Engels'

[7] See T. Benton's 'Natural Science and Cultural Struggle: Engels and Philosophy and the Natural Sciences', in J. Mepham and D.-H. Ruben, eds., *Issues in Marxist Philosophy* (Brighton: Harvester Press, 1979), vol. II.

commitment to a 'dialectics of nature' represents his commitment, in dialectical materialist terms, to the characteristically empiricist doctrine of 'the unity of science': the doctrine that the social sciences are or should be structurally similar to the natural sciences. Furthermore, these considerations suggest good ideological reasons why explicit acceptance of dialectical materialism would remain distinctive of Marxism. The 'historical contingency' of this fact would in reality be an ideological necessity: the necessity for bourgeois thought to oppose Marxism by resisting its claim to scientific status. Engels' account of dialectical materialism, as an argument in this field, has a polemical point and a rationale that is specifically political.

How then does dialectical materialism deal with that other problem I mentioned, the problem of the relation not of science to philosophy but of theory to (political) practice? Historically, two philosophical difficulties on this topic have been associated with dialectical materialism, both resulting from its tendency to represent Marxist social science as having the same general structure as natural science and thus as facing the same philosophical problems.

First, the conception of such a science as discovering causal laws explaining change, especially laws of a materialist kind, the material base determining thought and ideas, seems to imply an inevitability about the coming transformation of capitalism that makes political initiatives impossible and unnecessary, or at any rate merely epiphenomenal. This is 'economic determinism'. The revolution, on this view, appears less a political act, the culminating point of the class struggle, than simply the collapse of the capitalist system inevitably brought about by its own internal contradictions. This fatalism, apparently inconsistent with revolutionary politics, seems to be encouraged by Marx's own Preface to the first German edition and the Afterword to the second German edition of *Capital*. In the *Anti-Dühring* Engels offers a 'dialectical' solution of the problem seen as the problem of freedom and necessity.[8] He characterizes freedom as 'the appreciation of necessity',

[8] F. Engels, *op. cit.*, pp. 157–9.

arguing that the scientific discovery of natural necessities historically expands our freedom by expanding our control over ourselves and nature. Knowledge is power, and as it grows it thus extends rather than diminishes the possibilities for effective action. Now it is certainly the case that there is no inconsistency between deterministic inevitability and revolutionary politics, since revolutionary action itself may be inevitably determined. But the persistent appearance of inconsistency, here due to the tendency to exclude political action from the overall process of material transformation, needs to be explained. The explanation of that, I think, would also reveal why Engels' Hegelian argument, though a beginning, does not get to the root of the problem. For in the natural science model, the action we take in applying causal laws to the control of the material world is not itself the topic of those laws, and what is determined, therefore, appears as something other than such action. The problem is not solved if we take as typical the case in which the relevant knowledge is about the necessitation of something else. At the root of the problem is the question of precisely how that knowledge itself necessitates action: knowledge of other things may be power over those other things, but exactly how does that knowledge itself exert its power over us, i.e., over our own actions? The problem occurs because of the specific nature of that type of necessitation. It would not be inconsistent with a dialectical approach to regard that type of necessitation both as qualitatively different, and as historically emergent, from the causal necessity present in inorganic nature. But it requires a conception of social science that differentiates it in important ways from natural science, a conception I shall say more about later.

That conception and these considerations also have a crucial bearing on what, from the point of view of orthodox dialectical materialism, appears as a different, second, problem. Even if (Marxist) science is *compatible* with the effectiveness and rationality of (political) action, how can such a science *imply* any practical prescriptions and thus guide action? How can it, in other words, tell us what is to be done, whether to attack and destroy capitalism or to support and defend it? Marxism's commitment to science has always put it under strong intellectual pressure from the most powerful epistemologies and philosophies of science thrown up by the development of natural science in the Scientific Revolution, namely Kantianism on the one hand and empiricism and positivism on the other. Philosophically reflecting natural science's historical struggle for autonomy against the unified totality of the medieval view, and thus for independence not only from religion and perhaps philosophy, but also from morality, politics and art, both tend to represent science as value-free. Science is factual and theoretical, not evaluative and practical: scientific theories describe, explain and predict reality, and as such have a practical application as technology, prescribing means to ends, but in themselves have no other implications for practice, and in particular do not evaluate reality and are neutral with respect to moral, political and aesthetic values. A representative of this view from the first generation of Marxism is Rudolph Hilferding, one of the outstanding theoreticians of the Second International. In the introduction to *Finance Capital*, originally published in 1909, he characterizes Marxist theory as 'a scientific, objective and free science, without value judgments' and argues that 'insight into the correctness of Marxism, which includes insight into the necessity of socialism, is in no way a result of value judgments and has no implications for practical behaviour.'[9] Given this view of Marxist science, socialist political activity was thought to require, in addition to that science, a set of values, such as those of equality and freedom. Moreover, in submission to an idea essential to Kantianism, though shared by many forms of empiricism, namely that the ultimate arbiter of practice is morality, these socialist political values were often construed as *moral* values, sometimes Kantian,[10] sometimes utilitarian.[11]

These two philosophical problems are sometimes thought to result from a mechanistic or 'metaphysical' degeneration of Marxist materialism, i.e., from a failure to appreciate fully and

[9] R. Hilferding, *Finance Capital* (London: Routledge and Kegan Paul, 1981).
[10] See references in L. Goldmann, 'Is There a Marxist Sociology?', in *Radical Philosophy*, 1 (January 1972).
[11] L. Trotsky, in *Their Morals and Ours* (New York: Pathfinder Press, 1973), seems to rely on a type of utilitarian socialist morality.

properly its dialectical character. There is something in that. Nevertheless, that tendency is endemic to orthodox dialectical materialism as such because of its reliance on the orthodox model of natural science. I have already noted the general possibility of an ambivalence in Marxism towards natural science: respect for science as a progressive mode of thought, reservation about it as a classic product and intellectually dominant form of bourgeois culture. As I shall suggest later, the materialism of natural science, as standardly understood, is not compatible with its being fully dialectical. This materialism is the orthodox epistemological materialism of natural science, with its distinction between knowing subject and known object, the real material object of scientific thought in its existence independent, and in its nature the contrary opposite, of that thought (or any other); and its dialectic, as a 'dialectic of nature', therefore distinct from and independent of the dialectic of thought itself.

Marxist humanism and 'Western Marxism'

Dialectical materialism, which for Plekhanov and many other members of the first generation of Marxism was the Marxist philosophy that achieved its 'final shape' in Engels' *Anti-Dühring*,[12] became Communist Party orthodoxy after the Russian Revolution in the 'Comintern' period, the time of the Third International. But it was in that period that the orthodoxy began to be subjected to close critical scrutiny from within the Marxist tradition, as the second major conception of Marxist philosophy developed: its conception as Marxist humanism. Politically, this phase had some overlap with the thought both of the greatest of all Soviet 'dissidents', Trotsky, and of the outstanding Italian Marxist of the period, Gramsci. But as the

[12] G. Plekhanov, *Fundamental Problems of Marxism* (London: Lawrence and Wishart, 1969), p. 23.

distinctive stream of second-generation Marxism, this 'Western Marxism' began with Lukács and Korsch in the 1920s and continued through the work of the Frankfurt School and into the 'praxis' Marxism of contemporary Yugoslav dissidents, with Sartre's attempt to fuse Marxism with existentialist philosophy an extreme form of the tendency.[13] The significant political context was the watershed of the Russian Revolution itself and its aftermath: the failure of the Western European working class, the working class of advanced capitalism where the Marxist revolution was most expected, to follow the lead of Lenin and the Bolsheviks, and the subsequent (and partly consequent) failure of the Russian Revolution itself as it degenerated into Stalinist tyranny and party bureaucracy. Tsarist Russia had not been an advanced capitalist society. The antiquated and rotten condition of its state and economy both made successful revolution possible and necessitated afterwards, especially under the pressure of hostility and competition from surrounding capitalist states, a rapid and ruthless process of industrial modernization to bring the country to technological parity with its competitors. Meanwhile, in those Western European societies the prospect of working-class revolution receded and failed in the teeth of a type of economy and state, advanced industrial capitalism combined with either fascism or liberal democracy, that was very different from Russia under the Tsars, in particular more powerful, especially ideologically.

According to humanist Marxism, natural science is deeply implicated in these oppressive processes of modern societies, whether capitalist or so-called 'communist', and dialectical materialism is insufficiently critical of it. At the economic level natural science is involved as technology, and at all levels its technology is a process of manipulation in which power and

[13] See, e.g., G. Lukács, *History and Class Consciousness* (London: Merlin Press, 1971); K. Korsch, *Marxism and Philosophy* (London: New Left Books, 1970); M. Horkheimer, *Critical Theory* (New York: Seabury Press, 1972); M. Horkheimer and T. Adorno, *Dialectic of Enlightenment* (New York: Seabury Press, 1972); H. Marcuse, *One-Dimensional Man* (London: Routledge and Kegan Paul, 1964); G. Petrovic, *Marx in the Mid-twentieth Century* (New York: Anchor Books, 1967); J.-P. Sartre, *Search for a Method* (New York: Vintage Books, 1968).

domination are exercised over reality in general, including people. Indeed, under the sway of the objectivist materialism of natural science, especially in its mechanistic version, not only the mode of production but society in general becomes 'mechanized': social organization, as Weber argues, becomes rationalized and bureaucratic, and as Marx shows in his conception of 'commodity fetishism' people become less like subjects and more like objects or things. This is the process of 'reification', as Lukács calls it. Mass production, with its ideological counterpart in the ideological institutions of mass communication, the media and advertising, is the production not only of vast quantities of standardized articles of consumption but also of the masses themselves as consumers, the production of a workforce that is standardized and manipulable, and thus anti-revolutionary. Dialectical materialism may break with the mechanical philosophy, the traditional mechanistic materialism associated with the Scientific Revolution, but its continued dependence on the objectivist materialism of natural science, even in a dialectical form, represents the penetration of Marxism by bourgeois ideology. Diamat obscures the need for a Marxist critique of natural science and for the rejection of natural science as a model for Marxist social theory. In particular Marxism must be humanist: it must give central recognition to people as distinctively subjects not objects, i.e., as beings with consciousness and values. Those values are opposed to a science whose theoretical value-neutrality is a mask for its anti-humanist practice under capitalism. Marxist humanism recognizes strict limits on the role and form of any science in society, and opposes the technological manipulation and domination of people (and nature).

This humanism was thus not, like dialectical materialism, simply a philosophy within a Marxist theory that was predominantly scientific. It was, rather, a tendency for Marxist theory to be conceived as itself philosophy rather than science. This philosophy, then, was sharply distinguished not just from science but also from any 'philosophy of science' understood in the traditional and diamat manner. This sense drew on a tradition according to which, as natural science had historically developed as a study of a (primarily) non-human 'objective' reality, a study therefore itself objective, specialized, theoretical and non-evaluative, philosophy had not been superseded but had become (primarily) the investigation and defence, against science if necessary, of the distinctively human, specifically of the everyday, 'subjective', untheoretical and evaluative mode of thought about and understanding of themselves characteristic of the ordinary participants in society. If Marxist theory includes a science, that science must on this view be compatible with this general humanist philosophy, indeed must be embedded within it as a part of that philosophy.

The general culture in which these themes are unmistakably rooted is that of Romanticism. The Romantic reaction against Enlightenment rationalism and the mechanical philosophy associated with natural science and industrialization was a reaction on behalf of subjectivity against objectivity, art and values against science, consciousness, ideas, and feeling against brute matter, the organic against the mechanical. At the level of explicit philosophical theory the chief non-Marxist debt is to the philosophy closest to Romanticism, the German idealist tradition: on the one hand to Kant and Hegel, on the other to the *Geisteswissenschaften*, the hermeneutic version of social inquiry anticipated by Vico but developed chiefly in nineteenth- and twentieth-century Germany by such thinkers as Dilthey and Weber. Hegel conceived of history as the dialectical work of a subject of consciousness, indeed, idealistically as a work *in* consciousness. The hermeneutic philosophy of social inquiry stands in the non-Marxist philosophical tradition as the main alternative to empiricism and its doctrine of the unity of science. It argues that, contrary to empiricism, thought and theory about human and social affairs cannot have the same logic, methodology and epistemology as natural science. Understanding human and social affairs is less like causally explaining them in the manner of natural science and more like understanding ideas and language, i.e., grasping the internal relations that make language and ideas intelligible and meaningful. In fact the language of a society is one of its most fundamental and pervasive social institutions. The detached objective position of the observer, as in empiricism, must therefore be replaced by a closer relationship, involving 'empathy' with, or even full participation in, the matters under investigation. For participants in a society have an understanding of it, as they have an understanding of their own language, that no science can undermine. To the extent that that understanding is implicit rather than explicit, the approach must be philosophical. Whether it is implicit or explicit, that type of understanding is not scientific, at any rate in the natural scientific sense. Is it rational? Romanticism, at least in one of its most prominent versions, objects to reason itself. Weber identifies the culprit as scientific 'rationalization'. The possibility opened up is for a different and more adequate conception of reason than that provided by orthodox philosophy of science, especially of natural science, in particular by empiricism. It is this possibility that I shall pursue in analysing the general 'philosophical' structure of Marx's theory.

In outlining the development and nature of Marxist humanism as Marxist philosophy I have identified both its sociopolitical context and also its antecedents in non-Marxist culture. But there was for this development an equally important antecedent within Marxist culture itself, though one largely unknown to the first generation of Marxism, not generally discovered until after the Russian Revolution. This was the early work of Marx himself, much of which remained unpublished until the 1920s and 1930s. Moreover, Marx had begun his intellectual life as a philosopher, and in that early period had written much in and on philosophy. There was in Marx's life-work a transition from philosophy to science that seems to reflect those general historical transitions in European culture, in which natural philosophy gives birth to natural science and the social and political philosophy of the seventeenth and eighteenth centuries to social science. But the nature of those transitions is problematic. Is philosophy superseded by science? Does philosophy lay the epistemological, methodological, and perhaps ontological foundations of science? Or does philosophy put science in its place within its own totalizing view? Marxist humanism rejects the first and accepts the last suggestion. But whatever the answer, when Marx's early work began to be published the orthodox conception of the philosophy of Marxism as dialectical materialism was put under severe strain. Marx's 'early philosophy', as some had suspected, turned out to be different from the standard version of dialectical materialism. Most adequately represented by the *Economic and Philosophical Manuscripts* of 1844, that philosophy is essentially a type of humanism, strongly influenced by Hegel. One of its central ideas is Marx's version of the typically Hegelian concept of alienation, an apparently evaluative concept and one entirely absent from the *Anti-Dühring*. I will return to that.

In the last decade or two, this early work of Marx, and with it the humanist philosophy of the second generation of Marxism, has come under heavy attack from within the Marxist tradition. Since the second half of the 1960s, widespread radical political dissent has reappeared in the heartland of advanced capitalism, in Western Europe and America, and as the post-war boom of capitalism has conformed to type by staggering into crisis and slump Marxism has revived both inside and outside the Communist Parties, even in England, and even in, or on the margin of, English philosophy.[14] At the theoretical level the most influential tendency has been the reaction, associated with the Italian school of della Volpe, best known in England through the work of Colletti,[15] and with Althusser and his followers in France and elsewhere, against

[14] See the journal *Radical Philosophy*, and a number of books: I. Mészáros, *Marx's Theory of Alienation* (London: Merlin Press, 1970); R. Bhaskar, *A Realist Theory of Science, op. cit.*, and *The Possibility of Naturalism, op. cit.*; R. Keat and J. Urry, *op. cit.*; T. Pateman, *Language, Truth and Politics* (Jean Stroud, 1975); T. Benton, *Philosophical Foundations of the Three Sociologies, op. cit.*; D.-H. Ruben, *Marxism and Materialism* (Brighton: Harvester Press, 1977); G. Cohen, *Karl Marx's Theory of History* (Oxford: Clarendon Press, 1978); A. Wood, *Karl Marx* (London: Routledge and Kegan Paul, 1981); the series edited by J. Mepham and D.-H. Ruben, *op. cit.*; J. Krige, *Science, Revolution and Discontinuity* (Brighton: Harvester Press, 1980); and the series *Philosophy Now* edited by myself (Brighton: Harvester Press, 1976 onwards). My own ideas about Marxism are heavily indebted to these writings and to the Radical Philosophy movement, and on the subject of this article especially to J. Rée, 'Le Marxisme et la Philosophie Analytique', in *Critique* (August–September 1980).
[15] See L. Colletti, *From Rousseau to Lenin* (London: New Left Books, 1972) and *Marxism and Hegel* (London: New Left Books, 1973).

the Hegelianism and idealism of humanist Marxism. Althusser[16] has criticized both the humanist philosophy of this type of Marxism, and with it the high estimate of Marx's early humanist philosophy. For Althusser this early philosophy is neither an epistemological foundation of Marx's later science, the economic theory of *Capital*, nor is it a general matrix within which that science is put in its place. Marx's transition from his early philosophy to his later science, according to Althusser, is a transition from an immature form of thought that is rejected in favour of a development to a mature science. Althusser thus shares with the humanists he criticizes the view that Marx's early philosophy should be clearly distinguished both from his science and from philosophy of science. But this is not a rejection of philosophy as such. Althusser is himself a philosopher, and in his view genuine Marxist philosophy is implicit in Marx's later theoretical science, and can and should be made explicit by analysis. As with dialectical materialism, then, and in contrast to humanist Marxism, Althusser's conception of Marxist theory is that it is primarily and dominantly science, and that Marxist philosophy is 'philosophy of science'. This is not, however, as with diamat, a study of the content of the results of the advanced natural sciences that reveals, by a process of conceptual unification, a common world-picture that they share with Marxism, the world-picture of dialectical materialism. It is, rather, philosophy of science in a sense nearer to the orthodox discipline of that name, epistemology; though conceived by Althusser in a distinctively Marxist way, with theory a socio-historical practice of production, as 'theory of theoretical practice'. The tendency here is for this 'philosophy of science' to be understood as a Marxist *science* of science. But in his later self-criticism Althusser qualifies this doctrine with something that echoes further the humanist tendency he opposes: though still philosophy of science, Marxist philosophy differs from science in having a normative (ideological) character, specifically a political

[16] See L. Althusser, *For Marx* (Harmondsworth: Penguin Books, 1969) and *Reading 'Capital'* (London: New Left Books, 1970).

character. In distinction from Marxist science, Marxist philosophy is 'politics in the field of theory',[17] 'class struggle in theory'.[18]

Philosophy and science, idealism and materialism

There is a paradox in Western Marxism. Itself predominantly philosophical, it regards Marx's early work as philosophy. Yet though that early work begins as philosophy, as Marx's own subject and the one he conceives as having intellectual authority over all others, it soon develops a persistently anti-philosophical theme: the theme of 'the end of philosophy'. I have said that Marxism shares with non-Marxist thought the problem of the survival and identity of philosophy. It might seem that Marxism shares the empiricist view of the end of philosophy: that philosophy as a substantive discipline is superseded by science because the only substantive concepts and theories are empirical and thus not philosophical, so that philosophy turns out to have been an intellectual blind alley. That is not Marx's view. For him the end of philosophy is both its supersession and its realization. But his thinking on this subject reveals two distinct phases, and it is in the second that the theme develops a hostility to philosophy that is absent from the earlier phase.

Marx's early allegiance in philosophy was to a romantic idealism that followed Kant and Fichte, but he soon came under the influence of Hegel. This was a change from one idealism to another, but the difference is significant. His earlier idealism conceived the ideal and the real, 'ought' and 'is', as opposed but widely separated, and located philosophy itself on the side of the ideal as something withdrawn from and superior to a hostile and pedestrian reality. Under Hegel's influence 'I left behind the idealism which ... I had nourished with that of Kant and

---

[17] L. Althusser, *Essays in Self-Criticism* (London: New Left Books, 1976), p. 68.
[18] Ibid., p. 142.

Fichte, and came to seek the idea in the real itself.'[19] But for Hegel's disciples, the Young Hegelians, this Hegelian unity of ideal and real was ambiguous, and on the topic that preoccupied them, religion and its social and political instantiation in the Church, split them between a conservative right and a progressive left. For the former, the real was ideal or rational. For the latter, the unity that Marx spoke of seeking was compatible with a continuing hostility between ideal and real, a hostility in which philosophy, as rational ideal, retained its ancient supremacy, now over the real itself, and thus expressed its hostility to the real in the form of criticism. The aim of criticism was to bring the real into conformity with the ideal, that is, to realize philosophy and thus eliminate any further need for it. The end (aim) of philosophy was its end (finish), its disappearance in a process of transcendence. Thus Marx's earliest declaration of allegiance to the proletariat sees political emancipation as requiring the union of the proletariat with philosophy:

> Just as philosophy finds its *material* weapons in the proletariat, so the proletariat finds its *intellectual* weapons in philosophy... The *emancipation of the German* is the *emancipation of man*. The *head* of this emancipation is philosophy, its *heart* the *proletariat*. Philosophy cannot realize itself without the transcendence [Aufhebung] of the proletariat, and the proletariat cannot transcend itself without the realization [Verwirklichung] of philosophy.[20]

In its general form, as I shall show, this call for the unity of the theoretical and the material in the cause of political emancipation, and with it the realization and transcendence of the theoretical, never changes in Marx. What changes as he moves from this first to the second phase of his theme of the end of philosophy is that in the position of theory philosophy is replaced by science. Philosophy, which historically had helped

[19] From a letter to his father, published in D. McLellan, *Karl Marx: Selected Writings* (Oxford University Press, 1977), p. 8.
[20] K. Marx, *Introduction to a Contribution to the Critique of Hegel's Philosophy of Right*, in *Early Writings*, ed. L. Colletti (Harmondsworth: Penguin Books, 1975), p. 257.

to bring science to birth in the Scientific Revolution, in the process attacking the religion-dominated intellectual order of the feudal era, and which in the Enlightenment, especially in France, had carried the fight to the Church itself, shifted in German idealism and the Romantic movement into the defence of religion against science. Like Feuerbach, Marx rejected religion and came to reject idealism in general, Hegelian as well as Kantian, in favour of materialism. It was this rejection of religion and idealism and acceptance of materialism that he tended to represent as a rejection of philosophy as such in favour of science:

> Feuerbach's great achievement is:
> (1) The proof that philosophy is nothing else but religion rendered into thought and expounded by thought, hence equally to be condemned as another form and manner of existence of the estrangement of the essence of man.
> (2) The establishment of *true materialism* and of *real science* . . . [21]

> Philosophy and the study of the actual world have the same relation to one another as masturbation and sexual love. [22]

The thought here seems to be not that the transcendence of philosophy is its realization, nor that 'the study of the actual world' is founded on philosophy, but rather that philosophy as such is a sterile substitute for real thinking. But here are two slightly less hostile remarks:

> The philosophers have only *interpreted* the world in various ways; the point is to *change* it. [23]

> When reality is depicted, philosophy as an independent branch of knowledge loses its medium of existence. [24]

[21] K. Marx, *Economic and Philosophic Manuscripts of 1844*, ed. D. Struik (London: Lawrence and Wishart, 1970), p. 172.
[22] K. Marx and F. Engels, *The German Ideology*, ed. C. Arthur (London: Lawrence and Wishart, 1970), p. 103.
[23] K. Marx, *Theses on Feuerbach*, ed. C. Arthur as supplementary text to *The German Ideology, op. cit.*, p. 123.
[24] K. Marx and F. Engels, *The German Ideology, op. cit.*, p. 48.

The implication of this last quotation is that philosophy may in some sense survive, but not independently and as such, only within the medium of a different discipline in which 'reality is depicted', namely science. The former suggests that such a science, unlike philosophy, would not simply interpret the world but would help to change it. The theme of the end of philosophy thus comes to be understood not, as in the Young Hegelian period, as its direct realization in reality, but as its 'realization' at the theoretical level in a mode of inquiry that absorbs, transforms and supersedes it. This mode of inquiry is science. I shall point out various ways in which this seems to be an accurate description of Marx's own procedure.

There is a problem here. If idealism is philosophical, is it not the case that materialism also is a philosophy? Materialism was and is widely regarded as a philosophy, and according to Marx was given explicit form as philosophical doctrine by the English and French philosophers of the seventeenth and eighteenth centuries. If materialism supersedes philosophy, is it the case that philosophy can be superseded only philosophically?[25] If philosophy is idealist, materialism in Marx's sense cannot be a philosophy. How is it possible for materialism to be other than philosophy? Marx's argument is dominated by two considerations: first, all thought is other than material reality; second, of all *theoretical* thought-forms science is closest to material reality both in its mode of existence and epistemologically.

In its opposition to idealist philosophy Marx's materialism has a very general form as well as a specific realization in his science. It rejects idealism and dualism, but contrary to the tendency of philosophical materialism it is not reductionist. It does not, that is, assert that mind, consciousness and thought are reducible to material processes and thus ultimately identical with them. It holds, with dualism, that material reality and ideas are different, but against dualism it claims that this difference is not an ontological opposition and independence but rather a qualitative distinction compatible with causal interaction and the natural historical emergence of consciousness from matter.

[25] See A. Manser, 'The End of Philosophy: Marx and Wittgenstein' (University of Southampton, inaugural lecture, 1973).

As materialism it claims that existentially material reality is independent and consciousness dependent, and that historically, causally and epistemologically material reality is primary and consciousness secondary. In other words: there is a material reality whose existence is not dependent on any consciousness, human or divine; historically consciousness developed by natural processes out of and in causal dependence on this material reality; and specific causal dependence persists, that is, material reality in its specific forms and changes remains a constant causal condition of consciousness and its forms and changes, so that 'epistemologically', for instance, consciousness of or about this independently existing material reality is also causally conditioned by it. Now these materialist claims are all commonsense and/or scientific claims, not specifically philosophical ones. It is the scientific mode of investigation that is specifically adapted and suited to the investigation of material reality: it relies extensively on empirical methods, it confines its attention to what is spatio-temporal and subject to change, and its style of explanation of nature's processes is causal not teleological. Thus, though material reality is the basis of all thought, science is the only form of theory capable of recognizing this, so that in its case material reality is not merely its basic condition but its legitimating basis. As against this, a materialism that is philosophical is still really idealist. In accordance with philosophy's claim to cognitive authority over other subjects, it questions these commonplace materialist claims and argues for a materialist ontology and epistemology, thus seeking to go beyond material reality as the basis of science. Inevitably, it replaces this basis with an ideal one, with the *a priori* ideas that philosophy takes as its own: the empirical methods of science and commonsense give way to empiricism, and materialism survives, if at all, only in the form of the doctrine that this epistemology has an ontological basis, a basis not in material reality but in the necessary idea of material reality.

Science on Marx's view does not need, nor could it have, authorization by philosophy. On the contrary, seeking the justification of theory theoretically, at the ever more fundamental, abstract and general levels of theory itself, in philosophy, leads only to 'ultimate' theories, axioms, which in terms of this very problematic must be hanging idealistically unsupported in the air, either necessarily true *a priori*, or arbitrary. This is the well-trodden path to nowhere, to that oscillation between *a priori* dogmatism and a comprehensive and totally unreal scepticism that inescapably haunts modern philosophy, conceived as epistemology. Knowledge has no theoretical, i.e., philosophical, foundations. Philosophy's cognitive authority is an illusion, and all that survives is a descriptive 'epistemology' of a science whose real foundations lie elsewhere, in the material world.

Social materialism: practice

As so far outlined, Marx's materialism is in what I have called its 'general form'. In that form it recognizes what is true in the traditional materialism, including the epistemological materialism, associated with the rise of natural science: that the material reality of nature that is the object of scientific knowledge exists independently of our thought about it. This is a rejection of Hegel's idealism. But Marx's materialism has a specific character that rejects much else in that traditional epistemological materialism, and in doing so it follows Hegel instead, though at the same time transforming his philosophy into social scientific theory. What Marx rejects in traditional epistemological materialism is the subject-object relation at the basis of that epistemology, that is, the assumption that the cognitive relation is one in which the knowing subject directly confronts the material object, his or her thought passively reflecting that object. In the process Marx shapes his distinctive concept of materiality as a specifically *social* materiality different from the traditional 'matter' of the natural science paradigm: this social materiality, though not the object of natural science, is an inescapable condition of it, and for social science it is both condition and object. This is Marx's central concept of (material) *practice*. Marx's materialism insists on the need not only or primarily for materialist theory, a theory about practice, namely social science, but for practice itself; indeed, is itself a practice.

For Marx, Hegelian idealism in various ways represents an advance on traditional materialist epistemology. In rejecting the subject-object relation at the base of that epistemology, Hegel rejects the claim that knowledge and beliefs are acquired by individual subjects in direct and passive confrontation with material objects. Knowledge and beliefs are actively produced, and as such they are essentially social and historical products. Marx accepts that, but rejects the idealist and philosophical form of Hegel's doctrine. The idealist theory of knowledge as active was an attempt to solve an epistemological problem, the problem of how the mind can know a material reality that is other than, external to, and independent of the mind itself. The idealist solution was that the real object of knowledge is not material but ideal, a product of the mind's own activity. Marx rejects both the philosophical problem and the idealism it evokes. Knowledge is a socio-historical product, immediately a product of the activity of intellectual labour or work, of what Althusser calls 'theoretical practice'. But Marx puts two crucial gaps between his view and Hegel's. First, contrary to Hegel, the claim that knowledge is actively produced is compatible with the object's being material. Mental activity produces or constitutes knowledge, i.e., ideas and concepts. It does not produce or constitute the spatio-temporal objects that the knowledge is of. It does not even, in itself, change material reality. Second, not only is a proposition or theory, the content of an item of knowledge, an abstraction from the activity of thinking, but intellectual or mental activities are abstractions from material practices. Human beings are natural, material, objective beings whose material practices, involving both thought and physical action, presuppose and produce effects in a material reality existing independently of them. The most basic of such practices, on which all others depend, are the economic practices of producing the material goods necessary for life, such as food, shelter and clothing. These material practices condition mental practices. As an object of thought, the way material reality appears in thought reflects not only that material object but also the material practices of that thought's socio-historical context. Social practice, the condition but not the object of natural science, is however not only the condition but the specific object of social science. Society, the object of social scientific investigation and knowledge, is a structure of practices. Hegel's philosophical and idealist doctrine is here appropriated and transformed into social scientific materialism, the traditional problematic of thought and matter replaced by that of theory and practice.[26]

This contrast between thought or theory on the one hand and (material) practice on the other is more complex than the traditional problematic it replaces. Though theory may be assigned to the superstructure of society, as the product of the intellectual labour of specialist theorists, thought is common to all members of society and is 'spontaneously' involved, more or less, in any practice, at whatever level, including the most material, as when a shoemaker makes a shoe, his mind on the job. The materiality of society must therefore be different from the materiality of inorganic nature. The latter could exist entirely without thought, the former could not. Thought is part of the very nature of society, including its most material levels. In what ways, then, is consciousness secondary, for Marx? First, society exists independently of any concept of or thought about society. The thought that is involved in social life has neither created nor primarily shaped that life. There is a sense, as Marx stresses, in which people, in their directly material practices of production, also produce both themselves and society. But they do not do so deliberately. Moreover, just as in the case of food production they do not produce food out of nothing, as an act of creation, but rather out of some pre-existing raw material, as an act of transformation, both productive activity and product conditioned by the nature of that raw material, so the social structure historically pre-exists the practices of each individual and generation, conditioning those practices and moreover in such a way that their

[26] My views here owe much to the writings on this subject, regrettably so far unpublished, of W. Suchting of the University of Sydney.

'production' of society is generally speaking less a transformation than a reproduction of it.[27] In becoming agents of these practices the members of that new generation exercise agency less in the 'philosophical' sense, freely and rationally, than as bearers of those pre-existing structural relations, as their representatives. Their thought is shaped accordingly: generally speaking, it is not their thought that shapes their actions but rather their actions, themselves required by the pre-existing structure of social practices, that shape their thought.[28] Society masters us. But for Marx this situation is not to be understood as Althusser seems to understand it, 'philosophically', as a necessary and eternal condition of human bondage. On the contrary, the social structure has dynamism as well as inertia, and that condition is subject to historical change. Especially since the rise of natural science, thought and practice are beginning to exercise an increasing degree of control and mastery over nature. Nature will always be largely recalcitrant to such efforts, but just because society, unlike nature, is our own product, it is historically open to control and mastery without limit. This is the potentiality to be realized by socialism and its social science.

Hegel appropriated: alienation

We reach here, with these concepts of production, control and mastery, another crucial way in which Marx appropriates Hegel's philosophy and transforms it into a central element of his social science. We have seen that, confronted with the epistemological problem bequeathed to him by his forebears, the problem of our knowledge of the external material world, Hegel argued for a solution denying that reality is external to and other than consciousness. It is, rather, ideal, a product of

[27] See the excellent account in R. Bhaskar, *The Possibility of Naturalism, op. cit.*, ch. 2.
[28] L. Althusser, *Lenin and Philosophy* (London: New Left Books, 1971), p. 157f.

consciousness, produced by a process in which consciousness objectifies itself. This is the process of alienation. As C. Arthur has pointed out,[29] this concept of alienation is a central part of a move by which Hegel begins to shift epistemology, and philosophy generally, on to a new terrain. For alienation involves loss, loss of self, and it thus provides not only an interpretation of knowledge in terms of activity, but also the initial condition and rationale for a historical saga, in which spirit eventually recovers what it has lost, or at least reconciles itself to its loss by recognizing reality as its own alienated product. This new terrain, however, is still therefore, for Hegel, the terrain of philosophy and epistemology, the end of the saga being Absolute Knowledge. In appropriating this concept of alienation Marx retains a vital connection with epistemological concerns, but shifts the concept into a materialist and social scientific key, locating its application not only or basically in the production of ideas but in human practices generally, and basically in the sphere of material production in the economy, the production of material goods. Alienation is a historically specific process, relation and condition having a general form in which human products, the products of human powers, are alienated from, that is, separated from and lost to, their producers, who are consequently subordinated to the power and domination of what they have produced, in a process that involves the illusion that those items are not their products. Marx's materialism takes two forms in relation to this conception of alienation. He denies the general epistemology of Hegel's idealism, that material Nature is an (alienated) product of our ideas. But at the level of his scientific social theory Marx holds that in our material practices we produce material goods, and that in some modes of production, including capitalism, these products and modes of production are alienated. Moreover, in producing these material goods we produce that alienated mode of production and thus, as I have said, the social order generally. Society itself is an alienated product. Here too, then, there is a connection with epistemology, the connection

[29] C. Arthur, 'Objectification and Alienation in Marx and Hegel', in *Radical Philosophy*, 30 (Spring 1982).

involved in the fact that alienation involves illusion: even as a process that is material in Marx's sense, alienation is a material process in which ideas are generated, specifically ideas that are defective, i.e., illusions, mystification. When for Marx the production process is a practice whose special products are themselves ideas, an alienated mode of material production will tend to be reflected in an alienated mode of such mental production, as in religion, idealism and philosophy generally. Thus Hegel's own theory of alienation is itself alienated, an illusion of philosophical idealism induced by an alienated mode of material practice, and thus revealing, for those who can decipher it, some of the truth about society: a truth decipherable, however, not by philosophy itself but only by materialist science.

Analytical philosophy, Wittgenstein and Marx

The historical transition from the characteristically British empiricist conception of knowledge and ideas, in Locke, Berkeley and Hume, to the idealism of Kant and Hegel, and thence to the divide between the idealism of the hermeneutic conception of social inquiry and Marx's social scientific materialism, with its theme of the end of philosophy, has striking parallels with some of the dominant philosophical tendencies of twentieth-century English-speaking culture, the analytical movement and philosophy of science. That movement began at the beginning of the century with the attack by Russell and Moore on British Hegelianism and the development by Russell and Wittgenstein of the alternative of logical atomism. Russell united two streams of thought, British empiricism transmitted from Hume through Bentham to J.S. Mill, and the nineteenth-century renaissance of formal logic, through Frege. Russell's version of logical atomism was empiricist, and this aspect of the doctrine was developed by logical positivism into the criterion of meaning as empirical verifiability. Wittgenstein's contribution[30] was chiefly a theory of logic and of philosophy as logic. On this view truths of logic, unlike those of science, are analytic, verbal tautologies, and thus non-substantive, empty and uninformative about reality. Philosophical truths are a species of logical truths, and philosophy also, therefore, as a discipline now sharply distinguished from science, is analytic and uninformative. The end of philosophy is here its end as a substantive inquiry into the nature of reality, i.e., its end as metaphysics and its replacement, in that field, by the substantive discipline of science. In this way the analytical movement turned its back on much nineteenth-century Continental philosophy, especially its Hegelian forms, and saw itself as inheriting the classical modern philosophy of the seventeenth and eighteenth centuries, from Descartes to Kant, with its persistent attacks, particularly in the Enlightenment, on metaphysics as 'myth and superstition'. The major contribution that analytical philosophy saw itself as making, which in its view distinguished it clearly from the tradition, and which came to be thought of as 'a revolution in philosophy', was precisely its conception of philosophy. The classical modern period had tended to identify philosophy as a basic science. For the analytical movement it is logic, and thus non-substantive, non-scientific and certainly non-empirical. Specifically, philosophy in this form eliminates metaphysics by analysing language, explicating the meanings of concepts by revealing their logical interconnections. Metaphysics, accordingly, was seen as misuse of language, and in particular the result of the way in which the grammar (or 'surface' grammar) of the language tends to mislead philosophers as to its logic or meaning. For example, because the word 'mind' is a noun it is thought to name a thing, but since there is no physical thing that it denotes the mind is philosophically understood, or rather metaphysically misunderstood, as a non-physical entity. Such mistakes, misallocating words to their wrong logical types, are category-mistakes, and Descartes' dualism, with its doctrine

[30] L. Wittgenstein, *Tractatus Logico-Philosophicus* (London: Routledge and Kegan Paul, 1922).

that the mind is a non-physical thing, is a characteristic example.[31]

How could it be decided whether a word is being misused, and thus what its correct use is? Empiricism has an answer to this: a word is correctly used, and its meaning given, only in statements that are empirically verifiable (or perhaps falsifiable). But Wittgenstein was not an empiricist, and logical positivist philosophy of science never succeeded in showing that science, with its characteristically theoretical concepts, is empiricist: empirical, yes, but theoretical concepts proved strongly resistant to attempts to reduce them to observation concepts. In his earlier, logical atomist, period, Wittgenstein, like Russell himself and much of logical positivism later, took as his touchstone modern symbolic logic, which was thought to provide at least the syntax of a 'logically perfect language', a language entirely perspicuous in its meaning, and philosophically unmisleading. That view he later rejected. Though he retained much of his early theory of philosophy, the instantiation of linguistic and logical rectitude became for him, in a conception that in some respects echoed Moore and the Scottish Enlightenment philosophy of 'commonsense', ordinary language, language in its 'everyday usage'. Metaphysics was now the use, under the misleading influence of 'surface grammar', of ordinary words in extraordinary ways, and the job of philosophical analysis was to 'bring words back from their metaphysical to their everyday usage'. That everyday usage is 'in order as it is'. Metaphysical theories are thus 'houses of cards' in which language is 'on holiday' or like 'an engine idling', and people caught in these unreal thought-traps are like flies in fly-bottles. So philosophical 'therapy', in showing the fly the way out of the fly-bottle, or 'condensing metaphysics into a drop of grammar', 'leaves everything as it is'.[32] From Russell's point of view, the point of view of science and empiricism, ordinary language embodied 'the metaphysics of

[31] See G. Ryle, *The Concept of Mind* (London: Hutchinson's University Library, 1949), especially pp. 16–18.
[32] These quotations are drawn mainly from the account of philosophy in L. Wittgenstein, *Philosophical Investigations* (Oxford: Blackwell, 1953), §89–137.

the Stone Age'. From the point of view of the later Wittgenstein, empiricism is itself metaphysics and ordinary language is
totally non-metaphysical.

The rejection of metaphysics, the belief that science supersedes metaphysics, and the consequent theme of the end of
philosophy: all these Marxism shares with the analytical
movement, though with the difference already mentioned and
which needs further explanation. To approach that, we need to
note first that there are further resemblances between Marx and
the later Wittgenstein, chiefly on the nature of ideas. Wittgenstein's conception of philosophy and metaphysics is argued for
in his general theory of language, and in three important ways
this agrees with Marx: first, it rejects the empiricist conception
of meaning; second, language is essentially public not private,
and thus social not individual; third, words get their meaning
from their rules of use, from the practical language-games they
figure in, these language-games themselves being essentially
embedded in a general form of life. Both of these latter
doctrines appear anti-idealist and seem to echo Marx's materialism. Wittgenstein's attack on the possibility of a private
language is a criticism of Cartesian idealism and insists on the
necessity, for language in general, both of objects of reference
that are public, i.e., physical, and of language as a public
activity or practice with interpersonal criteria. This practice is
then itself said to be shaped by the general, social, form of life
of which it is a part. Yet in Winch,[33] Wittgenstein's philosophy
is made to yield a conception of social science that is
distinctively idealist in its hermeneutic conception of the
subject. For Winch argues that different societies have different forms of life and thus different ordinary languages,
languages whose meaningfulness and legitimacy are nevertheless guaranteed by that social context and which thus cannot be
undermined by philosophy or science: indeed, understanding
the language of participants is the chief part of understanding
that society, and this is an undertaking that is more philosophical than scientific, at any rate in the empiricist natural science

[33] P. Winch, *The Idea of a Social Science* (London: Routledge and Kegan Paul, 1958).

sense. In particular, the concepts of reality and rationality in societies may be very different from ours, but as part of a different form of life they are no less legitimate. The implication seems to be that there is no language-independent reality in relation to which concepts can be more or less adequate. This conceptual and epistemological tolerance is indistinguishable from sceptical relativism, and the possibility of objective cognitive assessment and progress seem threatened.

A parallel development has occurred in the philosophy of natural science. Logical positivist verificationism gave way to Popper's falsificationism, which argued that though scientific theories cannot be empirically verified they can be empirically, and thus objectively, falsified. The abandonment of this empiricism in Kuhn and Feyerabend, with the doctrine that science's theoretical concepts are not (wholly) empirical, so that even falsification is not possible by observation and logic alone, rejection of theories being to some extent arbitrary or 'ideological', has led here also to an idealism, this time specifically of natural science, that makes sceptical relativism unavoidable and seems incompatible with the possibility of scientific progress.[34]

These philosophical tendencies have found expression in social science itself, in particular in sociology, but in that field there is an older version of sceptical relativism that seems to be more materialist than idealist, and which in fact descends directly from Marxism itself. I mean the version in the subject called 'the sociology of knowledge'. According to this, since all ideas are generated in a social context, they are relative to, and in particular limited by, that social context. Objectivity is unattainable, and in particular no idea is objectively superior to any other.

To the extent that these arguments lead to sceptical relativism they are all susceptible to the paradox of that position: as an idea or theory itself, sceptical relativism claims to be true, or cognitively superior to its rivals, yet its content denies that possibility. Where is the mistake, and how does Marx avoid it?

[34] See, besides T. Kuhn, *op. cit.*, and P. Feyerabend, *op. cit.*, I. Lakatos and A. Musgrave, eds., *Criticism and the Growth of Knowledge* (Cambridge University Press, 1970).

The first thing that needs to be recognized is this: if we hold a view or theory about something, and thus claim it as true, or at any rate cognitively more adequate than its competitors, we should make sure that that theory's content is compatible with that claim. If the view or theory is about views or theories, it runs the risk of the self-referring paradoxes. Marx's theory meets this requirement: his materialist account of ideas is compatible with their being cognitively more or less adequate.

The problem in Wittgenstein's philosophy, which enables Winch to derive from it his idealism, is how to define 'everyday usage', 'language-game', and 'form of life' in such a way that they can mark theoretically the distinction between the conceptual meaningfulness and legitimacy of non-metaphysical language and the conceptual confusion of a metaphysical use of language. Clearly, a metaphysician's use of a word is still a use of it, and metaphysics is a language-game that belongs to a form of life such as religion, possibly to the form of life of a whole society if that society is dominated by and saturated with religion, as in medieval Europe and in some of Winch's examples of societies studied by anthropologists. It is significant that Wittgenstein's work, apparently so anti-metaphysical, has been taken as the foundation not only of Winch's theory of social science but also of a flourishing Wittgensteinian analysis of religious language, leaving that also 'as it is'. Further, is scientific language ordinary language? It is presumably not, as such, metaphysical. On the other hand, especially if empiricism is metaphysics, a science may be metaphysically contaminated, as Wittgenstein himself suggests about psychology.[35] But in that case, how can everyday language be totally immune to such contamination?

These problems are generated by two crucial claims in Wittgenstein's theory that Marx would reject: first the claim that the conceptual confusion constituting traditional (metaphysical) philosophy results from the detachment of words from their language-games and forms of life, as if idealism involved separation from the context of the social base; and

---

[35] L. Wittgenstein, *Philosophical Investigations, op. cit.*, II, xiv.

second the complementary claim that the use of language in its connection with its associated form of life guarantees its meaningfulness and conceptual propriety, something in itself sufficient to prevent conceptual confusion. On the former point, Marx's view is that just as philosophical materialism is really an idealism, so idealism (and thus philosophy) is materialist in this sense, that contrary to its own view of itself its very 'detachment' is rooted in a material form of life. For the idealism of philosophy is ideological mystification, and ideology reflects the material practices at the base of society, serving the class interests involved in those practices. That mystification is generated by the form of life itself. Thus, on the latter point, it can infect not only the ideological superstructure but also the commonsense ideas and everyday language of ordinary participants in those material practices. In a view that rejects Wittgenstein's sharp separation of metaphysics from ordinary language, Marx holds that the untheoretical and spontaneous ideas of participants in material social practices can involve a type of confusion that is crystallized in theoretical form in philosophy.

The ultimate underlying difference between Marx and Wittgenstein, which totally distinguishes Marx's radicalism from Wittgenstein's conservatism, and which I shall explain more fully later, is that for Marx a material form of life that generates ideas that are confused, at both theoretical and ordinary levels, is not merely confusing: it is itself confused. Wittgenstein and Winch take the 'rationality' of an established form of life for granted, or at any rate as beyond question. Marx does not. Thus, whereas according to his own account Wittgenstein's philosophical critique of philosophy and thus his conception of the end of philosophy 'leaves everything [else] as it is', both the rest of the linguistic and intellectual order and the social form of life in which those other forms of consciousness are rooted, Marx's scientific critique of philosophy, through a network of relations that I shall try to make clear, is also a critique of the whole social formation, theoretical and practical. Marx consequently draws the final materialist conclusion, that ('mental') criticism is not enough to eradicate these defective forms of consciousness. Far from being 'houses of cards', in which language is 'on holiday' and 'like an engine idling', they are solidly entrenched in social materiality, and they involve ordinary language in its normal state at work performing its common social function of mystification. What is needed to eradicate them is the practical overthrow of the defective forms of life they reflect.

For Marxism, then, Wittgenstein's philosophy of language, like Hegel's idealism, is itself ideological mystification, as its position in relation to the classical period of modern philosophy anyway strongly suggests. Though claiming to inherit that classical tradition, except for its conception of philosophy itself, this 'revolution in philosophy' thus also radically differentiates itself from the philosophy of that period. Similarities in problems and content mask a profound contrast in social and historical significance. The philosophy of the Scientific Revolution and Enlightenment was genuinely revolutionary: as the intellectual and ideological manifestation of the bourgeois revolution, it attacked and undermined the feudal world-view, replacing it with the new science and its mechanical philosophy, empiricist and rationalist epistemologies, and associated moral and political philosophies. By comparison, the twentieth-century analytical revolution in philosophy is in fact counter-revolutionary, philosophy's scope and status reduced to the conservatism of a subject that 'leaves everything as it is' and ordinary language granted philosophical immunity from criticism. It would be difficult to imagine a more striking example of the Marxist thesis that the continuities of a cultural tradition are compatible with a radical transformation in its political significance: the continuities those of the identity of the class whose interests it expresses, the transformation the historical change from that class's revolutionary rise to its conservative decline.

Analytical philosophy is a critique and supersession of philosophy that is itself philosophical. In declaring the end of philosophy it declares the end of philosophy as a substantive discipline, as metaphysics, but itself survives that end as a non-substantive discipline, in its pure specialist form as logical analysis. It is the attempt to preserve philosophy both in that 'purely logical' form and with a role that is critical, if only vestigially so, namely of metaphysics, that necessitates a general theory of meaning and produces the oscillation between empiricism and the later Wittgenstein's criterion of 'everyday usage'. As we have seen, that criterion has a strong tendency towards idealism and sceptical relativism and thus towards a toleration incompatible with criticism of any sort, however vestigial. For Marx, by contrast, the critique and supersession of philosophy is materialist and scientific. Specifically, the criticism of conceptual inadequacy and confusion is itself scientific, not philosophical, and its supersession is ultimately practical. Moreover the targets of this scientific criticism can thus include not only the high theory of the metaphysicians but also the untheoretical concepts of ordinary language and understanding. But Marx's allegiance to science, though aligning him with empiricism in these relationships, differs from that of empiricism in two ways. First, and more important, his allegiance to science is not that of a philosopher, who seeks to support science philosophically by formulating a demarcation criterion of scientificity and meaningfulness in general, but that of a practising scientist, whose distinction between adequate and inadequate concepts is drawn not in accordance with some such general philosophical criterion but in relation to the particular scientific appropriation of a specific subject-matter. Second, Marx's conception of science is not empiricist. These two ways are connected. The former leaves Marx space for the discovery and criticism of ideologically defective concepts within a particular science itself, such as political economy. But this in its turn is possible because Marx recognizes that science is not empiricist, i.e., that it has a conceptual content not reducible to empirical observation and consequently develops historically by raising and trying to solve conceptual problems, problems about the most adequate way to conceptualize the reality under investigation. It follows that the exclusive contrast between what is empirical and what is conceptual, according to which the analytical movement has tended to understand the distinction between science and philosophy, is invalid. Science certainly asks and tries to answer questions about reality, and empirical evidence is certainly necessary for that purpose. But as Engels saw in the passage already quoted from the 'Old Preface' to the *Anti-Dühring*, empirical evidence is not enough. The questions themselves can be and are questioned: those questions may be formulated, and thus invite answers, in terms of concepts that are in various ways inadequate to the field under investigation:

> Not only in their answers but in their very questions there was a mystification.[36]

Since the presupposition of conceptual adequacy in the question and answer cannot be taken for granted, every 'empirical' question also raises, or perhaps suppresses, a 'conceptual' question, and the one type of question cannot be answered independently of the other.

In rejecting empiricism from a scientific rather than a philosophical point of view Marx avoids the oscillation between empiricism's conception of an objectivist rationality and the tendency to sceptical relativism present in the idealist alternative. As I have pointed out, the contemporary philosophical critique of empiricism has standardly led to a conception of knowledge, including scientific knowledge, as basically arbitrary, evaluative, 'ideological', in a word non-rational: a tendency that shows both sides of the argument committed to an empiricist conception of rationality. Specifically, that conception of reason is theoreticist. The common assumption of all the forms of sceptical relativism I have mentioned as characteristic of twentieth-century thought, in Wittgensteinian idealism, the Kuhn-Feyerabend reaction to Popper, and the 'materialism' of the sociology of knowledge, is that if theory is not detached from but is in close contact with practice, if ideas are shaped by the structure of social practices and relations, ideas and theory must be to that extent non-rational or irrational. In other words, the context of material social practice is seen as *infecting* ideas with its own lack of rationality, as rendering them 'ideological' in a pejorative sense. Marx's materialism resists that tendency. More, it positively reverses it. His conception of the relation between

[36] K. Marx and F. Engels, *op. cit.*, p. 40.

ideas and material practice is not only compatible, in his understanding and practice, with rational scientific assessment and criticism of ideas, it allows for such assessment and criticism to extend to the structure of social practice itself. Marx's conception of rationality is not empiricist or theoreticist, it is scientific and practical, i.e., materialist.

Scientific realism, empiricism and hermeneutics

Recent developments in English philosophy of science have avoided both empiricism and idealism by elaborating a conception of science as realist, realist not in the Platonic but in the materialist sense; and as a number of philosophers have pointed out, one of the forms taken by Marx's scientific materialism is its realism in this sense.[37] For Marx, science is theoretical, and he rejects the empiricist doctrine of the reducibility of theoretical to observation concepts. Science has no epistemological foundations, in observation or anything else. What it has is a historical location, and the 'theoretical practice' of science, as Althusser has argued, is the intellectual labour by which the body of theories and concepts actually existing and accepted at the time is critically analysed and more or less gradually transformed into something cognitively more adequate. The presupposition of this notion of cognitive adequacy is anti-idealist: it is the existence of an independent object whose nature is cognitively accessible at the theoretical level. This conception of science is thus realist: the non-empirical theoretical concepts of science describe, more or less adequately, the material, i.e., spatio-temporal, reality that is the object of that science.

It follows that for Marx the material reality described by scientific theory is not empirical. On the contrary, with respect to that reality our senses mislead us, constituting a realm of

[37] R. Keat and J. Urry, *op. cit.*; T. Benton, *Philosophical Foundations of the Three Sociologies, op. cit.*; R. Bhaskar, *The Possibility of Naturalism, op. cit.*

appearances that veil and obscure, and even flatly contradict, the reality discovered by scientific theory. Marx is here appropriating the ancient philosophical distinction between appearance and reality, but again, as elsewhere, he decisively transforms it. He rejects the suggestion of ontological opposition between appearance and reality. He does not, that is, reject empirical appearances as subjective illusion. These appearances are appearances of reality, the way reality really does appear to us and is experienced by us. They represent, more or less accurately, an aspect of reality, namely its surface. On this view, then, reality is divided into strata. It has a superficial layer and deeper layers. But the relation between these 'phenomenal forms' and underlying 'real relations' is not simply a cognitive or epistemological relation, in which the former veil or obscure or contradict the latter. The relation is also a causal or explanatory relation, in which the phenomenal surface is an effect of the deeper levels. The task of science, then, is to penetrate theoretically to reality's underlying forces and structures and in the process to explain the way reality appears in terms of those forces and structures. At the same time this explanatory procedure is also critical. For it is the appearances of reality that are registered in the spontaneous untheoretical understanding and concepts that people have of the world, and in penetrating beneath them and explaining them science both comprehends and rejects as inadequate the ordinary language and concepts of the spontaneous understanding. It is this process of simultaneous criticism and explanation, rejection and comprehension, that defines 'critique'.

This account of realism so far is general enough to include natural science, and in fact I have so far situated it in opposition to empiricism and idealism as philosophies of natural science. But Marxist theory is social, not natural, science, and as such its realism provides it with the possibility both of a range of targets and of a mode of scientific explanatory criticism that are intrinsically political. The targets in the realm of ideas occur at two distinguishable levels.[38] First, as we have seen, is the type of understanding contrasted with theory as such: the spontaneous and untheoretical understanding that ordinary participants have of their activities, including workers in the material base, a type of understanding that registers only appearances. On the surface of capitalist society, including its economy, appears a systematically connected web of phenomenal forms, such as commodities, price, capital, money, wages, rent, profit etc., and these are what are represented in the everyday language and ideas of ordinary participants. Second are the ideas produced by intellectual labour in the ideological superstructure, including the more or less scientific theories of intellectuals such as the political economists, whose science may uncover some of the underlying reality while at the same time failing to be sufficiently critical of the superficial concepts of the unscientific consciousness. One such concept is wages as the price or value of labour. Marx's comments that '... "value of labour" ... is an expression as imaginary as the value of the earth' and that '... "price of labour" is just as irrational as a yellow logarithm' identify the mistake here, as Mepham has suggested,[39] as a 'category-mistake', a type of conceptual error familiar to philosophers, in which a concept of one logical category is misallocated to another. But for Marx such a conceptual mistake is substantive, due not to the superficial grammar of language but to the superficial appearance of reality, and his criticism is equally substantive, not philosophical but scientific. Philosophical theories of social inquiry in fact constitute part of this second level of ideas that Marxist social scientific realism takes as its critical target, in particular the two main alternative philosophical paradigms: on the one hand empiricism or positivism, on the other the idealism of the *Geisteswissenschaften* or hermeneutic doctrine.

In Marx's social scientific realism, this single conception of the distinction between social appearance and the underlying

---

[38] K. Marx, *Capital* (London: Lawrence and Wishart, 1954), especially the sections on 'The Fetishism of Commodities' (vol. 1, ch. I, section 4, pp. 71–81) and on 'The Transformation of the Value (and Respectively the Price) of Labour-power into Wages' (vol. 2, ch. XIX, pp. 535–42).

[39] J. Mepham, 'The Theory of Ideology in *Capital*', in *Radical Philosophy*, 2 (Summer 1972), p. 15.

social reality lays the foundation of an argument that simultaneously attacks both of these social philosophies and their influence on the tradition of Marxist philosophy itself. Empiricism, projecting the conception of a unified science in which social science, as in diamat, follows the natural science model, and in the process generating behaviourism and the general conception of the social sciences as 'behavioural sciences', misconceives both natural and social science, and their unity, because it treats phenomenal appearances as the whole of reality, failing to recognize the need for a critique of empirical concepts and the development of theoretical concepts. A hermeneutic approach not only makes the mistake of accepting an empiricist account of natural science and then supposing that because social understanding is not empiricist it must be different from natural science: in attributing to the ordinary language and untheoretical self-understanding of participants in a society a conceptual adequacy that theory cannot undermine, it fails to realize that those commonplace concepts are themselves predominantly empirical, registering only phenomenal appearances and not the real relations those appearances mask.

Ideas and politics: ideology and science

I said that this range of targets, and Marx's mode of scientific explanatory criticism of them, are intrinsically political. The general Marxist concept for the political role of ideas, for the class struggle at the level of the clash of ideas, especially those theoretical ideas produced by the labour of intellectuals, as part of society's superstructure, is that of ideology. There are few sites in the Marxist conceptual framework where the prejudices of bourgeois ideology have been so intrusive and clearly displayed as in this category of ideology itself. The commonest misunderstanding construes ideology as ideas whose practical political role, in particular their inclusion of values and political philosophy, render them cognitively defective in a radical and comprehensive way and thus essentially unscientific: ideology is 'false consciousness'.[40] The model for this misunderstanding of the category is the conception of metaphysics in empiricist philosophy; and bourgeois sociologists have even conceived of 'the end of ideology'[41] on the model of the empiricist conception of the end of metaphysics, as (social) science displaces (social) philosophy. As McCarney[42] has argued, contrary to all this, the use of 'ideology' in Marx does not imply cognitive defect. It denotes only ideas whose content gives them a political significance and use, and is epistemologically neutral. However, the illusion that 'ideology' implies cognitive defect perhaps has an explanation in something true, namely that Marx's interest in ideas that are cognitively defective and thus targets for social scientific criticism is itself governed by this concept of ideology. He is concerned, that is, with cognitive defect as a political category, with illusion, mystification and lack of scientificity as they function in the class struggle: in particular, with *bourgeois* ideology. It follows that though the concept of ideology is epistemologically neutral, scientificity, at any rate in social theory, is not ideologically neutral. The phenomenal forms generated by the underlying social structure play a necessary part in the reproduction of that structure: that is, the superficial ideas of ordinary participants and of bourgeois theorists, and the encouragement of that superficiality by bourgeois philosophy, whether empiricist or hermeneutic, tend to conserve the status quo. A genuine science of society such as Marx's, on the other hand, in critically opposing those ideas by exposing society's underlying reality, participates in the subversive transformation of the status quo. In other words, it aligns itself with the working-class socialist movement and represents at the theoretical level proletarian ideology. It recognizes that the consciousness of working-class participants tends to be dominated by conservative influences, on the one side by society's superficial appearances, on the

[40] This tendency is present in Althusser, as I argue in my 'Marx's Revolutionary Science' in J. Mepham and D.-H. Ruben, *op. cit.*, vol. III.
[41] The title of D. Bell, *The End of Ideology* (New York: The Free Press, 1960).
[42] J. McCarney, *The Real World of Ideology* (Brighton: Harvester Press, 1980).

other, in collusion with those appearances, by bourgeois ideologists and the ideological apparatuses of bourgeois society, church, education system, media etc. But it also recognizes that unlike the bourgeoisie in general workers are educable by Marxist science; for the interests and situation specific to the working class provide it with a point of view that has fundamental cognitive advantages over that of the bourgeoisie, and it is that point of view and those advantages that are incorporated in Marx's science and give it its cognitive superiority over bourgeois theory. The materialist involvement of ideas in the practical social and political context, specifically the conscious participation of social science in the working-class struggle, far from undermining scientificity, is a positive condition of it. It is not that Marx's science, being ideological, is none the worse for that. On the contrary, being proletarian ideology it is scientifically all the better for that.

Hermeneutics thus embodies a half-truth, or perhaps a quarter-truth. It is wrong in thinking that participation is sufficient for an adequate understanding of social life. Given the dislocation between social reality's phenomenal forms and its underlying real relations, participant understanding that is spontaneous and untheoretical can register only superficial and mystifying appearances. Scientific theory is necessary. But it too is not sufficient. Participation is also necessary. Participation need not be untheoretical and unscientific. Science need not be disengaged and neutral. What is required is the unity of the two. This is one mode of the Marxist unity of theory and practice, of science and political action. But hermeneutics is also wrong in suggesting that what is necessary is participation of any kind; and thus either that the unity of society is not a divided unity, or that if it is divided adequate social understanding is equally possible on either side of the divide.

It follows from all this that in its bearing on 'epistemological' matters, Marx's general materialist conception of ideas, as dependent on and conditioned by the material and practical social circumstances, is characteristically unphilosophical. His view at this level of generality is that with respect to any one of an indefinite range of items of knowledge, some circumstances are more favourable than others for its production and acceptance. Different social circumstances provide different degrees of cognitive access. Though in the search for knowledge of this or that sort some social circumstances are limiting and constricting and even make success impossible, it does not follow that all social circumstances of any kind whatsoever make knowledge of any kind whatsoever impossible, as if knowledge, objectivity and rationality required an impossibly idealistic detachment from materiality and practicality: that conception is an idealism whose growth has no doubt been partly responsible for the disappearance of that ancient and particularly materialist concept of knowledge, carnal knowledge. On the contrary, though some material circumstances and situations are cognitively limiting, others are cognitively liberating. In particular, when social matters are not only the condition but also the object of knowledge, access to such knowledge will depend on the way in which that social formation is cognitively stratified. What a social formation reveals and what it conceals can vary and change historically, as Marx points out in explaining how Aristotle, 'the great thinker who was the first to analyse so many forms, whether of thought, society, or Nature, and amongst them also the form of value', was unable to penetrate the nature of value as modern thinkers have done.[43]

Marx's materialism is of course *historical* materialism. His conception of thought and theory themselves is a historical materialist conception. That historical perspective is incompatible with dogmatism, but as a point of view that competes with others it is also incompatible with a comprehensive (philosophical) scepticism. In accordance with these two requirements, the polar opposition of the standard cognitive categories of truth and falsity, knowledge and ignorance, acceptance and rejection, must be qualified by a graded and comparative distinction, between what is more and what is less cognitively adequate, and specifically by a historical version of this, in terms of the possibility of cognitive development, advance or progress. The historical materialist conception of thought implies material social change as a crucial determinant of differential cognitive

[43] K. Marx, *Capital, op. cit.*, pp. 59–60.

access. Continuity in the social transmission of ideas makes plausible the concept of historical change as having the potential for cognitive progress, later generations benefiting cognitively from what has gone before. But within that general historical schema, for Marx, there occurs the distinctive reality of class differentiation and struggle, with its own implications for differential cognitive access. Class conflict involves conflict of ideas and ideology, and Marx's claim is that cognitive access is decisively differentiated by historical class position. A rising class is historically progressive, and its historically progressive character includes a point of view that gives it a fundamental cognitive advantage over the ruling class. In the present period the rising class is the working class, and only theory from its point of view can be fully scientific.

The working class, moreover, has a cognitive advantage over and above what it owes to being the rising class in the present epoch. As the class that needs no subordinate class to dominate, it is the only class that has the potentiality for classlessness and thus the power to effect the transition to a classless society. As such, its cognitive advantage will not be superseded by any other class.

Meanwhile, the ideas of the bourgeoisie, progressive and revolutionary when the class was rising, have now become conservative and reactionary. The bourgeois class position, originally cognitively liberating, is now a fetter on cognitive advance. The most general form of this cognitive deficiency is the unhistorical outlook of the ruling class. As the class whose interests depend on the maintenance of the existing social system, their overall tendency is to represent that system as natural and in its fundamentals not subject to change. The fundamental failure of classical political economy, 'so long as it sticks in its bourgeois skin',[44] is its inability to penetrate society's phenomenal forms deeply enough to recognize the underlying forces of radical social change and thus the transience of the capitalist mode of production and bourgeois society.

In considering the ways in which Marxist social science

[44] Ibid., p. 542.

opposes this bourgeois tendency and aligns itself with the working class, we can analytically distinguish three matters that Marx himself unites: first, Marxist science speaks of the fundamental changes that are actually occurring in society; second, it speaks of the power of people, specifically the working class, to change society by revolution; third, it speaks for, i.e., in favour of, such revolutionary change:

> Just as the *economists* are the scientific representatives of the bourgeois class, so the *socialists* and the *Communists* are the theoreticians of the proletarian class ... in the measure that history moves forward, and with it the struggle of the proletariat assumes clearer outlines, they no longer need to seek science in their minds; they have only to take note of what is happening before their eyes and to become its mouthpiece. So long as they look for science and merely make systems, so long as they are at the beginning of the struggle, they see in poverty nothing but poverty, without seeing in it the revolutionary, subversive side, which will overthrow the old society. From this moment, science, which is a product of the historical movement, has associated itself consciously with it, has ceased to be doctrinaire and has become revolutionary.[45]

The unhistorical outlook of the bourgeoisie, in representing society as natural and in its fundamentals not subject to change, is supported by the phenomenal appearance of society and social relations as fetishized and alienated objects. But fetishism is the representation of social relations and society generally not merely as natural material objects, fundamentally unchanging, but also as objects that are not our products and which, as fetishes, subordinate us, their producers, to their own power. In other words, they appear as unchanging because they appear specifically as things that we are powerless to change. But in employing these concepts for this purpose, Marx's science not only *interprets* the changing reality of society and

[45] K. Marx, *The Poverty of Philosophy* (New York: International Publishers, 1963), pp. 125–6.

the power of the working class to change that society by revolution: that science aligns itself with the working class by theoretically supporting the working-class movement, as its theoretical mouthpiece actually calling for such revolutionary change. It does so not simply in the way of orthodox science, by providing a 'pure' theory that has a practical application as technology. On the contrary, as I have already hinted, Marx's science has an evaluative, specifically a critical, relation to its object, bourgeois society. As such, it offends against that cardinal point of much bourgeois philosophy, that a properly constituted science must be value-neutral in relation to its object, confining itself to description, explanation and prediction.

The pressure of that doctrine, dominantly empiricist but also present in Kantianism, has at times, as I have already mentioned in describing 'diamat', led the Marxist tradition to suppose that in socialism Marx's social science, like all science value-neutral, must be supplemented with something non-scientific, 'ideology' or morality, to mediate its connection with socialist political practice. Kantian and utilitarian moralities have figured in this role. Yet Marx himself was contemptuous of morality, which he regarded as idealist and anti-revolutionary ideology, and in various ways and places claimed, in the words of *The German Ideology*, that 'the communists do not preach morality at all'.[46] Marx did not object to capitalism on moral grounds. Yet he clearly objected to it, and called upon the working class to revolt against it. Wood's account of non-moral goods in Marxism is important and persuasive.[47] What is philosophically crucial, however, is that Marx's critical attitude to capitalism is not something logically separable from, and simply conjoined with, his science. Nor is it simply a point of view from which become visible purely descriptive truths about capitalism. The subtitle of *Capital* is 'Critique of Political Economy', and the theory of capitalism in it is a critique of the theories of the political economists that is at the same time a critique of the political economy of capitalism

[46] K. Marx and F. Engels, *op. cit.*, p. 104.
[47] A. Wood, Karl Marx (London: Routledge and Kegan Paul, 1981), pp. 125–56.

itself. That theory contains critical concepts so central to and formative of its whole structure that they can reasonably be regarded as having categorial status in Marxism's conceptual framework. I have already mentioned the 'apparently evaluative' nature of the concept of alienation. This concept was central to Marx's earlier thought, when philosophy, though suspect, had not yet been superseded by a mature science. The word occurs much less frequently as Marx's science develops, and when it does it sometimes appears in scare-quotes as a typically philosophical word marking a rejected idealist concept.[48] What is dropped as unscientific, as Geras has argued,[49] is the philosophical anthropology in which the concept was originally embedded, a doctrine about the ideal essence of man, his 'species being', which alienation negates. But much of the structure of the concept remains. In his scientific work Marx analyses specific forms of the relation, e.g., in commodity fetishism, without the philosophical lumber. The concept that marks this relation at the basic, economic, level is the concept that occupies the commanding position in Marx's science: the critical category of exploitation. It is their direct experience of the negative effects of exploitation, in poverty, frustration and powerlessness, that gives working-class people that point of view from which the underlying character of the capitalist mode of production can be scientifically recognized, in particular its character as a system of exploitation. What obscures that recognition is the web of illusion and mystification that the system generates. The union of these two matters is crucial. As critical, the concepts of alienation and commodity fetishism involve the union of the two concepts of subjection and illusion, denoting an antagonistic relation in which people lack both freedom and understanding. As such, these concepts instantiate a more general critical but non-moral category in Marx's scheme, one essential to its scientificity, and it is through that connection that they enter the framework of Marxist science

[48] K. Marx and F. Engels, *op. cit.*, p. 56, and *The Communist Manifesto* in *The Revolutions of 1848*, ed. D. Fernbach, (Harmondsworth: Penguin Books, 1973), p. 91.
[49] N. Geras, 'Marx and the Critique of Political Economy', in *Ideology in Social Science*, ed. R. Blackburn (London: Fontana Paperbacks, 1972), pp. 288–9.

and claim scientific status. In explaining this I will try to shed light on the most difficult and outrageous of all Marx's affronts to orthodox philosophy, especially philosophy of logic, his materialist dialectic.

The materialist dialectic

The general item of knowledge that Marx thinks is accessible to the working-class point of view but not from the unhistorical point of view of the bourgeoisie is: that capitalism is changing and society will eventually be radically transformed by revolution. Marx follows Hegel in identifying a general pattern or mechanism of change, in particular of revolutionary change. Change is dialectical, the result of internal contradictions whose unified opposition gradually intensifies until a breaking-point is reached and a radical transformation of the whole occurs. Thus the bourgeoisie's unhistorical point of view, their failure to acknowledge the presence in society of forces of radical change, has a more specific form: their inability to grasp the dialectic, 'in its rational form a scandal and abomination to bourgeoisdom and its doctrinaire professors'. In the rest of that passage Marx explains why this is so, uniting two reasons where often only one is seen:

> because it includes in its comprehension and affirmative recognition of the existing state of things, at the same time also, the recognition of the negation of that state, of its inevitable breaking up ... because it lets nothing impose upon it, and is in its essence critical and revolutionary.[50]

This passage asserts that the materialist dialectic not only recognizes that the 'existing state of things' is changing radically, it is also 'critical and revolutionary'. Critical of what and revolutionary in relation to what? The passage seems to say

[50] K. Marx, *Capital, op. cit.*, p. 20.

that in virtue of his 'dialectic method' what Marx's science recognizes radical change in is also what it criticizes: 'the existing state of things'. How does the materialist dialectic make that possible?

Hegel regarded dialectic as a kind of logic and its central categories of unity and contradiction as categories of logic. The definitively dialectical claims are that reality is a unity that is contradictory and that historical change in reality is due to its nature as both unified and contradictory. Given his idealism, this implies that logical relations such as contradiction are relations between ideas. For orthodox philosophy this location of logic within ideas is generally acceptable. But much of that philosophy rejects Hegel's idealism and in its epistemology distinguishes between knowing subject and the real material object of that knowledge. In the process, locating logic on the side of thought, knowledge, ideas and language, it distinguishes logical relations from real relations. Real relations are spatio-temporal and thus chronological, historical and causal relations. Logical relations, such as contradiction, are not: they occur not within (material) reality, only within thought, and even, according to the anti-psychologism of modern analytical philosophy of logic, only within the abstracted contents of thought and language such as propositions, their essential character being that of truth-relations. Following Kant, logical opposition (contradiction) is to be distinguished from real opposition (conflict). Logical relations are thus non-substantive, merely verbal, holding solely in virtue of the meaning of the related terms. It is some such view that confronts with stark incredulity Marx's materialist dialectic,[51] with its claim that there can be contradictions not only between ideas but within a reality that is specifically material. According to orthodox philosophy, even if it made sense to apply logical relation concepts such as contradiction to reality, which it does not, Marx's dialectic would imply that contradictory propositions can be true of reality, when in truth all such propositions are necessarily false: contradictions in (material) reality are

[51] See K. Popper, 'What is Dialectic?', in *Conjectures and Refutations* (London: Routledge and Kegan Paul, 1963), pp. 312–35.

logically impossible. Avoiding absurdity, the effect of Marx's extension of the categories of unity and contradiction to material reality is thus to evacuate from their content their specifically logical character. Material contradictions are simply unified conflicts, in Kant's language real not logical oppositions. The project of a 'dialectics of nature', for reasons that will become clear, tends strongly towards the identification of contradiction with conflict, and classical dialectical material-ism is its philosophical expression.

I will outline an immanent critique of this orthodox objection to the materialist dialectic. As a first step to disentangling its confusions, let us concentrate on the admission that ideas and propositions at least, if nothing else, can stand in contradictory, including self-contradictory, relations. Then a statement assert-ing that one idea contradicts another, or is self-contradictory, will not itself be a contradictory statement. Contradictions within ideas are logically possible, and statements describing such contradictions can themselves be self-consistent.

Second, ideas, beliefs and assertions exist in reality. Their object, what they refer to or are about, may be a material reality, such as the solar system, but the traditional epistemo-logical distinction between ideas and their real object should not mislead us into supposing that ideas themselves are not real, do not exist as at least part of reality. Thus, if there can be contradictions between ideas there can be contradictions in reality. The logical relation of contradiction can be instantiated as a real relation of (logical) conflict. The anti-psychologism of modern analytical philosophy of logic would presumably object to this in the following way: contradiction and other logical relations hold only between the contents of ideas, beliefs and statements, and are (at least basically) truth-relations between 'propositions', not real relations, such as conflict, between psychological states and speech-acts. This tendency towards Platonic abstraction is characteristic of the tradition of the special discipline of formal logic and of philosophy of logic. It demarcates the boundaries of that specialism, but it should not be allowed to obscure the internal connections between content and act that make it possible for people as well as propositions to contradict one another. 'Contradict' is a speech-act verb, and when, for instance, on the question of whether the Earth moves, Galileo contradicted the Church he put himself into a position of real (logical) opposition to the Church.

Third, in natural science, which is a real social practice of intellectual labour, logical relations such as contradiction are instantiated as real relations and logical relation concepts are consequently applied as evaluative and specifically critical categories. They are not, as critical, applied to the material reality that natural scientific theories are about, especially when that material reality is inorganic, such as the solar system. But a theory in natural science stands in a double relationship: not only the relationship that has dominated traditional epistemology, the truth-relation, of correspondence or reflection, between theory and its real material object, nature; but also relations between that theory and other theories and ideas. These relations are logical, and as instantiated social and critical. When one theory or idea contradicts another, acceptance of one implies a commitment to the rejection of the other. Thus in the real social practice of natural science an argument is not simply, as formal logic represents it, a set of propositions, distinguishable into premises and conclusion, with some truth-relation such as implication holding between them. It is an activity of dispute, presupposing disagreement and opposition, in which some position is argued *for* and other positions are argued *against*. When such positions and ideas are actually constitutive of a specific social institution, such as the Church, argument against them is an attack on that institution.

Thus, contrary to much orthodox philosophy, values are implied by both logical truths and facts.[52] These are not *moral* values. They are, we might say, cognitive or epistemological values, values at the level of ideas and thought: the concepts of illusion and mystification are cognitively evaluative, in particular critical. More generally, as is signified by the categories of logic, these values are rational values. 'Reason' and 'rationality' are themselves, in these contexts, evaluative categories. When Marx, for instance, refers to his conception

[52] These arguments are presented at greater length, and in the style and method of analytical philosophy, in R. Edgley, *Reason in Theory and Practice* (London: Hutchinson's University Library, 1969).

of dialectic as dialectic 'in its rational form', by contrast with 'its mystified form',[53] he means to recommend it as more acceptable than Hegel's. The general defect of which self-contradiction is a specific form is: irrationality. It is because contradictions within a unity, self-contradictions, are defects, specifically irrationalities, that they need, in the language of dialectic, to be 'resolved', 'overcome' or 'reconciled' by what is, therefore, from a rational point of view, an advance or progressive change. If historically contradictions are motors of change they are motors not merely of change but of improvement or development. They are dialectically ambivalent.

Fourth, though all science, including natural science, must instantiate logical relations and thus be critical and evaluative in the way outlined, when we turn from natural to social science two important relevant differences are evident. On the one hand, the object of social science, society, itself includes ideas and theories. On the other, the rest of that social object, its material reality, is not the 'matter' or 'material substance' of traditional epistemology, with its paradigm of natural science, especially physics; it is, rather, for Marx, *practice*, specifically material practice. The materialism of Marx's social science is social materialism, in which the traditional philosophical problematic of thought and matter is replaced by the problematic of theory and practice. In accordance with the former point, a social scientific theory, in standing, like a theory in natural science, in a contradictory and critical relation to other theories and ideas about the same subject-matter, scientific or otherwise, will therefore, unlike a natural science theory, stand in that contradictory and critical relation to part of its real object, society. Moreover, in taking such ideas as part of its real object that theory will not only criticize them as cognitively defective, e.g., as self-contradictory or conceptually superficial and inadequate, it will also seek to explain them. For a materialist theory, that means tracing their features, including their defects, to their material conditions. Given that those material conditions causally and functionally necessitate those

[53] K. Marx, *Capital*, op. cit., p. 20.

defective ideas, and are thus themselves mystificatory, eliminating the illusions will require more than criticism of those illusions: it will require the practical transformation of their material conditions.[54] But for Marx such change is required not simply in order to eliminate confused ideas. Rather, material conditions in society cause defects at the level of ideas because they are defective in their own material way. In accordance with the latter point above, since the material reality of society is not inorganic matter but human practice, which involves thought, thought itself being a kind of practice or activity, that reality shares with thought some common values: in particular, practice, like thought, can be more or less rational or reasonable, more or less muddled and confused, more or less 'absurd'. If the connection between logic and words is not allowed to constrict the connection between logic and reason, practices and structures of practice, as more or less rational, can have logical relations and critical logical relation concepts can be applied to them. The dialectical category of contradiction has such an application, denoting a common structural defect that thought can share with a practice that is its material condition. Large-scale contradictions at the level of ideas are due to the irrationalities of a social structure of material practice that is self-conflicting, i.e., contradictory. The specific forms of these defects are thus united: illusion and mystification in thought, and lack of freedom in practice. In this way, moreover, self-contradictory thought can reflect the truth about a self-contradictory material reality. It does so not by explicitly asserting that truth and certainly not by asserting a logical impossibility, but rather by concealing it in its implicit structure, so that this 'secret', as Marx calls it, needs to be deciphered by science.

The general materialist connection between ideas and the rest of the social structure signifying a connection between the criticism of cognitive defect and the criticism of that social structure is formulated in Marx's early conception of religion:

The struggle against religion is indirectly the struggle against

[54] See R. Bhaskar's argument in *Radical Philosophy* 26 (Autumn 1980).

that world whose spiritual aroma is religion ... To call on
them to give up their illusions about their condition is to call
on them to give up a condition that requires illusions. The
criticism of religion is therefore in embryo the criticism of
that vale of tears of which religion is the halo.[55]

In the *Theses on Feuerbach*, the most concentrated account of
his views on this topic, Marx explicitly, in Thesis I, identifies
'revolutionary' with 'practical-critical' activity, and in Thesis
IV he summarizes the general relation involved in this activity
in terms of contradiction and self-contradiction:

Feuerbach starts out from the fact of religious self-
alienation, of the duplication of the world into a religious
world and a secular one. His work consists in resolving the
religious world into its secular basis. But that the secular
basis detaches itself from itself and establishes itself as an
independent realm in the clouds can only be explained by the
cleavages and self-contradictions within this secular basis.
The latter must, therefore, in itself be both understood in its
contradiction and revolutionized in practice. Thus, for
instance, after the earthly family is discovered to be the
secret of the holy family, the former must then itself be
destroyed in theory and in practice.[56]

I said earlier that Marx's science is critical, but not morally
critical, of its object, capitalist society, and is so through its
employment of a network of specific critical categories that are
integrated into his science by their connection with another that
is essential to its scientificity. That essential critical category is
contradiction in its dialectical form, contradiction in theory
united with contradiction in practice. The specific critical
categories I mentioned, such as alienation and fetishism, have
two characteristics that mark them as special forms of this
general dialectical category of contradiction. On the one hand
they are relational, and the general form of the relation they

[55] K. Marx, *Introduction to a Contribution to the Critique of Hegel's
Philosophy of Right, op. cit.*, p. 244.
[56] K. Marx, *Theses on Feuerbach, op. cit.*

denote is that of practical contradiction within a unity. On the other they bear critically on both thought and practice, involving both illusion and subjection. They thus represent unified structures of practical contradictions in which defects specific to practice and to thought, namely bondage in practice and mystification in thought, are themselves united. Emancipation – from both – requires the 'practical-critical' activity of revolution against those contradictions, that is, against the mode of production that is their basic instantiation and thus against that class whose interest it is to perpetuate that mode of production.

The end of theory and its dialectic

That revolutionary transformation of society into socialism and communism, in eliminating its basic structural contradictions, will also thereby eliminate its ideologically mystifying appearances. The appearance and reality of society will then coincide, rendering social scientific theory unnecessary and impossible.[57] Having been opaque and mystifying, society will become transparent and intelligible to its participants, their spontaneous and untheoretical understanding of their own practices adequate without benefit of science or any other kind of theory. Marx's realist account of society is not a philosophical ontology. Society's realist character is historically transient. And though hermeneutics (and its 'empiricism') has the last laugh, it does not do so as philosophy. What it philosophically and ideologically sees as an eternal element of the human condition is for Marx historically specific, something to be achieved, in the future, only by revolutionary struggle:

The religious reflex of the real world can, in any case, only then finally vanish, when the practical relations of everyday

---

[57] See the elegant argument in G. Cohen, *op. cit.*, pp. 326–44.

life offer to man none but perfectly intelligible and reasonable relations with regard to his fellowmen and to Nature.

The life-process of society, which is based on the process of material production, does not strip off its mystical veil until it is treated as production by freely associated men, and is consciously regulated by them in accordance with a settled plan.[58]

Thus the very existence of theory itself, not only religious and philosophical but even scientific and materialist, is inseparable from society's contradictory structure and its mystifying character. Indeed, involving socially as it does that central form of the division of labour, between manual and intellectual labour, theory, even Marx's own scientific theory, is an integral aspect of society's mystifying contradictions. Only a mode of practice that does not require to be understood by theory but can be comprehended spontaneously by its agents will finally eliminate that division. This is the ultimate sense of the VIIIth of the *Theses on Feuerbach*:

All social life is essentially *practical*. All mysteries which lead theory to mysticism find their rational solution in human practice and in the comprehension of this practice.[59]

Marx's materialism, his commitment to practice, here reaches its furthest extent and reveals itself as ultimately incompatible not only with idealism in religion and philosophy but with theoretical social ideas of any kind, even those of a materialist science. Philosophy has already in the present age lost its 'independent medium of existence' and thus its identity as a subject by contrast with science. Marx's own science also will disappear into the past of society's prehistory, superseded by a society whose rational form realizes in practice what science could only prefigure in theory.

But in the here and now, a necessary part of that process is the development and propagation of Marxist theory as science.

[58] K. Marx, *Capital*, op. cit., pp. 79–80.
[59] K. Marx, *Theses on Feuerbach*, op. cit.

I have tried to bring out the many ways in which Marx's science, as materialist and practical, is thereby political and not philosophical; the many ways in which its political and non-philosophical character is in fact essential to its scientificity. There are two reasons why it is not the case, as Althusser maintains, that 'class struggle at the level of theory' is philosophy. In the first place, for Marx it is science that is the theoretical form of revolutionary politics. In the second place, there is no Marxist philosophy. For Marx, philosophy is idealist ideology, and his relation to it exemplifies his materialist relation to bourgeois ideology in general: his rejection of it is by a process of critical analysis in which he deciphers and appropriates its secret truth about society's practical confusions and contradictions. Marx's science contradicts and criticizes many philosophical theories, and in the present situation 'Marxist philosophers' have the task, through their special knowledge of the resources of the philosophical tradition, of subjecting those theories to materialist critical analysis. But just as the philosophical theories Marxist science appears to accept it does not accept as philosophical, so its attack on the philosophical theories it rejects is not philosophical either. Conceptual, perhaps: but the argument for the necessity of the Marxist conceptual framework is not philosophical but scientific, and ultimately it can be 'proved' only materialistically, in and by a practice that in the course of history will nevertheless transform its necessity into superfluity and impossibility.

Chronology of Marx's Writings

Further Reading

Marx's Writings

K. Marx and F. Engels, *Collected Works* (London and New York, 1965ff), 50 vols. planned.
K. Marx, *The Essential Writings*, ed. F. Bender (New York, 1972).
The Marx-Engels Reader, ed. R. Tucker (New York, 1972).
K. Marx, *Selected Writings*, ed. D. McLellan (Oxford, 1977).

General Books

G. Lichtheim, *Marxism* (London, 1964).
L. Kolakowski, *Main Currents of Marxism* (Oxford, 1978).
D. McLellan, *Marxism after Marx* (London, 1980).

Culture

L. Trotsky, *Literature and Revolution* (New York, 1957).
E. Fischer, *The Necessity of Art* (London, 1963).
V. Lenin, *On Literature and Art* (Moscow, 1967).
F. Jameson, *Marxism and Form* (Princeton, 1971).
L. Baxandall and S. Morawski, eds., *Marx and Engels on Literature and Art* (St Louis, 1973).
M. Solomon, ed., *Marxism and Art* (New York, 1973).
V. Volosinov, *Marxism and the Philosophy of Language* (New York, 1973).
R. Williams, *Marxism and Literature* (Oxford, 1977).
E. Bloch *et al.*, *Aesthetics and Politics* (London, 1978).
G. della Volpe, *Critique of Taste* (London, 1978).

History

K. Kautsky, *Ethics and the Materialist Conception of History* (Chicago, 1918).

G. Plekhanov, *In Defence of Materialism. The Development of the Monist View of History* (London, 1947).

E. Hobsbawm, Introduction to K. Marx, *Pre-capitalist Economic Formations* (London, 1964).

G. Leff, *History and Social Theory* (London 1969).

M. Evans, *Karl Marx* (London, 1975).

V. Kiernan, *Marxism and Imperialism* (London, 1976).

G. Cohen, *Karl Marx's Theory of History* (Oxford, 1978).

W. Shaw, *Marx's Theory of History* (London, 1978).

D. Gandy, *Marx and History* (Austin, 1979).

Sociology

K. Korsch, *Karl Marx* (London, 1938).

I. Zeitlin, *Marxism: a Re-evaluation* (Princeton, 1967).

S. Avineri, *The Social and Political Thought of Karl Marx* (Cambridge, 1968).

T. Bottomore, *Marxist Sociology* (London, 1975).

A. Swingewood, *Marx and Modern Social Theory* (London, 1975).

T. Adorno *et al.*, *The Positivist Dispute in German Sociology* (London, 1976).

G. Therborn, *Class, Science and Society* (London, 1976).

M. Godelier, *Perspectives in Marxist Anthropology* (Cambridge, 1977).

K. Löwith, *Max Weber and Karl Marx* (London, 1982).

Politics

L. Maitan, *Party, Army and Masses in China* (London, 1976).

R. Blackburn, ed., *Revolution and Class Struggle. A Reader in Marxist Politics* (London, 1977).

S. Carillo, *Eurocommunism and the State* (London, 1977).

H. Draper, *Karl Marx's Theory of Revolution* (New York, 1977), 2 vols.

N. Harding, *Lenin's Political Thought* (London, 1977, 1981), 2 vols.

R. Miliband, *Marxism and Politics* (Oxford, 1977).

R. Bahro, *The Alternative in Eastern Europe* (London, 1978).

B. Frankel, *Marxism and the State. A Critique of Orthodoxy* (Melbourne, 1978).

J. Maguire, *Marx's Theory of Politics* (Cambridge, 1978).

Economics

P. Baran, *The Political Economy of Growth* (New York, 1957).

E. Mandel, *Marxist Economic Theory* (London, 1968).

R. Luxemburg, *The Accumulation of Capital* (London, 1971).

I. Rubin, *Essays on Marx's Theory of Value* (Detroit, 1972).

P. Sweezy, *The Theory of Capitalist Development* (New York, 1972).

M. Barrett-Brown, *The Economics of Imperialism* (London, 1975).

A. Bose, *Marxian and Post-Marxian Political Economy* (London, 1975).

M. Howard and J. King, *The Political Economy of Marx* (London, 1975).

R. Hilferding, *Finance Capital* (London, 1981).

Philosophy

F. Engels, *Anti-Dühring* (London, 1955).

R. Edgley, *Reason in Theory and Practice* (London, 1969).

K. Korsch, *Marxism and Philosophy* (London, 1970).

M. Horkheimer, *Critical Theory* (New York, 1972).

L. Colletti, *Marxism and Hegel* (London, 1973).

R. Bhaskar, *A Realist Theory of Science* (Leeds, 1975).

D.-H. Ruben, *Marxism and Materialism* (Hassocks, 1977).

J. Mepham and D.-H. Ruben, *Issues in Marxist Philosophy* (Hassocks, 1979).

A. Wood, *Karl Marx* (London, 1981).

Index

Index